ATTRACTING THE AFFLUENT

THE FIRST GUIDE
TO
AMERICA'S CHANGING
ULTIMATE MARKET

FROM
THE EDITORS OF
RESEARCH ALERT

FINANCIAL SOURCEBOOKS
NAPERVILLE, ILLINOIS

94-0764

Published by:

Financial Sourcebooks

A Division of Sourcebooks, Inc.
P.O. Box 313
Naperville, Illinois 60566
(708) 961-2161
FAX: 708-961-2168

Editorial: Ellen Slezak
Interior Design: Monica Paxson
Production and Layout: The Print Group
Cover Design: The Print Group

This publication is designed to provide accurate and authoritative information in regard to the subject matter covered. It is sold with the understanding that the publisher is not engaged in rendering legal, accounting or other professional services. If legal advice or other expert assistance is required, the services of a competent professional person should be sought.

From a Declaration of Principles Jointly Adopted by a Committee of the American Bar Association and a Committee of Publishers and Associations

Library of Congress Cataloging-in-Publication Data

Attracting the affluent : the first guide to America's changing ultimate
market / from the editors of Research Alert.
      p.   cm.
    Includes bibliographical references.
    ISBN 0-942061-23-3
    1. Rich as consumers--United States. 2. Marketing--United
States. 3. Marketing research--United States. I. Title: Research
alert.
HC110.C6.A85   1991
658.8'348--dc20   91-10939
                                                CIP

Printed and bound in the United States of America.
10 9 8 7 6 5 4 3 2

Contents

Preface

According to *Webster's Ninth New Collegiate Dictionary*, affluence has three definitions: "1a) an abundant flow or supply, profusion; 1b) an abundance of property, wealth; 2) a flowing toward a point, influx."

Those denotations reflect the intent of this book. The editors of *Research Alert* and *Affluent Markets Alert* have a wealth of information and a profusion of valuable facts about American affluents. We have dedicated ourselves to sorting out this abundance for you. We have synthesized the research information so that it flows toward a particular point—the location of the real-affluents, those with the affluent mindstyle.

We dedicate this undertaking to the connotation of affluence: plenty. America is a marvelous country with a historically unprecedented level of abundance. This potential has shaped the dreams of all Americans and much of the rest of the world's population. We dedicate this study of those who possess actual affluence to the hopeful dream of abundance that all people share. We hope our efforts will lead you to greater plenty.

One percent of the profits that *Research Alert* makes from this book will go to philanthropic causes that share America's bounty.

Eric Miller
Editor, Research Alert
Publisher, Affluent Markets Alert

Acknowledgments

Many companies, organizations and individuals have contributed to this book. I thank them all, and would like to acknowledge a specific few.

Many thanks to the many research organizations that have generated the fine research that has been used to inform and substantiate our findings. Foremost among them is, the Census Bureau. Although it is our tax dollars that fund its efforts, it is the high quality of its output (and its volume) that gives us tremendous tools with which to work. Many thanks also to the research firms, including Mendelsohn Media Research, Mediamark Research, Inc., Simmons, the Roper Organization, the Gallup Organization, and Management Horizons, who have shared their excellent work with us.

I also would like to thank the present and former editors at *Research Alert* and *Affluent Markets Alert* who have worked at great length and with care to create this book. I would particularly like to mention Tracy Calhoun, Ann Loughlin, Sharon Klotz, and Elisa Nudelman. Thanks also to Tom Black of *Smithsonian* magazine from whom I first heard the words "affluent mindstyle" and whose articulate insights prompted me to begin my investigations into affluence.

Finally, I would like to thank those who subscribe to *Research Alert* and *Affluent Markets Alert*. They foot the bill for our ongoing investigations into the real consumer trends in the United States. Their loyalty and praises are appreciated every day, and result in the high quality and excitement of our continuing work.

Part
I

Defining the Affluent Market

Introduction

Overview of the Affluent Market

Affluence drives America. This is true in more ways than just the obvious economic clout of the affluent sector. Even those who are not affluent live an affluent lifestyle—either in the parts of their lives in which they can manage it or in their imaginations. The economic power of the affluent fuels the nation's economy; the image power of affluence fuels the consumer style and lifestyle of the nation's population.

Everybody knows affluence; it's the American Dream. The dream is filled with images most Americans recognize—the BMW, the sailboat, the bottle of Absolut vodka, the cellular phone beside the swimming pool, and, of course, lots of time in which to enjoy these indulgences. Even those without the means of wealth seek to approximate affluence in any way they can—a fake-fur coat (though fur is rapidly losing its cachet), low-priced champagne, a holiday cruise. Americans feel that affluence is our national manifest destiny.

For American business, the affluent market is more than a dream. The reality is that not only do the affluent command the preponderance of U.S. spending power, but they also continually reinvent the image of the high life to which Americans aspire. Actually, these ever-changing icons of affluence are created in a kind of dance between the affluent market and affluent-focused businesses. Together they continually reinvent the images of affluence to which the rest of the nation, and, increasingly, the world, aspires. I have seen pictures of sports cars pinned to the walls of shacks in rural Indonesia and t-shirts with yacht club logos in Soweto.

The affluent market is the pot of gold many marketers want to find. But the end of this elusive rainbow is anything but easy to find. Finding the affluent market is a journey. I have noticed that many affluent marketers underestimate the difficulty of this journey. The target seems so easy to hit—they can locate rich people. Many marketers rely on the tools and gut feel used in earlier decades when reaching the affluent was a far simpler task. Many trust the first research numbers they see without placing them in context.

The journey to find the true-affluents is fraught with misleading and confusing information. The high stakes choices that many marketers must make are too often based on unexamined premises. For example, many marketers still view the affluent market as monolithic and cohesive. Once this was an acceptably useful view of the affluent; now it is disastrous. The affluent market has fragmented as much as the middle market has.

Using underexamined premises and imprecise thinking, many marketers will rely on demographic data to target the affluent. Demographics alone will not lead you to the real-affluents. Any demographic category will include those who live and spend like affluents as well as those who don't. In addition, using demographics has an entropic bias, as opposed to the limiting-of-focus that is the best way to reach the affluent. For example, choosing to target households earning $50,000-$75,000 per year will give you many more prospects than the real-affluents you want.

Finding the Real-Affluents
To locate the real-affluents you must triangulate. That may sound like a daunting cartographer's technique, but the principles are already familiar to you. You must find different kinds of research (preferably at least three) that cover the same terrain and look for the consumers who fall within the different groupings. You must consider, let's say, a demographic group with a psychographic identity in a geodemographic focus. This is the means to target the real-affluents.

The 64-billion-dollar question is who are the real-affluents? The answer we wish to give you is this book. The real-affluents are those who have an affluent mindstyle. Those whose ideas lead them to the values, lifestyles, and spending patterns of true affluence. Only in the journey to find mindstyle-affluents will you be able to bypass those who fall into some similar demographic and other research groupings but are not those who comprise affluent America. The dual-income couple earning $59,000 and living in a big apartment built onto a parent's house is probably not real-affluent. The single woman who just got her degree in architecture and is living in a small apartment in Chicago three successful years into her first job but earning only $27,500 may very well be a mindstyle-affluent.

Finding the real-affluents is just part of the problem—keeping up with them is every bit as difficult. Real-affluents are easily bored and are keen variety-seekers. Another reason it is essential to focus on the mindstyle aspect of affluence is that this is the way to begin to anticipate changes. This book will guide you toward the affluent, and will suggest the ways that you will be able to continue to find them as they change and evolve.

For a long time, marketers have taken the affluent market for granted. They have viewed it as a small, predictable, lucrative segment that doesn't change much. I've heard one critic of the practice describe it as marketing to the affluent by clicking your heels three times, and repeating to yourself that, "There's no place like a small, predictable, lucrative segment that doesn't change much." Such marketers believe that when the affluent market does change, outside influences (such as advertising images and market strategies) are more the cause than are pressures from within the market itself. You just can't afford the luxury of those views within today's affluent market. Marketers taking this approach have long since parted company with their real-affluent market. The affluents have roared past them, ignoring advertising and marketing that is not keeping up with the pace they set by deliberately pursuing their own idea of the affluent life.

The simplest fact is that the affluent market has changed from within. Dramatically. In the 1980s, it saw unprecedented growth. It has fragmented into specific target markets, just as other U.S. markets have fragmented into specific target groups. Marketers and researchers have applied their full creative arsenal of research and analysis techniques to the mass market. At the same time they have used standard marketing and advertising assumptions with the affluent.

The New Affluent Market

With the growth of the affluent market in the 1980s, and the continuing change it is generating, in many ways the affluent market is becoming the mass market. Affluents are swiftly and surely defining the tastes (and the appetites) of all U.S. consumers. They are, in fact, doing the marketer's and the advertiser's traditional job for them—simply by living the lifestyle of affluence. They are promoting the lifestyle and the mindstyle of affluence, and in the process, they are defining the way all consumers want to live—and spend.

In this light, affluence is as affluence thinks—and spends. Consumers want to be affluent; they want to think of themselves as affluent; they want others to think of them as affluent; and they want to be addressed as affluents. Like Narcissus preferring his own reflection to anything else he could see, affluent consumers love to see a reflection of themselves as affluents (this is true for wealthy and not-so-wealthy affluent consumers alike). Purchasing products they know are aimed at the affluent market allows average consumers to buy a piece of the dream. Purchasing an "affluent" product or service allows any consumer—if only for a moment—to live like an affluent. This is the real affluent market, regardless of household income, discretionary income, investments, houses, or property, and regardless of the traditional categories defining affluence.

Little wonder, then, that the real-affluents are such elusive prey, often defying some of our best and finest means of quantifying them. The successful marketer will not capture affluent consumers by merely quantifying the affluent market. The successful marketer will capture the imaginations, dreams, and dollars of affluent consumers by capturing the vision of the affluent mindstyle. Mindstyle will be your best guide for navigating the promising territory that lies between "living the good life" and "living the better life."

Redefine your idea of the affluent consumer because affluent consumers have already redefined themselves. Affluent consumers are not all wealthy; two very different types of affluent consumers could pass each other on the street and never imagine they are the same species of consumer. Forget the idea that affluent consumers are easy to spot by the amount of money they have to spend; remember that real "affluent" consumers think like "affluent" people.

Researchers have begun to realize that they must refocus the mass market microscope to study the affluent market. Beginning this study in earnest in recent years, they have made their first discoveries: 1) this burgeoning group is not a single market, but several very different subgroups and niche markets; and, 2) traditional market research techniques have been woefully inadequate in gaining insight into affluence. Current measurements of the affluent are imprecise; there is still no single reliable way to identify affluent consumers.

The Research Mess

The research on affluents is a mess. It is not necessarily wrong; it is just difficult to use and to rely on as an accurate view of affluence.

The simplest example of the problem is that there is little agreement on a subject as basic as the definition of affluence. Traditionally, affluents have been defined as households with $50,000+ in annual income. Today, however, a great many of these households are dual-earner households that are just getting by, so it's not a useful delineation anymore. If you have paid for a baby-sitter or a Broadway show in the last few years, you know this to be true.

In response, many researchers have scaled up the household income level floor they use to define affluence. Particular higher income stratifications have their adherents and opponents—some say $60,000 is too low, others say $100,000 is too high, and so forth. However, from our point of view, annual household income is a far from reliable indicator of the lifestyle, mindstyle, and qualitative aspects of affluence, which are more important with affluent markets than with any other.

No collectively acceptable definition or reliable kind of research has emerged, so different people continue to talk about different things when they discuss affluents. As we have said, the current research situation is a mess—the semantic confusion is even messier. In chapter 1 we will introduce you to eight of the current ways that research targets affluents. We will show you the strengths and limitations of each kind of research. We will then extract the best findings from all the different modes of research to present the essential affluent market—Americans who live life with the affluent mindstyle.

Much of the reason that affluents are so hard to measure is that they're less than thrilled with responding to market research. In fact, the essence of affluence is contrary to the experience of a questionnaire—affluents don't have the patience or the interest to plod through interviews. Consequently, researchers get very small numbers of them in many research samples, and they therefore get unreliable results. It takes clever and expensive lures to get a certain kind of affluent consumer to put up with an interview, often making quantitative research prohibitively expensive. It's reported that focus groups now pay over $200 to get some affluents to participate. This limitation, however, pales in comparison to the number of affluent consumers who need no lure, but who are never asked to participate—because they don't look like a researcher's traditional idea of an affluent.

Faced with the dearth of research, many marketers have relied on their well-developed instincts about consumer markets to target the affluent consumer. Use that 10 percent of creative inspiration, but follow it up with your 90 percent of perspiration: test your innovative idea about where an affluent market may be found by gathering data from a variety of research sources, leaving preconceived stereotypes about this market behind.

We believe that the affluent markets—all of them—are waiting to be discovered and defined. In this book we will:

- Put you on top of the ways in which affluents are currently being studied, with an analysis of the strengths and weaknesses of each technique;
- Elicit the best findings from each research technique, to create a composite picture of the real-affluents;
- Distinguish between the different segments of the affluent market, dispel common myths, and point to key segments;
- Present key attributes of the affluent lifestyle, mindstyle, media style, and consumer style;
- Detail the importance of the affluent market as it influences and drives the mass market;

- Make informed predictions about the future of the affluent market, pointing to key factors for keeping up with the most desirable of all consumers: the affluents.

Chapter

I

Current Research Perspectives
on Affluence

Market research currently gives us information on affluents from eight principle perspectives. In this chapter we'll take a look at the ways in which each perspective is in itself incomplete, and then we'll pull together the best information from the different points of view to create our own composite picture of who the affluent consumers really are. The fact that any single research technique doesn't deliver a *complete* picture doesn't mean that its findings aren't valid and useful; it only means that it will take an analysis of *all* the sources available to create a three-dimensional view of affluence. The different perspectives sometimes contradict one another, but, more often than not, different definitions of terms or methodologies account for discrepancies. We have analyzed those discrepancies to give you the best reliable data available.

Much of what is presented in this chapter (and the guiding benchmark in almost all discussions of affluence in current research) is based on statistics using the most basic and traditional definition of affluence: the $50,000+ household income. What we have seen concerning the upper income breakdowns of the affluent population leads us to state that this definition is outdated—or, at the very best, only marginally useful. Not only is the $50,000+ household income per year mark too low to hit the real level of affluence, but also, to make matters worse, no one can even agree on how many people qualify for it. Notice how four reliable sources differ in their calculations of the number of affluents who qualify for this most-basic measure. As exhibit 1-1 demonstrates, the counts from reliable research organizations differ by as much as 35% for this bottom line measurement.

Even the U.S. government—always interested in the wealth of its citizens—isn't exactly sure what constitutes affluence. It's not often that the Congressional Record is filled with a debate of who the rich are. But if you were C-Spanning your way through the latter part of 1990, you saw more definitions of "the rich" than you saw answers for how to take money from them. The resolution that the Congress arrived at is (no surprise) the same as the research community has settled for—no agreement.

We now present to you the best of the research we have found, discussing the advantages and drawbacks of both traditional and innovative methods of tracking the affluent consumer. But further research into the subsegments of affluence is of utmost importance. The affluent market is *not* monolithic; it is comprised of different economic segments, lifestage segments, and psychographic segments. Each has its own values, mindstyle, lifestyle, priorities, and consumer patterns. Currently, research of this depth and specificity is rarely available for successful niche marketing without commissioning expensive proprietary studies.

1. Education
"For the first time ever, the highest levels of education and concomitant opportunity for success, leadership and affluence became available to people according to their ability and talent rather than their parentage," according to *Smithsonian*'s Tom Black.[1] *The affluence explosion in this country has much to do with the education explosion which preceded it.* The number of college-educated Americans has increased dramatically since the G.I. bill was enacted on June 21, 1944, creating a population more educated than any population in history.

About 23.3% of the adult population had obtained *any* degree beyond the high school level by 1987; this is a significant increase over the

Exhibit 1-1. The 1988 estimates of number of adults with $50,000+ household income (by research organization)

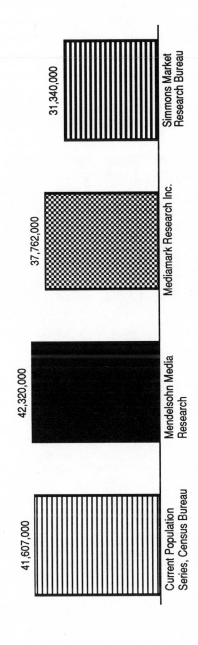

41,607,000	Current Population Series, Census Bureau
42,320,000	Mendelsohn Media Research
37,762,000	Mediamark Research Inc.
31,340,000	Simmons Market Research Bureau

Source: Affluence 1988-89, Mendelsohn Media Research, Inc.

level of 20.7% in 1984. While the average monthly earnings for
persons holding Master's, Bachelor's, or associate degrees significantly increased from 1984 to 1987 (after adjustment for inflation),
persons with no postsecondary degree, along with vocational degree
holders, experienced no real increase in monthly earnings.

Exhibit 1-2.   The educating of America (population 25+;
                figures rounded; medians based on households)

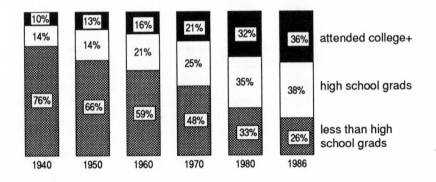

Source: Census Bureau, March 1986

Exhibit 1.3.   Average monthly earnings (by educational level)
                1984-1987

(1984 mean dollars adjusted to 1987, using inflation factor of 1.09)

| | Mean Earnings | |
Educational Attainment	**1984**	**1987**
Doctorate	$2,994	$3,637
Professional	$3,749	$4,003
Master's	$2,132	$2,378
Bachelor's	$1,679	$1,829
Associate	$1,294	$1,458
Vocational	$1,079	$1,088
Some college	$1,052	$1,088
High school grad. only	$ 924	$ 921
Not a high school grad.	$ 452	$ 452

Source: *What's It Worth? Educational Background and Economic Status:*
           Spring 1987, Census Bureau

Here are a few simple rule-of-thumb guidelines to calculate the effects
of continued education on learning:

- The earnings of those with a bachelor's degree are almost double the earnings of those with only a high school diploma.
- The earnings of those with a master's degree are well over double (150%) the earnings of those with only a high school diploma.
- The earnings of those with a professional degree are more than triple the earnings of those with only a high school diploma.

More recent Census Bureau data recording increases in monthly salaries demonstrates that this upward swing is continuing: the average monthly income reported by persons with professional degrees has increased to $4,323, followed by salaries of those with master's degrees ($2,776), bachelor's degrees ($2,109), and associate degree holders ($1,630). And a variety of research sources—though they may not agree on who the affluent are—seem to point to the same conclusion: the impact of higher education on income is obvious; higher education means higher earnings. Consider exhibit 1-4, which shows a direct correlation between the degree of education and the degree of affluence.

Exhibit 1-4.   Annual Income (by educational attainment of male head of household)

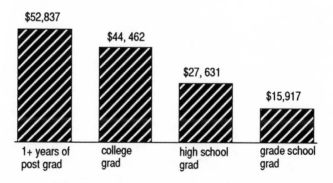

Source: *A Marketer's Guide to Discretionary Income*, Census Bureau/The Conference Board

Overall, affluents (described as $50,000+ annual household income) have 18% more years of schooling (median), are 56% more likely to be college educated (25% of affluents), and 130% more likely to have undertaken graduate study (26% of affluents) than the average American.[2]   Once again, though the exact percentages may not always agree, reports on the higher-end affluents point to the clear relationship between education and wealth. One study finds that for affluents with an annual household income of $75,000+, *education is the single highest correlation coefficient* (compared to other factors such as race, region, age, or marital status) in the equation for wealth—only 22% of the nation's total household heads have 4+ years of college, but a whopping 62% of affluent householders do.[3] Choosing the higher benchmarks of household income for charting affluent education and income levels, you'll still find the familiar correlation: the higher the income level (with the exception of the $200,000+ category), the higher percentage of affluents with four or more years of college.

Exhibit 1-5.   Educational degree and median personal income (by household income)

Annual household income	% College grad. or better	Median personal income
$50,000 - $59,999	32.7%	$28,900
$60,000 - $74,999	38.5%	$34,900
$75,000 - $99,999	44.1%	$39,900
$100,000 - $149,999	49.5%	$60,900
$150,000 - $199,999	52.7%	$73,700
$200,000 +	47.6%	$103,500

Source: *Affluence 1988 - 1989,* Mendelsohn Media Research, Inc.

So, as the country gets smarter, the affluent segment gets bigger. A college diploma also has a secondary impact on affluence. It is the handiest indicator of a consumer who is likely to have experienced and will probably adhere to an affluent mindstyle. Tom Black explains the mindstyle this way: "Once you graduate from college, you join the affluent fraternity, a group that has a wholly different set of values and habits than the mass market." Thus, it's not money alone that determines high-status purchasing; education consistently shows itself to be a correlated factor. The combination—forming a group of affluents described by author Michael J. Weiss as "Money & Brains"— makes for a demographic segment "almost cult-oriented toward conspicuous consumption."[4]

This consumption includes a ravenous affluent appetite for education itself; while affluent households comprise just 13% of the total number of U.S. households, they collectively account for 37% of all tuition dollars—and no other income group even comes close to their propensity for higher learning.[5] Education will be one of the biggest "experiential businesses" of the 1990s. It's just the ticket for affluents and potential-affluents: a life-long endeavor for self-improvement (not to mention a ticket into high-paying jobs).

With more people getting more education and more wealth, the mindstyle of the educated affluent becomes a key to the perpetuation of the species. According to a recent report from the Urban Institute, the more educated young will be "less likely to think that they have fallen behind the performance of previous generations. They will be insulated in part from the lackluster U.S. economic performance by relatively stronger wage growth, by a greater ability to enter the housing market and by substantially higher and more diversified net wealth holdings generally." Noting that the wealth of families headed by a young person with at least some college education is 66% higher than that of families headed by a young person with a high school education or less (keep in mind the quality of that wealth—Individual Retirement or Keogh Accounts, non-liquid assets like precious metals, jewelry, or art, and business assets), the report stresses the fact that while the more educated have higher debt for things such as investments, the size of their retail debt is considerably smaller than that of their counterparts with less education.[6]

However, research on educational attainment can also mislead; it is not a foolproof way to find affluents. For example, if you use the traditional affluent benchmark of $50,000 in annual household income, then some reports find that affluents have actually become a *less* educated group in recent years. But this phenomenon is mostly due to the increase of dual-income families and multiple wage-earners in nontraditional household settings.[7] And, as in so many of the hunting grounds in which researchers try to identify the tell-tale tracks of affluents on their way to the top, marketers with their nose to the ground can run head-on into each other with conflicting results.

Here's another painful example of the affluent research mess: two reports on affluence that dealt with education levels were issued in mid-1988. One claimed that a majority of affluents were college-educated, the other claimed exactly the opposite. Pretty basic stuff for such a contradiction. Yet because they were using different definitions of affluence, both were correct. Add to this some confusion about available data on the educated, and even the proponent of this angle towards affluence, Tom Black, says that none of the current syndicated research offerings can measure the educated market. Education levels provide a formula that seems to have potential, but doesn't always add up to the sum of affluence.

While the existing research methods and results may not be conclusive, what is abundantly clear to us is that education level is a very effective way of getting a handle on affluents and future affluents. If you raise your income benchmark of affluence to the $75,000+ household income mark (and we suggest that you do), the research fog clears a bit, and you are left with a picture of affluents painted in bold strokes: consumers with higher individual incomes and stronger and more diversified assets; and consumers schooled in the mindstyle of affluence, with greater potential not only to keep, but also to enhance their wealth. Increased access to education during the past decades—and the importance of the actual and *perceived* relationship between education and income—is producing consumers educated enough to know that they want the sum of the education/affluence equation.

2. Household income
As we've said, the traditional cutoff point to separate an affluent household from a nonaffluent has been a household income of at least $50,000 a year. This is by far the most common way of defining affluence in most of the research that's now available, and it is a tempting way to choose your target. Just seeing a dollar figure this high makes a marketer think that consumers are not going to miss at least a *few* dollars out of that sum Also, it delineates a huge market, many millions of prospective customers larger than a more narrowly-defined income cutoff.

However, $50,000 in income now targets neither affluence nor significant amounts of discretionary income. Anyone who regularly pays for parking and daycare knows that this delineation has lost its impact—the plumber and his first-grade-teacher-wife make $50,000 a year, and they would be the first ones to tell you that they are just getting by.

Some researchers are moving the affluent floor up to $60,000 or higher. *But there is still no agreement on an income level that means affluence. And for good reason.*

First things first. Let's say you do settle on the $50,000+ figure as the base you want to work with. In order to establish how many individuals or households you are targeting as your potential affluent market, you turn to some of the most prominent research organizations. But remember the hitch that we showed you at the beginning of this chapter—even settling for the broadest ($50,000+) definition of affluence, and using one of the most basic measurements (income), you can't find two sets of figures that agree. You can't know for sure just how many affluents there are out there.

Income is just one factor in the affluent equation—a factor that is affected by many variables. Taking recent Census Bureau statistics on the total U.S. population, we come up with the following useful (if general) information: Real per capita income reached an all-time high in this country in 1988, up 1.7% from 1987. Median household income and median family income were unchanged in 1988, at $27,230 and $32,190, respectively.

Although it seems contradictory for per capita income to go up while household income and family income are unchanged, both figures are correct. Per capita income includes all persons, while family income includes only related persons living in households. Decreasing family size (the American household currently is smaller than it has ever been) and increasing numbers of nonfamily households (unrelated people living together) are two trends affecting family income. The real income of married couple families increased by 1.1% in 1989 from 1988, while there was no significant change for families with a female householder, no husband present.

Reading these figures in an affluent frame of mind points to a few issues that the savvy analyst must face, if not resolve. The most obvious consideration is a research issue: we are presented with no fewer than three standard ways of measuring income—per capita, household, and family yardsticks. Each of these ways has a particular distinction for affluence, a distinct profile in comparison to the population. Obviously, few marketers will want to (or should) discard income measurement as a means for locating affluence. However, it is important to note two criteria: different standard income measurements exist; and, the affluent profile is different within the three different measurements.

For example, in one study, we read that although the average American family is decreasing in size, Upper Deck households (top 10% of earners) are above average in size—they are 15% more likely than the U.S. average to be comprised of three persons and 39% more likely to be comprised of four or more people.[8] If you consider that at least some of these "grown children" are working (and therefore affecting household income), you immediately come up with a new way to divide the income pie of that affluent household. In later chapters of this book, you will see that most affluents are married (79%, vs. 54% of the total U.S.). Furthermore, only half of affluents are single (12%), compared to the total number of consumers (24%), and a very low 4.3% are divorced, compared with 10% of total consumers. Also, there is no real trend among affluent households of unrelated people living together.[9]

Thus, you may conclude that affluent households, filled with higher numbers of adult family members, cast their own slant on household and family income figures. Again, we find that affluent households are not average households, and household or family income figures are limited in their usefulness. And again, the need for complex, pinpoint marketing research is greatest for marketers faced with defining and finding affluent markets.

Nevertheless, the income yardstick and some of its numbers are just too good to ignore. According to Mendelsohn Research, Inc., "The nearly 17,000,000 affluent adult households (household income $50,000+) amassed at least $1,480,000,000,000 in 1987 household income, an average of $88,200 per affluent household."[10] Also according to Mendelsohn Research, Inc., affluent households are increasing faster than the rate of inflation. In 1988, 12% of all U.S. households had incomes of $60,000+; by 1989, the number of $60,000+ households had risen to 13.1%.

Perhaps recognizing that aiming a marketing dart at $50,000+ household income and personal income figures is too much like hitting the side of an increasingly expansive barn, many services have zeroed in on the upper echelons of upper income, as well as the important distinctions within those rarified groups.

Getting down to the upper nitty-gritty, Find/SVP offers a breakdown of household income within affluent ($50,000+) households from Census Bureau data. The share of affluent households with a household income in the $50,000–$54,999 range is the largest percentage, 19.8%. Tied for second are those affluents with a household income of $55,000–$59,999 and a household income of $100,000 and over— each group accounts for 15.4% of the affluent market. The third percentage in double digits belongs to those households with a household income of $60,000–$64,999, who account for 12.3% of affluent households. Households earning between $65,000–$69,999 make up 9.7% of affluent households. For those with a household income of $70,000–$74,999, that percentage is 7.3%; for those with household income of $75,000–$79,999, that figure is 6.3%; and $80,000–$84,999 households represent a 4.6% share of affluent households. There is a very slight difference in percentage for the next two highest household incomes: $85,000–$89,999 households are at 3.6%, and $90,000–$94,999 households are at 3.5%. Just below the $100,000 household income mark are the 2.2% of affluent households with a household income of $95,000–$99,999. These figures represent percentages of a total of 19,333,000 affluent households.[11]

Such counts are certainly not useless, and to toss the income yardstick away would be to throw out the affluent Baby Boomer with the perfumed bathwater. But remember that although much of the research up to this point has used household income as the benchmark of affluence, household income is only the crudest way to measure what people have to spend on what they *really* want to buy. More problematic than settling on an income figure is the fact that *any* kind of income breakdown misses the yacht, because it takes no account of lifestyle and mindstyle factors. Yet, on the purchasing end, these factors are far more important to affluence than income level alone. Later in this book, you'll see a number of genuine affluent groups who don't even earn $50,000 in income, and you'll meet those earning a fortune who aren't among the real-affluent.

Income alone doesn't identify the real-affluent—they're the people who live the affluent lifestyle, hold affluent values, and buy products and services reflecting the images of affluence. These real-affluents live, believe, and buy affluently, regardless of their income. Of course, income influences spending, but the real-affluents will live the good life, fulfill the affluent image as much as they can, even without the means. (Consider the latest consumer installment debt figures.) They, too, can be considered members of affluent America. On the other hand, significant numbers of people who qualify in upper income categories don't have any other characteristics of the affluent market; all that glitters is not gold that will be spent, and money doesn't always burn a hole in the silk purses of those consumers with a high household income.

The mindstyle is what matters. Think about this—it's what your affluent consumers are thinking—those earning under $20,000 a year tend to think $100,000 is rich, while those already earning six figures think it takes about $1 million to be sitting pretty. To Americans on average, a $95,000-per-year income turns the rich switch.[12] The real bottom line of any mark defining this group is that it takes much more than a bank account to create an affluent American who will spend like an affluent consumer.

3. Net Worth

Net worth figures—ambiguous enough in their definition of wealth—must be combined with a variety of factors to achieve a true and well-rounded picture of the affluent consumer. *American Demographics* puts it this way:[13]

> Not surprisingly, net worth varies most sharply by household income. Households with incomes below $50,000 a year had a median net worth of less than $50,000 in 1986. But households with incomes of $50,000 or more had a median net worth of over $150,000. At the extreme, households with annual income of $100,000 or more had a median net worth of over $600,000. This affluent group receives 20% of the nation's income, but it holds fully 35% of the nation's wealth. That's why income data alone do not fully reflect the spending power of wealthy households.

There is already some information available from research that combines net worth figures with at least one other factor to arrive closer to the consumer who is able to spend in an affluent manner. The *Changing Times* Personal Prosperity Index, for example, figures that the average U.S. household ended 1989 some 2.2% wealthier (after inflation) than when it started the year. The index measures prosperity by combining household spending and household net worth. In 1989, the report concludes, it was net worth that gave the real boost to prosperity as the value of the average household jumped 2.4% to

$226,272.[14] Or, as in the case with exhibit 1-6, you can get a fairly specific breakdown of affluence within affluence by comparing the household income/net worth distribution levels among consumers with a household income of $60,000+.

Exhibit 1-6.   Household income compared to net worth
distribution

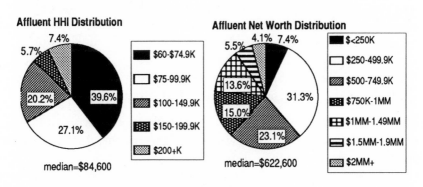

Source: *The 1989 Survey of Adults and Markets of Affluence*, Mendelsohn
Media Research, Inc.

There is, in fact, no real shortage of information reporting net assets, net wealth, and net worth. A nationally representative study of 800 Americans in households with a minimum of $100,000 in gross annual income, representing the top 2.5% income level, shows that their average household income is approximately $194,000. Besides the primary residence, their personal assets come close to a quarter of a million dollars; 63% report net assets greater than $250,000; 24% report net assets greater than $1,000,000; 8% report net assets greater than $2,000,000.[15]

While these figures measure *something*, it's important to keep many questions in mind before you decide to net consumers armed only with worth figures. In other words: examine the research before you examine the affluent consumers it measures. The following questions represent some aspects of the total net worth package of information you should consider carefully, especially when hunting the highly desirable but often camouflaged affluent spender.

How does the research define net worth?

It's safe to say that much of the current research citing net worth figures relies on one or more of these familiar factors: home equity, financial portfolios (including stocks, mutual funds, bonds, checking, savings, and money market accounts, etc.), personal assets (precious metals, jewelry, art, etc.), household assets (expensive equipment in the home, automobiles, etc.); it may also include *actual* earnings and income, *potential* earnings, *real* earnings . . . starting to get the picture now? Sometimes the image of net worth itself can be as clear as mud, made muddier by the variety (and there are many) of different calculations of what an individual, a family, or a household is worth. And you only make life harder for yourself if you try to compare (or average) net worth data from a couple of different sources; no one has yet had much success combining apples and oranges into one fruit.

Clear data that defines its terms is available, but difficult to find. Exhibit 1-7 is particularly useful in that it clearly defines its terms, and it takes a comparative look at its own data as well.

Exhibit 1-7.   1986 Financial profiles (by age group, values are medians)

Financial characteristics	All households	Baby Boomers	Pre-Boomers	Elderly
Liquid assets*	$3,000	$2,000	$4,200	$5,601
Net worth	$42,630	$20,634	$70,542	$59,898
(without home equity)	*($14,365)*	*($9,480)*	*($22,628)*	*($16,427)*
Income**	$21,137	$22,333	$28,662	$12,115
Savings rate***	10.0%	9.2%	14.2%	7.0%
(without home equity)	*(4.7%)*	*(5.3%)*	*(4.8%)*	*(1.0%)*

* Liquid Assets include: stocks, mutual funds, bonds, checking/savings accounts, money market accounts, and CDs.
**Income is the average of the median 1983,1984, and 1985 annual incomes. It could be viewed as "permanent income."
***Savings rate is calculated as the change in household net worth from 1983 to 1986 as a percent of household income from 1983 through 1985. The first rate includes changes in home equity; the second rate does not.

Source: *1983 and 1986 Surveys of Consumer Finances*, Board of Governors of the Federal Reserve System (tabulations of unpublished data) listed in *Demographics in the U.S.: The Segmenting of Housing Demand*, National Association of Realtors.

How does the most common denominator of net worth affect the measurement of affluent net worth?

Though the previous chart is uncommon in its clarity and specificity, its emphasis on home equity is a common theme in research statistics on net worth. Home equity is the most important component of net worth for two-thirds of all U.S. families who live in a home they own, but economic forecasts suggest that home ownership may not drive a family's net worth growth in the nineties. The more diversified your financial portfolio (and affluents are no stranger to this idea), the better your chances to keep—and probably enhance—your net worth. Married homeowners—across all age groups—have a greater net worth than their renting counterparts, with or without home equity included (and affluents are more likely to be married than the total U.S. population).[16]

Again—with affluents in mind—we can see how education plays a major role in factoring current and projected net worth: 67% of net worth for those homeowners with a high school education or less is based on home equity, compared to 55% for those with a college education who have a diversified portfolio.[17] This particular example demonstrates two key ideas about translating general and net worth statistics into a descriptive formula of affluence:

- You can't lose by cross-referencing at *least* one other factor (marital status, the affluent habit of keeping a diversified financial portfolio, education) with any single figure (net worth) you evaluate; and,
- When you add one of these additional factors to your own calculations, you turn off the beaten path to keep up with the affluents, who will probably not follow the general trend of things (net worth decreasing as home equity falters in a weaker economy).

How does net worth affect spending?

The bottom line: not reliably. If you've ever gone out to a nice restaurant with a wealthy friend or relative, if you've ever watched them as they ordered the cheapest thing on the menu, and if you've ever watched *them* watching *you* at the end of the meal, waiting for you to pull out your emergency stash of cash, then you've learned the painful lesson: the haves are sometimes the spend-nots. On the other hand, you've probably gone out to a very fancy restaurant at a time you didn't consider yourself affluent, because you felt like doing something special. In both of these instances, affluence is a state of mind, a style of living—and spending.

No measure of net worth will enable you to predict (with any accuracy) which consumers will spend affluently; it won't always tell you who has the money to spend, because we've all somehow found the money for purchases that seemed outrageously luxurious and suddenly absolutely necessary. Sizeable portions of the affluent market have more ambition, savvy, spending power, and credit than they have net worth. The widow with $500,000 in ten dollar bills in her mattress, which would no doubt qualify her as the owner of at least one considerable household asset, is not as real-affluent as the 26-year-old Assistant Editor at Harper & Row who is unmarried, has no home equity, never manages to save (let alone invest) her money, and earns $27,000 a year, but drives a late model Prelude with the CD player blasting on her way to the shopping mall. All of which leads us to our next category of measuring affluence: discretionary income.

4. Discretionary Income

At first glance, this chunk of consumer cash, especially for those marketers offering goods and services beyond the basic requirements of food and shelter, seems like an ideal way to measure what money affluent consumers can choose to spend in any way they like. Not to be confused with disposable income (after tax income, but used to pay bills for essentials), discretionary income is a *portion* of the disposable income of a household.

Discretionary income is also additionally (and more specifically) defined as the amount of money which would permit a family or an individual to maintain a standard of living comfortably higher than the average for similar families or individuals. But beware of concrete definitions of discretionary income. Comparisons between one household's discretionary wealth and another's depend upon a host of psychographic and demographic variables (for example, it is difficult to calculate how wealthy or comfortable someone with a high income feels; also, childless couples tend to have higher percentages of spendable income, as do singles). *The amount of spendable cash that is left over for luxuries and excitement can have little to do with how much income is earned, even less to do with how much of that money an affluent will feel he or she can spend, and, often, nothing whatsoever to do with what an affluent will buy.*

Nevertheless, you will frequently encounter this concept and measurement of income that consumers will supposedly spend at their discretion. It is therefore useful to examine the leading interpretations and most commonly accepted measurements of discretionary income, if only to enable you to pick and choose what you can use and what you can discard. We will step in to press our point about how discretionary income figures must be used in combination with other consumer profile factors, pointing out key areas where quantitative measurement of discretionary income overlaps with consideration of the affluent mindstyle of discretionary income.

Exhibit 1-8.   Profile of affluent income groups with discretionary income (DI), by share and index

(U.S. average=100 Index, all figures rounded)

	$50,000-74,999	$75,000-99,999	$100,000+
Share of all U.S. households	11%	3%	2%
Share of DI households	32%	11%	8%
Index to all DI households	279	346	346
Share of all spendable DI	29%	21%	29%
Index of avg. amount of DI per household	93	185	384

Source: *A Marketer's Guide to Discretionary Income*, Census Bureau/The Conference Board

---

According to *A Marketer's Guide to Discretionary Income*, one-third of all U.S. households have discretionary income (DI). For those with DI, the average amount is $12,300 a year-money to burn, play with, invest, express themselves with. Most likely to have DI are: the well-educated (5+ years of college education defines 60% of those with discretionary income, averaging $18,250 per household); dual-income married-couple households (41%, averaging $13,300 per household); those aged 55-59 (35%, averaging $14,600); and homeowners (35%, averaging $13,300).

Households earning more than $50,000 per year possess the lion's share of these extra dollars—79% of the United States' $319 billion total discretionary dollars are in their hands. Not surprising is a positive correlation between total income and discretionary income. What perhaps comes as news is the extreme concentration of these "luxury" dollars in affluent hands. Half of all discretionary dollars are controlled by households earning more than $75,000; a third, by those earning more than $100,000. These findings underscore the concentration of discretionary income among the upper affluent: $75,000+ households represent 19% of all households with discretionary income, but they control 50% of all discretionary dollars; $100,000+ households represent 8% of all discretionary income households, but they control 29% of discretionary dollars.

Exhibit 1-9.   Upper income group households: total number, pretax and post-tax income

Annual household income	Number of households	Average before tax income	Average after tax income
$50-74,999	10,085,000	$59,437	$45,172
$75-99,999	2,938,000	$84,725	$61,440
$100,000+	1,984,000	$142,032	$85,475

Source: *A Marketer's Guide to Discretionary Income*, Census Bureau/The Conference Board

---

Some take the increases in DI in the 1980s as a clear expression of an affluence explosion. To get a sense of the dramatic increase in discretionary income in the U.S., put together the increase in the number of households with discretionary income and the mean amount received—a 22% increase in four years ('83 to '87), from $262 billion to $319 billion. The mid-1980s saw an unprecedented leap in the affluent segment's size and resources for luxury spending.

On an absolute basis, in 1988, affluents spent $48,718 of their estimated $67,199 income, or 73%. Average consumers spent $25,892, or 91% of their $28,540 income. The most obvious assumption is that non-affluents spend out of need—the basics are covered, leaving little for luxury or discretionary spending. On the other hand, affluents devote larger portions of their outflow dollars to non-necessities like apparel (6.2%) and entertainment (5.9%). Education and donations are also high on the affluent spending agenda, claiming 1.5% and 3.8% of discretionary dollars, respectively.[18]

The first letters in dual income may stand for discretionary income to some researchers. A word of caution here: as we mentioned earlier, beware of taking dual income measurements at face value; some dual income households may have strong working legs and weak financial legs—or *more* legs representing more people in the house to feed. Just over two-fifths (45%) of all U.S. households have 2+ persons working, but almost three-fifths (65%) of discretionary income households have two or more workers. The nation's average household pretax income is $30,800, vs. $56,605 in discretionary income households. Here's a statistic that could make you rethink the household income benchmark of $50,000 as too *high* to encompass all of your potential affluent market, if you're concentrating on discretionary income alone: while homes with annual earnings of $40,000+ constitute just over a quarter of the population, they account for well over two-thirds of those in the discretionary income brackets, and they control almost 90% of all discretionary income.[19]

Another way to present the potential spending power of high-income households is to look at what portion of those in each income bracket have extra, discretionary dollars (exhibit 1-10).

Exhibit 1-10. Measurements of discretionary income (by household income)

Annual household income	% with discretionary income	Average discretionary income per household
<$15,000	0.7%	$ 1,014
$15-19,999	7.5%	$2,304
$20-24,999	11.7%	$3,438
$25-29,999	21.5%	$3,737
$30-34,999	31.8%	$4,700
$35-39,999	37.4%	$5,841
$40-49,999	55.5%	$6,746
$50-74,999	80.8%	$11,493
$75-99,999	100%	$22,818
$100,000+	100%	$47,320

Source: *A Marketer's Guide to Discretionary Income*, Census Bureau/The Conference Board

Now that we've measured how much discretionary income is out there (as well as where it's hiding, even in some of the atypical income categories), it's time to trace discretionary dollars back one step further. The wallet is connected to the hand bone, and the hand reaching for the wallet is connected to the . . . *mindstyle*. Examining Simmons' Get Set, a group of consumers selected on the basis of their actual buying behavior, not income (see the Psychodemographic section later this chapter), research reveals that high income may not translate into high spending. Other factors that may be more important than the size of the household coffers: attitudes toward money, circumstance affecting cash flow, and low disposable income (due to other financial commitments).[20] While 37% of affluents (household income $50,000+) describe themselves as "not too careful about spending,"[21] only 1% of us freely label ourselves as rich. A Gallup Poll of Americans (affluents and non-affluents alike) indicates that people say the following reasons are very important reasons for wanting to be rich: not worrying in an emergency (81%); college for children (79%) and giving to charity (63%); a big house ranks high for 16%, *followed* by expenses like an expensive car (10%), maid/servants (10%), expensive clothes (8%), or lavish entertainment (6%).[22] Another survey finds that only 14% of affluents feel that they're very well off. Forty percent say they don't feel financially secure; 20% don't even feel well off; just one-quarter feel they have "made it." Furthermore, two-thirds feel some guilt about being affluent.[23] Yet the Gallup Poll also reveals that many Americans could live with that kind of guilt; the poll says that the majority of those questioned said they would rather be rich than not.

The human elements—the mindstyle elements—of these findings throw a monkey wrench into the smooth running of the discretionary income calculator. If the primary reason consumers want to be rich is to achieve some kind of security for themselves and for their families, the reality of the situation could be explained to them by the 40% of affluents who do not feel financially secure.

- Do these affluents nevertheless spend freely, "not too careful about spending"? (You have to check spending and savings patterns.)
- Do non-affluents, denied the security of a substantial amount of wealth they would not have to touch to cover their everyday expenses, settle for purchasing products and services that *represent* affluence—and security? (You have to check a list of products and services that they actually buy, not just what they imagine they would buy if they felt wealthy.)

- Do the three-fourths of affluents who don't feel they have "made it"—not to mention the two-thirds of affluents who say they feel some guilt about being affluent—want to continue living in the "insecure" and "guilty" way they are now, for just as long as they can? (You bet they do; you have to check other research. A case in point: when asked if "being able to maintain my current lifestyle in retirement" was an "important goal" to them, 89% of those with a household income of $50,000–$74,999, and 92% of those with a household income of $75,000+ agreed that it was an important goal.)[24]

Another wild card to consider, especially in times of an economic recession: one consumer's luxury is another's necessity. For affluents, luxuries have a curious way of turning into necessities; they may be *necessary* to the lifestyle they enjoy. For non-affluents (with that healthy chunk of discretionary income), distinctions between necessity and luxury may vacillate, more closely tied and sensitively tuned to shifts in their personal wealth or movements in the general U.S. economy. And you have to keep your eye on the busy affluents—constantly defining and redefining the definition of luxury—who can make a seeming intangible like time into a curious commodity. The luxury of time (and the products and services that offer affluents more of it) becomes a necessary element of continuing the good life. *Definitively* labeling what things are necessities and luxuries is impossible, and drawing the definitive line separating disposable and discretionary income leaves a parallel degree of ambiguity.

In the spirit of what we think will be the wave of research on affluents in the future, we've found a report that covers discretionary income with a variety of variables in mind. You've seen that some estimates of wealth are strictly objective (income, home value, bank balance), while some are strictly subjective (self-perception, lifestyle choices, goals). The two have come together in a marketing theory that depends on both total family income (TFI) and subjective discretionary income (SDI). [25]

Created in part by William Wells, executive vice president and director of marketing services at DDB Needham Worldwide Advertising, the joint TFI/SDI approach to defining affluence presumes that "a subjective assessment of discretionary income can capture some of the variance that traditional family income measures leave unexplained." Combining income data with subjective, phenomenological data yields a highly refined picture of consumer habits. Within the class of objective wealth (a measure of what people have) lie subclasses of subjective wealth (a measure of what people feel about what they have). Either measure alone is not as powerful an indicator of behavior as the two combined. But "combining SDI and TFI helps explain consumption of certain kinds of goods and services." Because the affluent are not homogenous in their spending patterns, highly-predictive variables like the combination of SDI and TFI "help to explain individual differences within income groups." Consumers with low incomes sometimes behave like consumers with high incomes and vice versa.

Consider fast food items. In the case of Burger King, McDonald's, and pizza restaurants, it is the higher TFI but lower SDI groups who are most likely to eat at such restaurants. "Patronage is predicted by a higher income combined with a feeling on the part of the purchaser that he or she has less to spend. Perhaps higher income predicts a greater likelihood of eating out, but lower SDI predicts that the meal will be at a place considered less expensive." Similar conjunctions of TFI and SDI explain consumption of video games. Higher incomes make purchase more likely, but perception of lower discretionary income (perhaps associated with many children at home) predicts less expensive forms of entertainment—like video games. For food items such as bologna, hotdogs, packaged spaghetti, and dry pizza mix, SDI alone (without TFI) is a significant predictor of purchase. "The data show that consumers of those four products (considered 'economy' purchases) represent all income levels, but the heaviest users are consumers who have lower levels of SDI."

In all cases where SDI is the significant factor, the relationship is a negative one implying that "the feeling that one is not relatively well off may be a more precise indicator than the feeling that one has a lot of extra money to spend." We couldn't agree more.

5. Lifestyle

Designations such as the "Upper Deck" and the "Up Market" sound affluent, and they *are* affluent—if you look at the economic status of those included; however, segments within each of these categories, with different needs and tastes, are bound to spend differently.

Although lifestyle can only measure how consumers are currently living affluently (and not necessarily what they might purchase to more closely match the way they live with their image of the way they want to live), lifestyle begins to approach the intangible mindstyle of affluence.

The following are examples of research techniques that rely less on strict demographics, but use them to target lifestyle features of affluents and segments.

The Upper Deck[26] from Mediamark divides the top 10% of U.S. household income groups into the following segments:

- The Good Life—no employed persons, or head of household not employed;
- Well-Feathered Nests—at least one high income earner and children present;
- No Strings Attached—at least one high-income earner and no children;
- Nanny's in Charge—two or more income earners, none high, and children present;
- Two Careers—two or more income earners, none high, no children present.

Lifestyle is probably the first category we've examined so far that depends upon a variety of factors, some of them very specific, to provide a more well-rounded rubric for cross-referencing affluents. It also enables you to find affluents who might otherwise be shut out from what are usually reliable starting points. For example as shown in exhibit 1-11, if you start from the springboard of education, you will leap right over the Good Life segment—this is the generation that grew up in the Great Depression, and most of them didn't attend college (Index=132, when compared to other consumers with no college experience). Those in The Good Life segment, however, represent 8% of the Upper Deck; they are older, unemployed, and likely to be widows living in $200,000+ homes. Even though their income and net worth are substantial, they're not prowling the mall with shopping list in hand—they've already acquired most of their household goods and feel no need to either replace them with posher products or impress the Joneses. They're basically thrifty, but *still indulge in carefully selected luxuries* (their primary joy being foreign travel). They're the restrained rock of ages types that most of us forget if we think of affluents as dressed-for-success Yuppies. They are in the top 10%, and don't necessarily behave affluently; but they might, depending upon your product or service. (The more affluently-oriented households No Strings Attached and Two Careers will be explored in chapter 5.)[27]

Exhibit 1-11. Indexes for Upper Deck psychographic groups (Index of 100 = median for all Upper Deck households)

	Good Life	Well-Feathered Nests	No Strings Attached	Nanny's in Charge	Two Careers
Male	98	96	115	87	97
Female	103	105	83	115	103
Age: 18-24	61	35	45	180	198
25-34	66	109	77	93	130
35-44	27	199	75	105	38
45-54	49	94	137	86	93
55+	355	16	173	39	63
Single	98	19	60	137	212
Married	93	135	111	86	60
Other	176	36	130	106	109
Post-grad	61	142	126	76	53
College grad or more	67	125	122	80	71
Some college	107	100	83	104	113
No college	132	72	86	120	124
Any child in household	45	234	—	234	—
Home owned	106	107	103	102	86
Value of home over $200,000	140	115	128	56	65
Northeast	79	86	86	114	130
North Central	70	106	93	109	106
South	123	109	112	88	77
West	119	97	105	93	96

Source: *The Upper Deck Report*, Mediamark Research, Inc.

The Management Horizons Consumer Market Matrix defines the Up Market[28] as the upper income quartile of households. The Up Market and its six lifestages are used as a framework for examining the buying behavior of the upper end of the income spectrum. Analysis of the demographics of the Up Market shows:

- 35% are dual-income households;
- 70% are married;
- 55% are childless;
- 37% have two members in the household;
- 38% are married with children;
- 32% are married with no children;
- Up Market male and female household heads are more than twice as likely to be college grads as non-Upper household heads;
- Younger males and females are more educated than their older counterparts.

Typically, affluents are married, parents of teenagers, urban, full-time workers in two-income households. Affluents also live in larger-than-average households—3.2 members, vs. 2.5 for non-affluents. They tend to work harder, play harder, and seek new experiences more actively than do nonaffluents.[29] But something happens to affluents (household income $75,000+) when they hit their mid-forties. Their frantic pace of activity drops, and they start to pay more attention to their communities, their families, and their planet. This transition takes on added significance, of course, as the demographic monolith of Baby Boomers enters its forties. This will be further detailed in chapter 7.

The *Lifestyle Market Analyst* provides a stop-action snapshot of affluents, combining lifestyle activities with considerations of age. Most of today's 18-to-34-year-old affluents will, in time, evolve closely into their current-day older counterparts. Many transitions in values and priorities derive from the maturation process. Examining age-preferred lifestyle segmentation can reveal both today's and tomorrow's trends. Notice the disparity in activities between the junior and senior upscalers (exhibit 1-12).

The Ultra Rich—as defined by Vance Packard in his book *The Ultra Rich, How Much Is Too Much?*—are Americans in the $50 million to $8 billion range, with a 1987 average net worth of $330 million (making them "centimillionaires," if you're lucky enough to need the term to describe your customers). As a matter of fact, this word may describe at least a few of your customers. For according to Packard, "in two or three cases their lifestyles were preposterously unrelated to their great wealth."

Exhibit 1-12. Affluent lifestyles ranked by index—across age spectrum (U.S. total = index of 100)

18-34 Years Old, Income $75,000 and Over

Lifestyle	Index
Snow Skiing Frequently	355
Real Estate Investments	313
Tennis Frequently	294
Racquetball	260
Wines	243
Running/Jogging	222
Career-Oriented Activities	219
Stock/bond Investments	209
Foreign Travel	208
Boating/Sailing	199

35-44 Years Old, Income $75,000 and Over

Lifestyle	Index
Real Estate Investments	299
Tennis frequently	265
Snow Skiing Frequently	262
Personal/home computers	229
Wines	218
Stock/bond Investments	206
Career-Oriented Activities	203
Foreign Travel	202
Running/Jogging	198
Racquetball	183

45-64 Years Old, Income $75,000 and Over

Lifestyle	Index
Real Estate Investments	337
Foreign Travel	278
Stock/Bond Investments	267
Tennis Frequently	246
Wines	226
Attend Cultural/Arts Events	201
Fine Arts/Antiques	189
Golf	184
Personal Home Computer	182
Gourmet Cooking/Fine Foods	174

65 Years and Older, Income $75,000 and Over

Stock/Bond Investments	396
Foreign Travel	352
Real Estate Investments	327
Golf	223
Grandchildren	219
Current Affairs/Politics	214
Attend Cultural/Arts Events	205
Community/Civic Activities	199
Tennis Frequently	186
Fine Arts/Antiques	180

Source: *The Lifestyle Market Analyst,* National Demographics and Lifestyles/SRDS

Another example of why you shouldn't make fast assumptions with the affluent: Arthur Jones, inventor of Nautilus exercise machines, delivers a bomb to the net worth theory and pumps up the lifestyle method of gauging affluents when he is quoted as saying, "I could live on $10,000 to $15,000 a year. I eat very little—maybe $30 a week on food. I don't have an extensive wardrobe. I don't have any hobbies. Occasionally I do go to the movies. I read a lot but often I buy pocketbook editions or borrow from someone and change them around with my employees. Any parties are strictly business."

Some statistics from Packard for your wishbook: "The Federal Reserve Board, in one accounting, labeled people in the top 10% as the Rich, the Very Rich and the Super Rich. The starting point for being merely Rich in 1983 was $419,000 per household (net worth). Below the Rich were the 90% labeled Everybody Else. During the preceding 20 years the net worth of the merely Rich had grown 47% faster, in constant dollars, than that of Everybody Else."

6. Psychogeodemographic Clustering

Assuming that an address reveals more than a resume, Claritas[11] developed the PRIZM system of target marketing. This system breaks down every one of the 36,000 zip codes in the nation into one of 40 categories. The clusters that appear within each zip code, taken together, create "a pecking order of affluence," a spectrum of wealth. The basic assumption is that five factors influence every buying decision made: social rank, mobility, ethnicity, family life cycle, and housing style. The study claims that "although no neighborhood is strictly homogenous in all respects, the system works because the differences among the neighborhoods are more significant than the differences among households within the neighborhoods."

Combining Census data, nationwide consumer surveys, and interviews, the cluster approach to the quest for reliable indicators and determinants of consumer habits "pigeonholes people according to their attitudes and aspirations." Neighborhoods given monikers like Blue Blood Estates, Money & Brains, Furs & Station Wagons, and Urban Gold Coast—the highest on the list of Zip Quality rankings—ccount for only 6% of the American population, but they comprise the most affluent. The results span from the number one cluster, Blue Blood Estates (median annual household income $70,307), to the

40th, Public Assistance ($10,804), creating a national mosaic, a psychogeodemographic paint-by-zip-code.

As the number one cluster, **Blue Blood Estates** (1.1% of U.S. households) is the one to which most Americans, in their dreams, aspire. This cluster holds one-third of the nation's private wealth, 60% of America's corporate stocks, 30% of all interest-bearing assets, and nearly a tenth of the country's real estate. Blue Bloods are the white, college-educated, corporate kingpins and white-collar professionals (like heart surgeons and entertainment lawyers) who paved their way to affluence along roads of hard work: 16-hour days, seven days a week. Marketers will find them in places such as Beverly Hills, CA, Scarsdale, NY, and McLean, VA.

Money & Brains (0.9% of U.S. households) makes for a demographic group "almost cult-oriented toward conspicuous consumption." This second-ranked cluster is comprised of Americans who are highly success oriented, obsessed with health (three times as likely as the average American to shop in health food stores), and who "regard food as a fashion."

The "executive hearth" neighborhoods—**Furs & Station Wagons** (3.2% of U.S. households)—house a career-oriented group who, unlike Money & Brains, save for the future. As a general tendency, *less* affluent clusters look for instant gratification (play the lottery) while the *more* affluent plan and save (invest in long-term stocks and real estate).

The high-rise residents of **Urban Gold Coast** neighborhoods (.5% of U.S. households) are major consumers of all forms of culture—plays, theater, books. Situated in metropolitan areas, Gold Coasters spend much of their time away from home. Sports enjoyed by this urban elite "tend to be any that are expensive, inconvenient, and practiced only in distant places—like the slopes of St. Moritz." Exhibits 1-13 and 1-14 give detailed information on these clusters.

If you don't have the time for a neighborhood evaluation of your fast-paced market of urban affluents, National Demographics and Lifestyles/Standard Rate & Data Service offers a quick-reference ranking of "affluent-populated cities," as shown in exhibit 1-15.[30]

Exhibit 1-13. Profiles of the rich & clustered (national average = 100)

Cluster	High usage		Low usage	
Blue Blood Estates				
1.1% of U.S. households	U.S. Treasury notes	521	Tupperware	47
Primary age range 35-44	Car rentals	398	Chewing tobacco	37
Super-rich suburbs	*The New York Times*	599	*Sports Afield*	22
Single-unit housing	*Architectural Digest*	499	*Ebony*	4
Politically conservative	Rolls Royce	2554	Chevy Impala	47
Sample neighborhoods:	Jaguar	1758	Dodge Diplomat	28
Beverly Hills, CA 90212	Natural cold cereal	179	TV dinners	61
Scarsdale, NY 10583	Lowfat milk	133	Powdered fruit drinks	55
McLean, VA 22101	"Late Night w/ David Letterman"	127	"People's Court"	47
". . .the pinnacle of success to which Americans traditionally aspire. . ."	"Tonight Show"	123	"American Bandstand"	4
Money & Brains				
0.9% of U.S. households	Classical Records	289	Motorcycling	41
Primary age range 45-64	Sailing	252	CB radios	24
Posh in-town neighborhoods	*Forbes*	442	*Field & Stream*	33
Single-unit housing	*Gourmet*	358	*True Story*	14
Politically moderate/conservative	Rolls Royce	1683	Chevy Chevette	48
Sample neighborhoods:	Jaguar	1119	Plymouth Gran Fury	41
Georgetown, Washington, DC 20007	Whole wheat bread	131	Canned meat spreads	74
	Liquid nutritional supplements	131	Canned stews	22
Princeton, NJ 08540	"At the Movies"	138	"Facts of Life"	48
Coral Gables, FL 33146	"Murder, She Wrote"	135	"As the World Turns"	27
". . .well-off intelligentsia, leaders of science, academia, and management. . ."				
Furs & Station Wagons				
3.2% of U.S. households	Country club membership	445	Nonfilter cigarettes	54
Primary age range 35-54	Depilatories	370	Travel by bus	64
Executive communities	*Bon Appetit*	241	*Jet*	32
Single-unit housing	*Forbes*	216	*Grit*	0
Politically conservative	BMW 5 Series	480	Pontiac Phoenix	69
Sample neighborhoods:	Audi	460	Plymouth Gran Fury	64
Pomona, CA 91765	Rye/pumpernickel bread	222	Non-dairy creamers	80
Reston, VA 22091	Lowfat milk	125	Meat tenderizers	80
Plano, TX 75075	"60 Minutes"	122	"Highway to Heaven"	59
". . .the nesting ground of the American executive. . ."	"Nightline"	120	"Friday Night Videos"	51
Urban Gold Coast				
.5% of U.S. households	Aperitif/Specialty wines	1243	Powerboats	0
Primary age groups 18-24, 65+	Pregnancy tests	378	Fishing Rods	19
Upscale urban enclaves	*Metropolitan Home*	2227	*Car Craft*	0
High-rise housing	*Atlantic Monthly*	1756	Hunting	0
Politically liberal/moderate	Rolls Royce	352	Chevrolet Nova	1
Sample neighborhoods:	Ferrari	172	Oldsmobile Omega	0
Upper East Side, Manhattan, NY 10021	Tomato/vegetable juice	150	Pork sausages	35
	Fresh chicken	124	Canned corned-beef hash	24
Upper West Side, Manhattan, NY 10024	"Nightline"	154	"Lifestyles of the Rich & Famous"	35
Fort Dearborn, Chicago, IL 60611	"Late Night w/ David Letterman"	152	"Dance Fever"	0
". . .metropolitan lifestyles. . .limousine liberals. . ."				

Source: *The Clustering of America*, by Michael J. Weiss, Harper & Row

Exhibit 1-14. Zip Quality rankings, by PRIZM cluster (zip quality is based on income, home value, education, and occupation)

Zip Quality/cluster	Median income	Median home value	% college grads
1. Blue Blood Estates	$70,307	$200,000+*	51%
2. Money & Brains	$45,798	$150,755	46%
3. Furs & Station Wagons	$50,086	$132,725	38%
4. Urban Gold Coast	$36,838	$200,000+*	51%
National median	$24,269	$64,182	16%

*The upper census limit for home values is $200,000+, therefore these figures are estimates

Another tack for pinpointing consumers on the affluence map is to zero in on whole regions at a time by using a kind of buying power ritcher scale to calculate a particular *market's* ability to buy (see exhibits 1-16 and 1-17). *Sales & Marketing Management (S&MM)* outlines this approach in its "1988 Survey of Buying Power." *S&MM* has developed an exclusive classification, Effective Buying Income (EBI—all personal income less personal tax, nontax payments), which they claim is more sensitive than what is customarily referred to as disposable or after-tax income because it subtracts any compensation paid to military or diplomatic personnel stationed overseas. *S&MM* has also constructed a Buying Power Index (BPI) for metros, counties and cities throughout America. This index combines properly weighted data on population, EBI, and retail sales, thus calculating a particular market's ability to buy relative to the United States as a whole (U.S.=100).

Crunching these numbers with population figures (also charted) can produce a Performance Index (PI) as well as customized BPIs that help set sales goals/quotas and define sales territories, develop marketing strategies, and select test markets.

The latest edition of the same survey, using the $50,000 cutoff in EBI (personal income less taxes) to categorize a total of 16.3% of all U.S. households, lists metros with high spending power. The majority of metros listed in exhibit 1-18 also rank in the top 25 areas based on total affluent population, which means a marketer can reach a large audience composed largely of affluents.

Exhibit 1-15. Cities with high affluent frequencies (by age range, household income $75,000 or more)

		City	Index
Age: 18-34	1.	Washington, DC	270
	2.	Boston, MA	210
	3.	New York, NY	200
	4.	San Francisco, CA	200
	5.	Charlottesville, VA	160
	6.	Los Angeles, CA	160
	7.	Hartford, CT	150
	8.	Atlanta, GA	130
	9.	Austin, TX	130
	10.	Miami, FL	130
Age: 35-44	1.	Washington, DC	236
	2.	Boston, MA	186
	3.	San Francisco, CA	177
	4.	New York, NY	168
	5.	Charlottesville, VA	164
	6.	Hartford, CT	159
	7.	Atlanta, GA	150
	8.	Los Angeles, CA	145
	9.	Dallas, TX	141
	10.	Baltimore, MD	136
Age: 45-64	1.	Washington, DC	241
	2.	New York, NY	195
	3.	Boston, MA	187
	4.	Hartford, CT	167
	5.	San Francisco, CA	164
	6.	Baltimore, MD	141
	7.	Los Angeles, CA	141
	8.	Charlottesville, VA	138
	9.	Detroit, MI	131
	10.	Atlanta, GA	128
Age: 65+	1.	Palm Springs, CA	414
	2.	West Palm Beach, FL	400
	3.	Sarasota, FL	357
	4.	Ft. Myers, FL	329
	5.	Charlottesville, VA	243
	6.	Washington, DC	243
	7.	Miami, FL	200
	8.	New York, NY	200
	9.	Richmond, VA	186
	10.	Santa Barbara, CA	186

Note: Data ranks cities by density of affluents, not by absolute numbers of affluents. Read: "the ratio of 18-34-year-old affluents to total population is 2.7 times greater in Washington, DC, than in the nation as a whole." etc.

Source: *The Lifestyle Market Analyst*, National Demographics and Lifestyles/SRDS

Exhibit 1-16. Regional summaries of retail sales for 1987 (figures rounded)

Retail Sales by Store Group

	1987 Total Retail Sales (millions)	% of U.S.	Retail Sales per Household	Food (millions)	Eating & Drinking Places (millions)	General merchandise (millions)	Furniture/ Furnishings/ Appliances (millions)	Automotive (millions)	Drug (millions)
New England	$102,981	7%	$21,473	$20,267	$10,749	$10,671	$4,646	$22,254	$3,245
Mid Atlantic	$236,256	15%	$16,775	$52,694	$21,776	$25,629	$14,539	$48,105	$8,569
East North Central	$255,552	17%	$16,426	$48,999	$24,822	$32,680	$13,314	$57,699	$10,311
West North Central	$109,601	7%	$16,410	$21,781	$10,202	$14,389	$4,686	$25,723	$2,982
South Atlantic	$272,739	18%	$17,292	$56,094	$25,470	$31,871	$15,879	$62,956	$10,520
East South Central	$81,880	5%	$14,513	$16,723	$6,653	$10,725	$4,192	$19,981	$3,557
West South Central	$163,117	11%	$16,739	$38,045	$15,058	$19,148	$8,146	$35,406	$4,744
Mountain	$80,943	5%	$16,255	$18,351	$8,060	$9,068	$4,364	$16,026	$2,598
Pacific	$241,829	16%	$17,790	$48,980	$27,765	$26,387	$14,256	$49,931	$9,527
Total U.S.	$1,544,897	100%	$17,005	$321,934	$150,555	$180,569	$84,022	$338,080	$56,064

Source: "1988 Survey of Buying Power," *Sales & Marketing Management*, Bill Communications, Inc.

Exhibit 1-17. Regional summaries for 1992 projections (figures rounded)

	1992 total EBI (millions)	% change 1987-1992	1987	1992	1992 total retail sales (millions)	% change 1987-1992	1987	1992
New England	$291,804	47%	$41,473	$57,926	$154,587	50%	6.6	6.1
Mid Atlantic	$792,333	43%	$39,276	$54,231	$344,909	46%	16.3	15.7
East N. Central	$798,360	47%	$35,007	$49,896	$373,529	46%	16.9	16.5
West N. Central	$335,164	48%	$33,892	$48,287	$160,499	46%	7.1	7.0
South Atlantic	$804,549	54%	$33,070	$46,442	$422,717	55%	16.9	17.4
East S. Central	$240,660	54%	$27,755	$40,572	$123,010	50%	5.3	5.3
West S. Central	$471,075	55%	$31,195	$45,171	$235,417	44%	10.1	10.2
Mountain	$248,692	59%	$31,412	$44,747	$122,341	51%	5.1	5.3
Pacific	$819,684	52%	$39,813	$55,271	$369,610	53%	16.1	16.5
Total U.S.	$4,802,322	50%	$35,255	$49,682	$2,306,618	49%	100.0	100.0

Source: "1988 Survey of Buying Power," *Sales & Marketing Management*, Bill Communications, Inc.

Exhibit 1-18. Metros with the highest percentage of house-holds with EBI of $50,000 or more

Metro	% of HH with EBI=$50K+	Median EBI	Number of HHs in thousands with EBI=$50K (rank)
San Jose, CA	40.2%	$41,717	204.8 (15)
Bridgeport-Stamford-Norwalk-Danbury, CT	40.2%	$40,537	120.7 (27)
Middlesex-Somerset-Hunterdon, NJ	38.7%	$41,254	134.8 (24)
Nassau-Suffolk, NY	38.4%	$41,534	337.3 (7)
Bergen-Passaic, NJ	36.4%	$38,404	176.3 (21)
Washington, DC	36.3%	$38,489	508.1 (3)
Trenton, NJ	34.9%	$37,057	41.7 (69)
Oxnard-Ventura, CA	33.7%	$37,196	71.9 (44)
Anaheim-Santa Ana, CA	33.6%	$37,096	271.5 (9)
Newark, NJ	32.3%	$34,806	224.1 (12)
Manchester-Nashua, NH	32.0%	$36,437	39.5 (74)
San Francisco, CA	31.5%	$34,227	212.6 (14)
Oakland, CA	31.3%	$34,640	243.4 (10)
Monmouth, NJ	29.9%	$33,742	112.6 (32)
Lake County, IL	29.4%	$35,398	49.1 (59)
Boston-Lawrence-Salem-Lowell-Brockton, MA	29.3%	$33,558	411.3 (5)
Anchorage, AK	29.2%	$33,627	24.3 (95)
Hartford-New Britain-Middletown-Bristol, CT	28.2%	$34,135	117.4 (30)
New Haven-Waterbury-Meriden, CT	27.0%	$32,636	79.8 (41)
Honolulu, HI	26.8%	$31,666	71.8 (45)
Seattle, WA	26.6%	$32,665	198.8 (16)
Kenosha, WI	26.5%	$33,820	11.8 (166)
Portsmouth-Dover-Rochester, NH	26.4%	$33,444	32.7 (83)
Los Angeles-Long Beach, CA	25.8%	$29,561	816.9 (1)
Santa Rosa-Petaluma, CA	25.0%	$30,812	36.6 (77)
U.S. Total	16.3%	$24,488	15,013.3

Source: "1989 Survey of Buying Power," *Sales & Marketing Management*, Bill Communications, Inc.

Also offered in the survey are the latest projections for the wealthiest metros of the future, with a specific breakdown of metro area and state (exhibit 1-19).

Exhibit 1-19. Tomorrow's wealthiest metros: average EBI (DI) in 1993

Metro	1993 Average EBI
Bridgeport-Stamford-Norwalk-Danbury, CT	$78,675
Middlesex-Somerset-Hunterdon, NJ	$72,197
Nassau-Suffolk, NY	$72,038
San Jose, CA	$71,105
Bergen-Passaic, NJ	$70,691
Trenton, NJ	$69,303
Lake County, IL	$67,650
Washington, DC	$67,178
Newark, NJ	$65,449
Anaheim-Santa Ana, CA	$65,035
Oxnard-Ventura, CA	$64,305
San Francisco, CA	$63,809
Monmouth-Ocean, NJ	$62,891
Manchester-Nashua, NH	$62,700
Boston-Lawrence-Salem-Lowell-Brockton, MA	$61,981
Oakland, CA	$61,180
Honolulu, HI	$60,618
Hartford-New Britain-Middletown-Bristol, CT	$60,302
Kenosha, WI	$59,098
Anchorage, AK	$58,954
New Haven-Waterbury-Meriden, CT	$58,470
San Diego, CA	$57,584
Portsmouth-Dover-Rochester, NH	$57,506
Seattle, WA	$56,845
Los Angeles-Long Beach, CA	$56,607

Source: "1989 Survey of Buying Power," *Sales & Marketing Management*, Bill Communications, Inc.

Using any Psychogeodemographic clustering method of marketing to the affluent is a bit like grabbing your trick-or-treat bag and heading for the neighborhood with the biggest houses: you don't know for *sure* that the treats will be better (or more plentiful), but you figure that they *should* be; at the very least, you know that they *could* be.

7. Spending Patterns

Super Innovators
This group is a Mediamark[31] psychographic subsegment of consumers eager to try new products in several product categories. Supers do not necessarily fit into traditional affluent-income strata, but they very nearly define the new affluent consumer mindstyle. In terms of share of buyers of a variety of products, Super Innovators command a marketing value worth three to five times their size (exhibit 1-20). The number of Super Innovators, however, has declined in the five years since the initial study. Jerry Ohlsten, director of product development

at MRI, has a hunch that it's not a change in the market but a change in the products offered—they're not new enough. When the thrill of the hunt is gone, Supers wait until something really exciting appears.

Exhibit 1-20. Super Innovators selected product ownership (100=average U.S. adult)

	U.S. Adults	Super Innovators	Super Innovators' share
Total population	174,900,000	12,869,000	7%
	Percentage	Index	Percentage
Home products			
burglar alarm	7	315	23
greenhouse, sunroom	1	327	24
solar heat/hot water	1	302	22
skylights	1	397	29
phone answering machine	13	332	25
water filter	6	307	23
Electronics products			
compact laser disc	5	332	24
home personal computer	14	319	24
modem	2	419	31
monitor	6	410	30
software (personal finance, taxes, investments)	3	509	37
video camera	3	312	23
Leisure products and sports participation			
home gym system	3	398	29
sports watch, chronograph	3	374	28
Financial			
own investment property	4	325	24
travel & entertainment credit cards	9	310	23
financial planning	5	423	31
money market funds	7	351	26
Leisure activities			
aerobic exercise	10	301	22
electronic games	7	340	25
electric trains	3	295	22
health clubs	9	380	28
photography	14	281	21

Source: *Consumer Innovators*, Mediamark Research, Inc.

Super Innovators are on the young side (57% are age 25 to 44, with heaviest representation among 35 to 44-year-olds), educated (65% attended or graduated from college, vs. 35% of all U.S. adults; exhibit 1-21), married (nearly half, 47%, have been married 10 years or more, vs. 42% of all adults), and have children of all ages, with preteens and teens particularly evident in the household. They aren't the wealthy— less than half (47%) have $50,000+ annual household incomes, with two wage-earners being the norm. Supers don't have jobs, they have careers, and they're heavily concentrated in suburbs of large counties in the West (with above-average numbers in the East).

Exhibit 1-21. Super Innovators education index (100 = average U.S. adult)

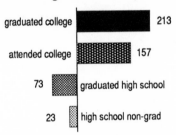

Source: *Consumer Innovators*, Mediamark Research, Inc.

They're the community movers and shakers, belonging to business, civic and religious organizations. Besides being exceptionally active, visible, and articulate citizens, they are also opinionated. They get their ideas published; they write and visit public officials; they address public meetings. They're also far more involved with fund-raising and volunteer work than the average U.S. adult.

Spenders

For years the older consumer was assigned low points on the outer rim of the marketer's dartboard. The older consumer was generally viewed as set in his or her ways and sufficiently established as to not inspire images of the "shop 'til you drop" marketer's dream. Times have changed and the consumer aged 45–64 has been documented and credited with bulls-eye status. In general, this age group has reached the point of highest earnings potential.

Impact Resources has surveyed more than 24,000 people in high-traffic retail centers. *Spenders (45-64)* contains a profile of 38,791 consumers surveyed through self-administered, anonymous questionnaires in 35 U.S. markets. It compares that category labeled Spenders with consumers 18+ (a total sample size of 186,912), providing marketers with a comprehensive view of these Spenders' demographics, lifestyle, shopping, and media habits (see exhibit 1-22). Here are the findings in the categories as noted:

Employment

- more likely be professionals/managers.

TV News

- news watchers—TV *news* viewership during all times of the day, particularly early evening broadcasts, is greater than the average consumer (18+), as is viewership of religious programming (Index = 124).

Radio

- particular about radio listening, preferring formats such as Big Band (Index=181), Classical (Index=126), Easy Listening (Index=184), Country (Index=124) and News/Talk (Index=145); however, listening to the radio is less than average at all times of the day.

Newspapers

- are more likely than the average consumer to read the local news, business/finance, editorial, and national/foreign news sections of the newspaper; reading of ad circulars in newspapers is similar to the average adult.

Shopping

- are more likely to use coupons than the average adult and slightly more likely to shop by catalog/direct mail; convenience stores and TV home-shopping programs hold little allure (Index=72 each).

Fast Food

- eat at McDonalds, although it's not as popular with Spenders as with the general population; Spenders are more likely to have no preference.

Sit-down meals

- nearly half spend $30 for two people one or more times a month at a full-service restaurant.

Investing

- are investors—a higher percentage of Spenders have financial investments, such as money market funds and CDs, compared to the average consumer (18+).

Cars

- partial to American-made cars, most of all to Lincoln/Mercury, and Buick/Oldsmobile; their cars are usually less than five years old.[32]

The Get Set

In recognition of the affluent-mindstyle path to tracking affluence, Simmons Market Research Bureau has corralled the Get Set,[33] a group comprised of those whose income levels don't necessarily qualify them for affluent status when using the $50,000+ benchmark, but who "think spending is their inalienable right, their American heritage." These "zestful purchasers of premium products and services" must be considered affluent mindstylers even though the most commonly used traditional criteria is not met. These are trendsetters, experimenters, those who will lead the masses in more upscale-style purchasing habits. The Get Set is:

- skewed to males: 55%, vs. 45% females;
- tend to be employed in professional/managerial occupations; however, 20% don't work at all;
- college grads: 44%; more than 30% have never attended college;
- have average household income of more than $35,000—but fewer than half of Get Set households earn $50,000 or more, confirming that behavior rather than income is the clearer determinant of affluence.

According to the 1988 Simmons Study of Media and Markets, the Get Set accounts for only 16% of the population, but also accounts for the upscale purchasing habits noted in exhibit 1-23.

Exhibit 1-22. Profile and comparison of Spenders age 45 to 64 & 18+ U.S. adults

■ Spenders
◩ U.S. adults

Spenders' above average occupations

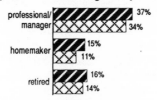

professional/manager 37% / 34%
homemaker 15% / 11%
retired 16% / 14%

Newspaper sections regularly read

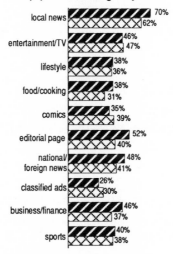

local news 70% / 62%
entertainment/TV 46% / 47%
lifestyle 38% / 36%
food/cooking 38% / 31%
comics 35% / 39%
editorial page 52% / 40%
national/foreign news 48% / 41%
classified ads 26% / 30%
business/finance 46% / 37%
sports 40% / 38%

Investments

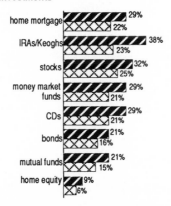

home mortgage 29% / 22%
IRAs/Keoghs 38% / 23%
stocks 32% / 25%
money market funds 29% / 21%
CDs 29% / 21%
bonds 21% / 16%
mutual funds 21% / 15%
home equity 9% / 6%

Source: *MA*RT Spenders (45-64)*, Impact Resources

Exhibit 1-23.   The Get Set's upscale purchasing habits

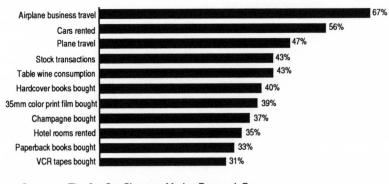

Airplane business travel	67%
Cars rented	56%
Plane travel	47%
Stock transactions	43%
Table wine consumption	43%
Hardcover books bought	40%
35mm color print film bought	39%
Champagne bought	37%
Hotel rooms rented	35%
Paperback books bought	33%
VCR tapes bought	31%

Source: *The Get Set*, Simmons Market Research Bureau

Get Setters are highly correlated to "Actualizers," "Achievers," and "Fulfilleds," categories we'll explore later in this chapter. You can also approach them by knowing what they are not:

Experiencers

- Get Set Index 77—young, vital, enthusiastic, impulsive, and rebellious. Highly ambivalent about their beliefs, they seek variety and excitement, savoring the new, the offbeat, and the risky. Experiencers are avid consumers of clothing, fast food, music, and videos.

Strivers

- Get Set Index 44—seek motivation, self-definition, and approval from the world around them. They are striving for a secure place in life. Unsure of themselves, they are deeply concerned about the opinions of others. They live conventional lives and respect authority. As consumers, they favor established products that convey status.

Makers

- Get Set Index 39—practical people who have constructive skills and value self-sufficiency. They live within a traditional context of family, work, and recreation and have little interest in what lies outside that context. They are unimpressed by material possessions other than those with a practical purpose (tools, pickup trucks).

Believers

- Get Set Index 35—conservative, conventional people with strong beliefs and attachments to traditional institutions: family, church, community, and nation. They follow established routines and, as consumers, are highly predictable, favoring American products and established brands.

Strugglers

- Get Set Index too small to determine—chronically poor, ill-educated, and low-skilled people without strong social bonds. Strugglers show little evidence of self-orientation and are often despairing and passive. Their chief concerns are for immediate security and safety. They represent a very modest market for most products but are loyal to favorite brands.

Exhibit 1-24 illustrates what the Get Set *is*.

The Exclusive Set

And now, Simmons Market Research Bureau, the same company that developed the Get Set profile, has focused its research on the highest-income consumer echelon. Presenting: the Exclusive Set. Qualifying household income: $75,000. Simmons' Exclusive Set marks an important break from past studies in that the $75,000 benchmark, while ultimately reducing the affluent population base, defines a clear separation from the general market. As we've said, we expect this higher income qualification to be the general trend in almost all types of research on the affluent.

Because of its relatively tight perimeter, this narrower but immensely valuable segment of the population differs markedly from those earning less than $75,000. They are 2.7 times more likely to be professionals or managers, 2.8 times more likely to have graduated from college, and 1.5 times more likely to live in a metro-suburban area. Those in the Exclusive Set are 8 times more likely to have an individual income of $40,000 or more and are nearly 50 times more likely to have an individual income of $60,000 or more. Among marginally affluent households (earning near or slightly over $50,000),

---

Exhibit 1-24. Get Set statistics (U.S. average index=100)

Public Activities	*Index*
Addressed public meeting	278
Had something published	264
Wrote to public official	247
Active in civic issues	234
Visited public official	224
Contributed to public radio	253
Contributed to public TV	249
Memberships	
Environmentalist group	327
Country club	301
Art association	288
Business club	284
Civic club	280
Health club	265
Religious club	250
Religion	
Jewish	229
Episcopal	212
Presbyterian	147
Lutheran	125
Leisure activities	
Photography	237
Adult education	213
Musical instrument	194
Stamp collecting	183
Woodworking	177
Reading books	175
Cooking for fun	172
Indoor gardening	169
Coin collecting	168
Self-concept	
Amicable, benevolent	152
Intelligent, smart	136
Organized, efficient	135
Creative, inventive	118
Trustworthy, competent	118
Open-minded, liberal	117
Self-assured, confident	115
Kind, good-hearted	114
Buying style	
Cautious; no unknown brands	121
Brand loyal	116
Plan ahead	111
Style-conscious	108
Events during last year	
Sold or changed home	162
Collected from investment	137

(cont.)

(Ex. 1-24 cont.)

Youngest child left	127
Paid off home	114
Events during next year	
Youngest child will leave	151
Will sell or change home	147
Will change jobs	135
Will collect investment	123

Source: *The Get Set*, Simmons Market Research Bureau

it is often the combined earnings of two or even three lesser earners that qualify the household as affluent. What the Exclusive Set reveals is that for higher-income households ($75,000+), it's more likely that a single earner is responsible for the household's affluent status.

A demographic profile shows that the Exclusive Set, as compared to the rest of the population, tends to be older, male, and well-educated (see exhibit 1-25). Simmons estimates there are about 17.5 million consumers in the Exclusive Set, which translates into 7% of the U.S. population.

Power Purchasers and Progressive Patrons

Consumers & Innovation[34] says that consumers who are highly creative and who exhibit novelty-seeking behavior are more likely to spend on innovative products. Adopters of innovation tend to be better educated, economically advantaged, employed in high status occupations, and urbanized/suburbanized. They have frequent exposure to new goods and services due to their high shopping frequency and media exposure, especially print (specifically magazines). The two shopper typology groups that exhibit these characteristics most of all when out to buy are: Power Purchasers and Progressive Patrons, who also happen to be the two shopper types most heavily concentrated in the Up Market and the two heaviest consumption groups of the shopper typologies.

- Power Purchasers are defined as self-indulgent, variety-seeking, and risk-taking.
- Progressive Patrons are also defined as variety-seeking and risk-taking, but are more open-minded, imaginative and more experientially oriented than are Power Purchasers.

Exhibit 1-25. Demographics of the Exclusive Set compared to households earning less than $75,000 per year

	Exclusive Set	HHI <$75,000	Index
Male	52%	47%	110
Female	48%	53%	91
Age 18-24	18%	14%	122
25-34	17%	25%	71
35-49	36%	26%	140
50+	29%	36%	83
Graduated college	46%	16%	279
Attended college	23%	18%	128
Graduated high school	25%	41%	62
Didn't graduate high school	6%	25%	25
Individual Income of <$20,000	16%	33%	48
$20,000-$40,000	18%	23%	79
$40,000+	40%	5%	802
$60,000+	25%	0.5%	4920
Professional/Managers	40%	15%	272
Technical/Sales/Clerical	25%	20%	123
Craft/Precision production	5%	8%	158
Other	5%	18%	27
Metro central city	27%	31%	89
Metro suburban	66%	45%	146
Non-metropolitan	7%	24%	27

Source: *1989 Simmons Exclusive Set*, Simmons Market Research Bureau

Power Purchasers and Progressive Patrons exhibit consistent preferences across many product categories for department stores, off-price stores, and specialty stores. They are willing to sacrifice time, convenience, money, and risk factors for quality. Appeals based upon fine craftsmanship are appropriate for most Up Market segments.

When trying to attract this sophisticated segment, marketers should keep the following in mind:

- Professionals and/or dual income Up Market households, especially those with children, are time-constrained, but when shopping for high-risk items, time-convenience loses importance. Reducing perceived risk and/or increasing convenience are keys to shortening decision-making time.

- Promoting products/services solely on their functional attributes is less effective than focusing upon experiential attributes.
- Better service gains importance in older segments of the Up Market. As the Baby Boom ages, service will become a more important patronage factor.

8. Psychographics

Actualizers, Achievers, Fulfilleds. Psychographic segmentation of the affluent is explored in SRI's VALS II[35] program. Actualizers are on top of the VALS chart. They are: "successful, sophisticated, active, take-charge people with high self-esteem and abundant resources ... image is important, not as evidence of status or power, but as an expression of taste, independence, and character . . . their lives are characterized by richness and diversity. . . their possessions and recreation reflect a cultivated taste for the finer things in life." (When the VALS program is correlated to Simmons' Get Set, analysis shows that Actualizers are three times more likely than average to be Get Setters, with a Get Set Index of 298; U.S. average=100.)

Achievers (Get Set Index=241) are successful career and work-oriented people who like to, and generally do, feel in control of their lives. They value structure, predictability, and stability over risk, intimacy, and self-discovery. As consumers, they favor established products and services that demonstrate their success to their peers.

Fulfilleds (Get Set Index=181) are mature, satisfied, comfortable, reflective people who value order, knowledge, and responsibility. Content with their careers, families, and station in life, their leisure activities tend to center on the home. They are conservative, practical consumers concerned with function, value, and durability in the products they buy.

Achievers, Strivers, Pressured, Adapters, and Traditionals. Kinder? Gentler? Think again. This forecast calls instead for a vortex of materialism to continue building here and around the globe. Its winds will blow an even wider space between the haves and the have-nots, with the former indulgently clamoring for ultraluxury, preferential treatment, sophistication, and self-reward. Swollen as the banks of greed may be, levels will rise. Ever-more-specialized upscale market niches will be the rage, as new standards of having it all shift to higher ground. In fact, the relativization of success means the mountain of luxury has no summit. Who is leading the consumer expedition?

Backer Spielvogel Bates (BSB), with an eye on worldwide consumer attitudes, gives an answer. The combined results of GLOBAL SCAN, TREND SCAN, and FUTURE SCAN, analytic models of current and future consumer behavior, reveal BSB's worldwide class of Achievers whose values determine others', whose desire for control and success is ubiquitous, and whose tendency toward pampering is more passion than predilection. Furthermore, this social class will reign into the next millennium.

BSB's 14-country, 5-continent mammoth study finds 22% of those countries' populations to be Achievers. Though that same percentage applies in the U.S., other countries have different breakdowns. For example, in Japan, 17% of the people are Achievers, and in the United Kingdom, 18%. The U.S., the U.K., and Japan are actually very similar in psychographic makeup, but other countries, like Australia and Spain with their above-average rates of Achievers, differ in profile. BSB is currently cropping their results to service country-by-country research.

Exhibit 1-26. Worldwide breakdown of consumer types (the 5% "unclassified" are omitted)

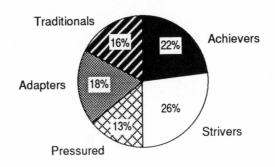

Source: *GLOBAL SCAN*, Backer Spielvogel Bates Worldwide

Achievers

- Sophisticated, the attitude leaders; they shape mass values. Affluent, assertive, and still climbing.

Strivers

- Young (average age 31) on the run, hard-working, seek immediate gratification. Short on time, energy, money—they optimize convenience.

Pressured

- Mostly women who are wedged between the twin responsibilities of income and family. Pressureds have little latitude for pleasure.

Adapters

- In these older consumers, new ideas and trends commingle peacefully with traditional standards. Content with themselves, Adapters contend well with change. They even seek out new activities to enrich their lives.

Traditionals

- Strongly rooted to the past, these consumers resist change, preferring familiar territory over new ground. Their values echo the oldest codes of their countries and cultures.

Achievers comprise a plurality of consumers for luxury goods, exotic vacations, sophisticated drinks, deluxe hotels, premium anything and everything. U.S. Achievers snatch up, for example, 43% of this country's expensive jewels and cars. Japanese Achievers (17% of the population) buy almost half (47%) of that country's expensive jewels and cars. Fancy cameras, nifty ski trip packages, novel fun...all attract Achievers.

The key seems to be the superlative. Almost any service or product can be escalated into a hyperbolic region of personal luxury. Content is secondary to category. The marketer's challenge in seducing Achievers is to take a product to its extremes—the highest endpoints of quality, sophistication, prestige, indulgence, and luxury are where the Achievers want to be. They will buy what either takes them there or proves they are already there. Of course, "there" is a moving target, thus the dance between consumer and marketer promises to be ever-changing.

By projecting current data along future demographic trajectories, BSB evolves GLOBAL SCAN (a picture of what is), into FUTURE SCAN (a picture of what will be). Its prophecy of rampant materialism (which, by the way, runs counter to the findings of many other studies) predicts that today's Achievers will pioneer two new classes in the coming decade: the Accomplished and the Elite. The Accomplished will be mature consumers who are prepared to harvest the rewards of lives spent working for ultrasuccess. Indeed, the middle-aged will, in large part, control affluence. Some younger Achievers will be the first members of a small but very affluent class called the Elite. Together, the Accomplished and the Elite will command center stage, becoming the upper crust of the haves. Glimpses of these lifestyles-in-the-lead will fuel others' hunger for affluence.

Desire for the highest quality of life will intensify, creating new niche industries for both men and women. If it smacks of personal indulgence, pampering, or ego-massaging, it has a place in the future marketplace. The socio-economic hierarchy, which the Achievers now lead and the Accomplished and Elite will lead in the future, creates a psychology of reward. The top recognizes itself as such, partly from the emulation and effusive attention it receives from the rest of society. The affluent internalize this awareness as a strong sense of entitlement, a self-evident right to have "the best." It is through the continual search for ultimate luxury that inroads into new, ultraindulgent markets will be made.

BSB suggests that materialism will flourish as today's Baby Boomers pass their values down to their children. While other social groups will continue to contend with the fear and pressure of material scarcity, Achievers will continue to do just that: achieve. Though everyone confronts walls of frustration and pressure, Achievers readily scale such barriers, amassing renewed confidence and control in the process. Others, especially Strivers, continually collide with their boundaries, and eventually become resigned and helpless and perhaps a little bitter that the glitter is on the other side. Note that a Striver's dollars will often hibernate in a savings account, while an Achiever's dollars will do battle in the uncertain territories of stocks and bonds.

Highly sophisticated Achiever tastes will fuel demand for premium products in all industries. Especially attractive: high-style perfume, cosmetics, indulgent sweets, and "light" foods. Also, today's Achievers will enjoy more entertainment, more vacations, and more dining out in the future. For the escapist have-nots, food is usually a mood-lifter. For Achievers, food is another weapon in their quest for the best. They don't eat just any ice cream, they eat the best. All over the world, Achievers try to eat natural foods (yogurt, herbal tea), yet they yearn for new taste sensations. So, while health is a priority, relentless pursuit of super-sensuous foods will eventually show up as inches on Achievers' waists. Once calories are crucial, they'll look for "light" versions of premium tastes. Those inches, however, can always be melted away at a deluxe health spa.

Self-determination is a battle cry of the affluent. Products and services which reinforce or enhance consumers' control over their lives will succeed. The desire for control however, stretches beyond individual lives into government halls and troubled skies. Achievers are particularly concerned about the environment. They feel strong hostility towards perpetrators of societal ills: corporate polluters and apathetic governments. They won't allow the planet to suffer much longer and want goods, and packaging, to be safe for the globe.

Influentials

Affluence is usually about money and spending mores. There's another form of wealth, though, distributed among the consumer base: the influence of the consumers the Roper Organization has labelled as the Influentials.

While affluents are characterized by dollars, Influentials are characterized by attitudes and actions. From some perspectives, of course, the two intersect. Both consumer groups are wealthy, well-educated, and professionally powerful. The distinctive mark of Influentials, however, is their fervent activism. Simply stated: Influentials act and believe with a passion that they make a difference.

Influentials are interested, aware, connected, striving, celebrating, responsible, and self-determined. Their opinions are strong, their mindset fierce. They see the whole globe—not just their corner of it. They believe in the power of change and in their ability to foster it: they are philosophical freedom fighters. These consumers value creativity and self-actualization as a way of life.

Prime-of-life aged, wealthy, well-educated, professional, and family-oriented, Influentials look much like affluents in demographic make-up. Exhibit 1-27 compares key demography for Influentials and the total population:

Exhibit 1-27.   Demographic profile of Influential Americans vs. total public

Age	Influentials	Total
18-29	20%	28%
30-39	26%	21%
40-49	22%	17%
50-59	14%	12%
60+	18%	22%
Annual Income		
<$15K	13%	27%
$15-$24.9K	18%	23%
$25-$34.9K	23%	21%
$35+	46%	29%
Employment		
Executive/prof.	48%	27%
White collar	26%	28%
Blue collar	25%	44%

Source: *The Influential Americans: Who They Are, How To Reach Them,* The Roper Organization, Inc.

What distinguishes Influentials from the rest of the consumer base is their supreme connectedness to their surroundings. For example, 68% are very interested in worldwide current events, as compared with 33% of all consumers. More than half (53%) can name both of their state senators—only 35% of all Americans can do that. Their values—family, religion, work, education—reflect a sense of interdependence and achieving.

Summary of Research Methods

We've explored the primary tools currently available to profile the affluent. As you have seen, certain tools are far more important than others. Those approaches that segment lifestyles and lifestages within

---

Exhibit 1-28. What bores Influentials

	Influentials	Total
House cleaning	57%	46%
Most entertainment shows on TV	39%	21%
Paying bills	36%	35%
Sports on TV	33%	27%
Grocery shopping	32%	29%

Source: *The Influential Americans: Who They Are, How To Reach Them,*
The Roper Organization, Inc.

---

an overall economic framework, paying particular attention to spending habits, more accurately target affluent American segments. The overlapping between categories—Get Set consumers categorized in both the Spending Patterns and Psychodemographic sections, for instance, and the blurry lines between geographic and psychographic plotting—are symptomatic of the vagaries of the current research climate.

They are also, on the other hand, indications of what the best research on affluence will look like in the future: complex subsectoring; complex (but more accurate) pinpoint equations. You will see even higher-tech approaches to locating affluent consumers that tip their hats to the value of qualitative data by making it as quantitative as possible.

An example of what we mean: "The Affluence Model" from Donnelly Marketing Information Services. This computerized affluence-predictor uses a combination of inputs: databases plus demographics. Information on income, assets, attitudes, consumption, and employment is injected with detailed statistics from Donnelley's Master Residential File, which covers 90% of all U.S. households (the model can be used to generate data on specific households or neighborhood clusters). This method is all over the place—encompassing many of the separate traditional categories of research—yet it will deliver an answer to the question of how to locate the affluent.

Nevertheless, no matter what numbers are available, it is inevitable that advertisers and marketers will end up relying on instinct to some degree when marketing to the affluent. That reliance is partly habit, and partly a consequence of inadequate research data. Yet, few executives in today's competitive business climate are comfortable making major financial commitments based on gut feeling. We'll continue to look at this affluent market from other angles to better educate the instincts that will eventually have a major say in affluent market decisions.

Part

II

Living the Affluent Life

Chapter

II

Money

The decade of the 1980s saw an increase, polarization, and concentration of wealth in the United States, leaving a smaller middle class. What was once considered a monolithic middle-class mass market has now shrunk to about one-third of the nation.

Census Bureau statistics tell us that the traditional definition of middle-class as those with household income between $15,000 and $35,000 per year now includes many fewer Americans. Measured in 1988 dollars, the proportion of whites who fit into that category is now less than 35% (down from 40% in 1972); the proportion of blacks is now 33% (down from 37% in 1972); and the proportion of Hispanics is now 39% (down from 49% in 1972).

As the money migrated toward the income poles in the 1980s, a greater number of Americans moved into affluence than moved into poverty. On the up side a quintile of household income earned 47% of all U.S. income, a substantial increase from 43% in 1969. On the down side we recognize that the technical poverty line is artificially low, and does not reflect the reality of urban life today. We feel that the actual poverty rate is about 33% higher than the official counts, and many middle-class families are struggling not to lose ground.

This change in national income distribution is profound. Just as the graphic shape used to depict the age groupings of the U.S. population is rapidly changing from the traditional triangle (the many young at the bottom declining to the few old at the top) to a rectangle (equal numbers in all age groups), so, too, is the shape and scope of U.S. income levels changing. What was once a rectangle is evolving into an hourglass.

The affluence explosion carried right through the 1980s. In 1989 the *Changing Times* Prosperity Index rose 2.2% after inflation; this was the largest gain since 1986 when it rose 2.8%. *But if the 1980s was the decade of increase, the 1990s will be the decade of stabilization.* As you will see in this chapter, the affluent sector at the top of the hourglass will be very concerned with the preservation of its money and lifestyle. Households that joined the ranks of the affluent in the 1980s will be doing everything they can to keep from getting squeezed back down to the middle.

The flood of affluence in the 1980s, filled the glass only to the middle. In the 1990s, upward mobility may be more difficult for those near the bottom and the thinning middle, but the affluent market will be full of people with more wealth than they've had in the past. You will no doubt face more of a challenge separating the affluent (and the "wannabee" affluents) from their dollars, but since people will always *want* to be affluent, and people will always spend money, you will be able to get it.

Take your cue from signs of how much money is out there, how the media play a part in affluent spending, what goals and lifestyles will be valued in a period of stabilization, and how these goals of security, *careful consumption*, and preserved wealth will manage to trickle down even to the bottom of the glass. Use this report to gather information—all kinds of information—about what will be valuable to the consumer in the coming decade. *The habits of spending and the appetites for products and services nurtured in the eighties will not disappear overnight; they are more likely to go through a period of realignment and readjustment. Use the data on these aspects of affluent spending in the past to inform your marketing decisions of the future.*

In the next few chapters, we'll present the best of the available data on affluent consumer activity in the recent past, concentrating on the four main categories, money, values, lifestyle, and media, that encompass the most important aspects of affluent resources, behavior, and mindstyle.

Within these chapters, you'll find specific information that you can use in your own equation of affluence. We'll point out the real trends—well-established, or just in the beginning stages—that you should keep your eye on. We'll also label some of these ballyhooed trends for what they are—nothing more than fads, creating a marketing minefield that will flare brightly for a moment, but will make a mess of any long-term plans for successfully reaching the market you want.

The research mess means that you can't target your best affluent customer with an off-the-shelf package of research. None of the current research targets the real-affluent, the mindstyle affluents. To find them you have to put the available research together in new ways.

A mindstyle researcher, has to be wary and well-informed. You have to sharpen your instincts and back-up your hunches, those gut instincts that guide many a successful marketer, and you have to adjust your own mindstyle to the climate of the new affluent market. It may seem like a paradox, but we believe that you will see in the following pages what we have come to believe: *even in times of economic recession—or perhaps especially in times of recession—the size of the affluent market and the power of the affluent mindstyle should not be underestimated.*

Finding the Money

Money is the raw clay of affluence. As individuals sculpt their lives, they accumulate and shape the clay to their own designs. Even those without enough to sculpt an affluent lifestyle still strive to create part of their design with an affluent flair. The importance of affluence begins with money; money that the affluent consumer has to spend, or the money that the average consumer will spend to approximate or approach some aspect of affluence. Don't forget the basic golden rule: *them that's got the gold make the rules.*

In this chapter we will look at money and the affluent: at their accumulation of it, their income and financial situation. Understanding how much money is out there, where it's concentrated, and how more money is being generated will help you define the structure of the affluent market. Examining how affluents manage their money goes a long way in explaining how affluents control their consumer tools. Money is obviously the single most important factor in the survival of the affluent consumer species; its existence won't insure that it will be spent, but knowing where it exists and how it's treated will enable you to pinpoint the *potential* of your particular market.

If you are counting dollar bills, the good news is that there are more of them among affluents. The decade of the 1980s has fostered two basic shifts in the movement of money: it is piling up rapidly, and it is piling up at the top.

All income measures tell us that more households now qualify for the $50,000+ household income benchmark. This figure alone is not cause for celebration, for two simple reasons: 1) it often takes two incomes to reach this mark; and 2) it takes more money to buy even the basic necessities these days, and $50,000 per year does not mean a family isn't struggling to keep afloat. However, there is also more income among the upper echelons of affluents (household income $60,000+), and this trend *is* significant in marking increasing wealth among existing affluent consumers.

Affluents know that affluence doesn't come easy, except to a lucky few. Most affluents achieve that status the old fashioned way, they earn it. In the following chapters, you will see that they are willing—even eager—to work for more than their daily bread. Many of them have caught the entrepreneurial bug; most of them choose a career over the less-satisfying prospect of a 9-to-5 job. But if they work hard for their money, they want their money to work hard for them. They actively seek (and find) ways to diversify their financial holdings; they are interested in safe and profitable ways of keeping and expanding their wealth. They are business-savvy, they are money-savvy, and they are anxious to continue and improve their affluent status. They also know better than to depend on "old" money to prop up "new" wealth.

Look for the ways they handle their money. This will give you some insight into how affluents are likely to spend (or to save) their gold. It will also give you some idea about the security of the future of affluents, how the nature of their capital—and the way they plan to save and increase it—compares with the best predictions of future economic growth and security (less home equity, more diversified portfolio, for example) of all U.S. consumers. It will also clue you in to how affluents feel about their gold, and how they cover their own bottom lines.

More affluence

According to Mendelsohn Media Research (MMR), the affluent ($50,000+ annual household income) quintupled their numbers during the Reagan years.[36] Since 1984, the number of adults with a household income of $60,000+ has doubled—and these have been low-inflation years, so the increase in numbers is genuine. In addition, about 1.5 million households have a net worth of over $1 million. Nearly one out of four adults (24%) live in households earning $50,000+ annually—they earn half the nation's income and control two-thirds of its discretionary income.

In 1985, 35% of affluent ($50,000+) households reported household income at $60,000–$99,000; in 1988, this percentage grew to reach 40.6%. Because affluence is spreading to a wider proportion of the population, MMR has raised the bottom dollar cutoff point for affluence to $60,000, to more closely capture the truly affluent (other research organizations will follow). Using the $60,000+ benchmark for affluence, MMR finds that in 1988, 12% of all U.S. households qualified as affluent; by 1989, that number had risen to 13.1%. (You might do well to bank on these figures—in 1989, MMR's numbers jived with U.S. Census data to within .5%). For 1990, based on their $60,000+ cutoff, MMR says that the total number of affluents in this country has risen to 37,000,000; that's 9 million more than in 1985 (a 32% increase in five years). All indications are that their ranks will continue to grow.

In 1989, the highest income quintile received 47% of the total income received by all households, higher than the comparable figure for 1969 (43%). This change was accompanied by somewhat lower shares going to the lowest 20% and middle 60% of households. [37] Exhibit 2-1 illustrates a similar pattern of change between 1977-88.

Exhibit 2-1.　Selected income decile groups, income change 1977 to 1988 (constant 1987 dollars)

Income decile	% change in average after-tax 1977-1988 income	$ change
U.S. total	+9.6%	+$2,310
First (lowest)	−10.5%	−$375
Second	−1.3%	−$94
Fifth	+.2%	+$33
Ninth	+7.9%	+$3,087
Tenth (highest)	+27.4%	+$19,324
Top 5%	+37.3%	+$33,895
Top 1%	+74.2%	+$129,402

Source:　Congressional Budget Office

Corroborating the findings of the MMR report, Donnelly's *Affluence Report* also expects the percentage of U.S. affluent households to increase in the future (exhibit 2-2).

Exhibit 2-2.　Household income distribution, 1989 and projected 1994

	1989	1994
0-$9,999	9.8%	7.0%
$10,000-$14,999	5.9%	5.2%
$15,000-$24,999	13.7%	10.3%
$25,000-$34,999	13.5%	10.7%
$35,000-$49,999	18.2%	15.3%
$50,000-$74,999	19.6%	19.9%
$75,000-$99,999	9.3%	14.0%
$100,000-$149,999	7.1%	10.8%
$150,000-$199,999	1.7%	4.3%
$200,000+	1.2%	2.4%

Source:　*The Affluence Report*, Donnelly Marketing Information Services

Exhibit 2-3 illustrates just how dynamic the growth in the affluent market is. The two Management Horizons[38] reports previously mentioned are a reflection of the changing states of affluence. Their lowest limits for inclusion in the Up Market rose considerably in just two years. In defining their method of inclusion, a higher household income was necessary in their 1988 report than was needed in their 1986 report.

Exhibit 2-3. Raising the floor on affluent research

	Consumers & Innovation (1988)	The Up Market (1986)	Amount change
Younger singles	$37,500+	$32,500+	+$5,000
Younger couples	$60,000+	$45,000+	+$15,000
Younger parents	$45,000+	$37,500+	+$7,500
Mid-life families	$60,000+	$50,000+	+$10,000
Mid-life households	$50,000+	$45,000+	+$5,000
Older households	$27,500+	$22,500+	+$5,000

According to a study sponsored by *Town & Country,* households with incomes of $75,000+ are growing faster than any other; the number of these households is projected to grow to more than 14.8 million by 1994—what the study points out is a *fourteenfold* increase over 1980 figures (exhibit 2-4).

Exhibit 2-4. Percent of U.S. households with HHI over $75,000 (numbers in millions)

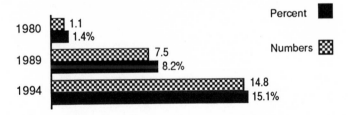

Source: "Era of the Influents," *Town & Country*

Polarization of Wealth

As more households have become affluent, the affluent have gotten richer. In the 1980s, the poor got poorer; the middle class fought hard to maintain its standard of living and many members lost ground; and the upscale segment grew and prospered. In the tightening economy of the 1990s, the poor will continue to get poorer, the middle class will lose ground, the lower-upper class will fight to hold on, and the top dogs will do very well indeed.

Census data released in late 1988 (compiled by Fairchild Publications in their study *Consumer Market Developments*[39]) shows that the highest quintile of total income in 1986 earned 46% of all pretax income, vs. 45% in 1984 and 44% in 1980 (exhibit 2-5). Real household net worth, per capita, reached a record $53,600 in 1987, up almost $10,000 from 1982. The share of the nation's wealth held by the richest 1% of the population increased from 27% in 1973 to almost 36% in 1987. Forbes' 1989 annual survey of the 400 richest Americans found that the group's collective net worth in 1988 was $220 billion, a $4 billion gain in just one year. And the number of billionaires in the study jumped from 26 to 49 in the same year.

Exhibit 2-5. Share of total income by fifths of households, selected years: 1980, 1982, 1984, 1986 (based on 1986 dollars)

	1986	1984	1982	1980
Number of HHs (000)	89,479	85,407	82,368	80,776
Income before taxes				
lowest fifth of HHs	3.7%	4.0%	4.0%	4.1%
second fifth	9.7%	9.8%	9.9%	10.2%
third fifth	16.2%	16.4%	16.5%	16.8%
fourth fifth	24.3%	24.6%	24.6%	24.8%
highest fifth	46.1%	45.3%	45.0%	44.2%
Income after taxes				
lowest fifth	4.4%	4.7%	4.7%	4.9%
second fifth	10.8%	11.0%	11.3%	11.6%
third fifth	17.2%	17.2%	17.5%	17.9%
fourth fifth	24.8%	24.8%	24.8%	25.1%
highest fifth	42.6%	42.3%	41.8%	40.6%

Source: *Consumer Market Developments*, Fairchild Publications

For all but the wealthiest 1% of the nation, new and improved taxes mean simply more and more taxes, according to a new study by the Democratic Study Group. While most Americans have indeed had their federal taxes cut, the benefits have been more than offset by state, local, and payroll taxes—leaving most of us where we were ten years ago. The uppermost affluent, however, have culled the benefits of federal cuts but have not been stung by localized increases. The result is that in comparison to 1980, the nation's tax burden is still carried by the middle and lower classes.

Exhibit 2-6 shows changes in personal and payroll taxes as percent of income from 1980 to 1990 for each income quintile. The last column, net change, clearly displays the tax advantage of the wealthy, with the net 1980-1990 tax difference for the richest 1% averaging more than $12,500 per household.

Exhibit 2-6.   Changes in average tax payments per family, 1980-1990, resulting from changes from 1980-1990 average tax rates

	Average Income	Pers. income taxes as a % of income		Payroll taxes as a % of income		Average change in taxes both pers. and payroll resulting from change '80-'90
	1990	1980	1990	1980	1990	Net Change
Lowest 20%	$7725	-0.4%	-1.5%	5.4%	7.6%	$85
Second 20%	$19,348	4.5%	3.5%	7.9%	10.1%	$232
Middle 20%	$30,964	8.1%	6.7%	8.7%	10.7%	$186
Fourth 20%	$44,908	11.0%	9.0%	8.7%	10.6%	-$45
Top 20%	$105,209	17.1%	15.6%	5.9%	6.8%	-$631
Top 10%	$144,832	18.9%	17.3%	4.7%	5.5%	-$1159
Top 5%	$206,162	20.7%	18.9%	3.5%	4.0%	-$2680
Top 1%	$548,970	23.9%	21.5%	1.5%	1.6%	-$12,626

Source: *Shifting Tax Burdens Leave All But Wealthy Worse Off,* No. 101-30, Democratic Study Center

For all income groups, personal income taxes as a percent of income dropped by an average of about 2.0%. At the same time though, payroll taxes increased, more for lower quintile, less for upper quintiles. Hence the persistent imbalance. For the richest-rich, the payroll tax increase was virtually negligible while personal tax decrease was substantial.[40]

It may come as no surprise that affluents do not see the extremism and polarization which others lament; they don't carry a bitter sense of imbalance between rich and poor. On a national level, the estrangement between the classes is perceived to be increasing, but most affluents do not agree (exhibit 2-7).

The change in family income measured over the decade between 1977 and 1988 and shown in exhibit 2-8 provides one of the most graphic depictions of what a lot of people have known all along: the poor are growing in numbers, the middle class are, proportionally, getting squeezed even harder (and often find themselves on the upper end of the bottom), and the upper income families are not only holding on, but doing *better.*

Exhibit 2-7.   It's true that the rich get richer while the poor
get poorer (percent who completely or mostly
agree) 1987 ■ vs. 1990 □

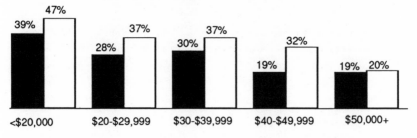

39% 47%	28% 37%	30% 37%	19% 32%	19% 20%
<$20,000	$20-$29,999	$30-$39,999	$40-$49,999	$50,000+

Source: *The People, the Press, & Politics 1990: A Times Mirror Political
Typology* ,Times Mirror Center for the People & The Press

Exhibit 2-8.   Change in family income 1977-88 (in 1987
dollars)

Income Decile	% change	$ change
First	−14.8%	−$609
Second	−8.0%	−$665
Third	−6.2%	−$813
Fourth	−6.6%	−$1216
Fifth	−6.3%	−$1507
Sixth	−5.4%	−$1619
Seventh	−4.3%	-$1,577
Eighth	−1.8%	−$798
Ninth	+1.0%	+$577
Tenth	+16.5%	+$16,913
Top 5%	23.4%	+$31,473
Top 1%	49.8%	+$134,513
All Families	2.2%	+$747

Source: *The Politics of Rich and Poor*, The Urban Institute

Work and Entrepreneurship

Affluence very often means working long hours. The *Affluent Hand-book*,[41] in comparing European and American households with in-come over $75,000, finds that the head of an affluent household averages nearly 50 hours of work per week, and 42% have a partner/ spouse who also works. In fact, households with two or more people earning a paycheck account for 65% of all discretionary dollars.[42]

Many affluents own their own businesses, and few American workers put in longer hours than entrepreneurs. As we all know, the entrepreneur became the "buzz person" of the 1980s—even more so than the yuppie (more media creation than market reality). *Working Woman* magazine,[43] in a recent article says, "The largest single source of wealth creation in the world is entrepreneurial activity. In the 1960s there was a total of perhaps 7 or 8 million companies in the country— 200,000 new annually. In 1989 we had a total of 19 million companies, with roughly one million start-ups last year alone. By 2000 we're going to have 30 million enterprises. It all feeds on itself: each company is another customer for somebody else, so the more of them there are, the more opportunities multiply."

The high costs of retirement, the increasing numbers of those who retire early, and widespread corporate downsizing will have many Americans thinking about becoming their own bosses. A recent *Wall Street Journal* article predicts that "Boomers will continue to form new companies at a furious rate in the decade ahead" despite the conventional wisdom that says they'll become more risk-averse as they age.[44] The reverse is true for the Baby Busters who, because of their smaller numbers, will be in more demand, and will, therefore, command higher salaries.

The chance that one will become an entrepreneur increases substantially if one is already in a dual-income household. "Futurists forecast that more than 52% of all married couples are expected to be two-wage-earner couples by 1990, up from 28.5% in 1960. The availability of a second income lessens the risks of entrepreneurship by providing at least some security during the time the business is being developed."[45]

A trend in entrepreneurship comes in a premixed and tested format (just add money and hard work)—franchising. It's one of the fastest growing business routes to affluence. "The Commerce Department expects franchising sales of goods and services in more than 509,000 outlets to reach almost $640 billion in 1988, about 7% higher than in 1987, and outpacing the level of sales at the start of the 1980s by about 91% . . . Movement by U.S. franchisers to foreign markets continues to grow at a rapid rate."[46] Franchising opportunities are more available to those in the middle-class who want to move up, and they are one of the most successful routes for minority entrepreneurs to attain affluence.

"Mom and Pop" businesses are giving way to savvy, lucrative franchises, with older and more affluent Boomers at the storefront. Today's franchise buyers are better educated and have more business know-how than yesterday's buyers: the typical franchisee has a college degree and a yearly income of $67,356.[47]

The 1990s will see a rise in the number of prospective franchise buyers. Professionalism and value will be key marketing points for these upscale Boomer franchisees of the 1990s. They will thoroughly research deals before they commit and will likely require more legal assurances and documentation from sellers than past or current franchisees. Boomers will take their passion for quality into every arena they enter, franchising included. Over the past five years franchise sellers have found that franchise buyers have higher incomes, higher net worth, and are better educated (exhibit 2-9).

Exhibit 2-9. Percent of franchisors who agree with the following statements regarding franchisees

	% of franchise sellers
Income level higher than five years ago	80%
Net worth higher	83%
Education level higher	61%
Business experience greater than five years ago	69%

Source: *The Franchise Marketing & Sales Survey 1989-'90*, DePaul University and Francorp, Inc.

Many consumers are eager to steer their own entrepreneurial bandwagon. For 27% of Americans, winning $1 million would go a long way in boosting their enterprising fantasies towards reality.

The numbers have become impressive—as we entered the 1980s, 27% of affluents came from the corporate ranks. But now that figure is below 11%; half of new affluents own their own businesses; 80% of U.S. millionares are first-generation millionaires. In addition to their financial importance to the affluence explosion, entrepreneurs will emerge as a 1990s leaders because their values perfectly express the needs of the 1990s—a blend of the thrill of the 1980s, with values akin to preservation.

Exhibit 2-10. What they would do if they won $1 million
(percent choosing)

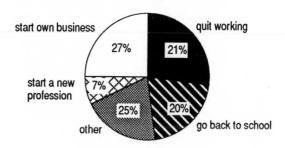

Source: Chex Cereal survey of 500 adults, as cited in *USA Today*

- They believe in hard work, family, and seem to represent having control of life.
- They are optimistic, and symbolize the power of the individual.
- They stand for equal-opportunity: women are the fastest-growing segment of entrepreneurs (and will comprise half of the self-employed by the year 2000); minorities are opening businesses faster than Caucasian males. Women and minorities tend to "hire their own"—thus factually enhancing the image of entrepreneurism as the land of opportunity.[48]

Finances

Affluents generally regard themselves as good money managers, and those who have a household income of more than $75,000 think more highly of themselves than do those in the $50,000 to $74,000 range. However, 35% to 40% think they're not so hot in the management department and therefore turn to the experts. And judging by their behavior, they'd much rather turn to specialists than to banks.

Financial institutions have to work harder to reach the affluent. High-income earners don't trust that banks appreciate their business and don't think banks have a real interest in their financial health. The affluent consider themselves to be more aware of the various services and accounts offered by banks and are more confident that they could get a loan if they needed one. Exhibit 2-11 shows how affluents' attitudes compare with others.

Exhibit 2-11. Ratings of financial institutions (average score for each income group; 5=strongly agree; 1=strongly disagree)

	<$20,000	$20,000-$74,999	$75,000+
Your institution is open when you want	4.06	3.92	3.76
You understand the different kinds of accounts offered by your institution	4.07	3.98	4.20
They appreciate your business	4.23	3.79	3.73
Doing business with them is easy and convenient	4.34	4.08	4.09
They have a personal interest in your financial well-being	3.66	3.25	3.19
It would be easy to borrow money from them if you had a good reason	3.89	4.04	4.16

Source: *Quality of Service Study June, 1989*, The Gallup Organization/ Bank Advertising News

Personalized Marketing

After years of concentrating on cost-cutting and profit-building, financial service companies will have to shift to a consumer-centered outlook if they are to succeed in the 1990s. So, get closer to your customer. Consumer values are changing, and marketing that doesn't reflect such change will fall on deaf ears, said Joe Plummer, executive vice president at DMB&B, at the 1989 American Marketing Association Financial Services Marketing Conference. Consumers are becoming:

- more sophisticated;
- smarter about financial services;
- more enlightened about money and materialism;
- more focused on experience and less on things;
- more connected to communities and less self-centered.

These traits distill to an emphasis on trust. Bankers can be friends, too. The consumer looking to integrate a disenfranchised life will welcome companies committed to customers—not to themselves. The flip side of gaining trust is displaying respect. An example of such respect is offering older financial services customers transportation to the place of business rather than nifty, splashy gadgets or promises that don't have impact on their lives.

If the goal of a financial services company is to enhance the quality of its customers' lives, it can't help but stay close to the consumer and can't help but gain a following. What a company also needs besides a working philosophy of "Better, not Cheaper" is a sense of responsibility to the customers it serves.

Older consumers are worried about health care and retirement. They may have more simple needs and outlooks. The hi-tech gee-whiz banking that moves a young consumer will bore or intimidate an older one. Older customer, might appreciate large-print pamphlets instead of bells-and-whistles stocks.

Boomers heralded the shift in values from loyalty, stability, security, and faith in heroes to self-centeredness, short-cuts, and aggressiveness. Despite of, or maybe because of, their fierce fight to win, Boomers are more discontent than others. They are still fundamentally optimistic but are a little queasy at the prospect of providing for retirement and taking care of aging parents. Financial services and resulting marketing messages that speak to these issues will find vast consumer resonance. Boomers have overextended themselves financially and are looking for subtle limits and confident guidance.

Addressing the needs of women

The growth in the numbers of women in the marketplace will slow but only because demographics of professionals are evening out. Companies will need to keep on top of changing family trends and changing roles and opportunities. "Financial services are going to really have to do a better job than just showing women in their ads."[49]

Financial plans

As expected, wealthier, better-educated folks are more likely to buy a financial plan. Over a quarter (28%) of those earning $75,000+ have one, compared to 16% of those earning $40,000 to $75,000, and 11% of all respondents; however, only 9% of affluents without a plan express any interest in heading to a bank for financial advice. Instead of the bank, affluents go to the specialists: financial planners. According to the SEC,[50] the average financial planning client is married (80%), a professional (56% are professionals of the business, technical, or medical sort), and well-educated (44% have college degrees, as do 48% of their spouses, and 34% also have graduate or professional degrees). In general, clients are male (67%), but the higher-income clients are more likely to be female (53% of them). Annual average combined (both spouses) income of financial planning clients is $87,039 with a median combined earned income of $57,623.

A new study sponsored by the Security Industry Association shows that when it comes to investing, affluents do show a degree of loyalty to their brokers. This survey of affluents (total investments, minus house, of $100,000 or more) finds that the majority (57%) hold an investment account with only one firm. A third (30%) use more than one firm but have a primary service provider that they use most often. Only the remaining 13% do not have a principal brokerage firm. Primary advisors get high marks for basic competence and advice (exhibit 2-12), but some affluents would like to see lower fees and more convenient locations.

Exhibit 2-12.   Affluents' rating of primary financial advisor
(4=excellent; 1=poor)

Professional competence	3.44
Good explanations	3.42
Places customer interests first	3.35
Offers variety of investments	3.27
General advice	3.25

Source: *The Affluent Investor*, SIA/Nuveen Research

When they need help with investment decisions, affluents turn most often to stockbrokers and accountants, though, as shown in exhibit 2-13, a quarter of those surveyed depend on themselves or their spouse.

Young Affluents

Young affluents (under 50 years of age) will hold strong loyalty to a good financial advisor—an indication of their relationship-orientation. In comparison to the over-50 traditional generation, new affluents are a little more confused about how to find good financial advice and are more likely to use money as a measure of success. They'll go into debt to invest, leveraging themselves in the hopes of making a profit. Perhaps ironically—given their intense drive towards financial success—young affluents just plain don't enjoy the whole investment-decision process as much as the traditionals do. Exhibit 2-14 illustrates additional differences between new and traditional affluents.

About a third of all affluents—young and old—place a high value on service and relationships, even to the point of foregoing immediate

Exhibit 2-13.   People relied upon for investment advice

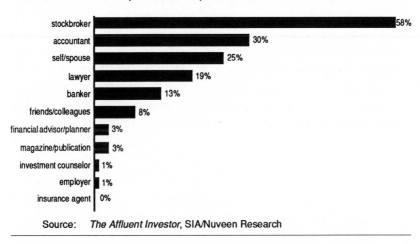

stockbroker	58%
accountant	30%
self/spouse	25%
lawyer	19%
banker	13%
friends/colleagues	8%
financial advisor/planner	3%
magazine/publication	3%
investment counselor	1%
employer	1%
insurance agent	0%

Source: *The Affluent Investor*, SIA/Nuveen Research

Exhibit 2-14.   Financial attitudes

	New generation	Traditional market
Enjoy investment decisions	53%	62%
Successful at decisions	62%	70%
Will take investment risks	52%	46%
Comfortable investing borrowed money	28%	18%
Believe quality advice costs	54%	59%
Want one main advisor	72%	67%
Need advice for major decisions	45%	37%
Loyal to advisor, not firm	83%	79%
No time to manage money	27%	28%
Don't know how to find advice	32%	27%
Money is measure of success	40%	35%
Advisory firms overcharge	36%	34%

Source: "The New Generation of Affluent Consumers," *Private Banking Winter 1990*

profits or interest rate advantages. Such affluents are good candidates for private or personalized banking, but most have no idea how such a banking connection can help them: 86% of "new generation" affluents and 89% of "traditional" affluents are "not sure what a private banking unit can do for me."[51]

Mutual Funds

According to *American Banker*,[52] current mutual fund owners and those most likely to buy them are those who have a household income of $75,000+ (42%), hold a graduate degree (36%), are age 65+ (31%), are in the upper-middle-income bracket, $40,000–$75,000 (30%), and those who are college graduates (28%). Once again, the affluent tend not to buy them at banks, preferring to deal with the mutual fund directly. As household income *rises*, the tendency for affluents to purchase mutual funds at a bank, in fact, *decreases*—while 45% of all Americans who don't own funds say they would not consider buying them at a bank, 57% of consumers earning over $50,000, and 64% of those earning over $75,000 would not buy mutual funds at a bank.

Credit Cards

Almost every affluent gets to say "charge it"—98% own some sort of credit card, with VISA in the hands of nearly three-quarters of those with a household income of $60,000+. More than 60% count on MasterCard to make purchases, and 41% "don't leave home without it." The basic no-frills card membership is the most popular—especially for VISA and MasterCard. Eighty percent of VISA holders and 75% of MasterCard holders have the regular cards, while 65% of AmEx's affluent members have its version of basic green. Exhibit 2-15 and 2-16 give more details about the cards affluents carry in their wallets.

Exhibit 2-15.   Percent of affluents with credit card

American Express (total)	41%
green	27%
gold	16%
platinum	1%
Optima	4%
VISA (total)	74%
regular	60%
gold	18%
MasterCard (total)	61%
regular	46%
gold	20%

Note: totals are inconsistent due to multiple card ownership

Source: *1989 Survey of Adults and Markets of Affluence*, Mendelsohn Media Research, Inc.

Other credit cards haven't got the appeal of the Big Three, though Discover is making headway into the affluent wallet—19% of affluents carry it. Diner's Club (5%) and Carte Blanche (.6%) have much smaller affluent bases. Three-quarters of affluents carry a department store card, and half carry gasoline or telephone cards. They're also somewhat likely to carry airline travel or car rental cards.

Exhibit 2-16.   Percent of affluents with other cards

Airline travel card	12%
Auto rental	10%
Department store	75%
Gasoline	54%
Telephone	53%

Source: *1989 Survey of Adults and Markets of Affluence*, Mendelsohn Media Research, Inc.

The card that's in their wallet may not be the first card in their mind (exhibit 2-17). It is interesting how quickly the recognition factor drops off after the Discover card (though MasterCard is in the big three in terms of affluent cardholders).

Exhibit 2-17.   Which credit or charge card advertising first comes to mind? (numbers rounded)

Affluent ($75,000+ annual household income)		General public	
American Express	37%	VISA	31%
VISA	31%	MasterCard	20%
Discover	10%	American Express	18%
None	10%	None	14%
MasterCard	6%	Discover	10%
Other	2%	Other	4%
Don't Know	1%	Don't Know	3%

Source: *American Awareness of Advertising for Charge or Credit Cards, May 1989*, The Gallup Organization/Bank Advertising News

---

Stocks/bonds

Currently, affluents think real estate and stocks are the most attractive ways to make their money work for them—45% in the $50,000-$74,999 range hold stocks/bonds compared to 60% in the $75,000+ range.[53] Rising investment level is a predictor of greater reliance on real estate and less on stocks (exhibit 2-18).

Exhibit 2-18. Type of investment considered especially
attractive (percent agreeing by investment level)

Type	<$150,000	Current value of investments $150,000-$199,999	$200,000+
Real estate	6%	14%	13%
Stock market	13%	5%	5%
Mutual funds	9%	8%	4%
CDs	8%	8%	1%
Municipal bonds	3%	2%	7%
Tax-free (general)	2%	8%	6%
Utilities	2%	5%	4%
Tax-free bonds	3%	3%	2%
Treasury bonds	2%	2%	2%
Government bonds	2%	2%	1%
Money market	1%	0%	1%
Blue chip stocks	1%	2%	1%
Commercial real estate	1%	0%	1%
Limited partnership	1%	0%	1%
Other	8%	11%	13%

Source: *The Affluent Investor*, SIA/Nuveen Research

The "greed is good" image of the 1980s was promulgated by the Boesky and Milken sagas of overnight millions and no ethics. Contrary to the popular wisdom that has filtered down from these myths, investors care very much about a company's long-term focus and strategy; short-term results are only important for 1% of them. Many corporate strategists believe that investors, often affluent, want a quick return and structure management policy accordingly. This creates a satisfaction gap wherein an issue which is crucial for the investor is addressed unsatisfactorily by management. Concerns with the largest negative gaps are: clear strategy, workplace efficiency, and long-term results. Management overcompensates, creating large positive gaps, meaning corporations work too hard on issues unimportant to investors, when it comes to short-term results, willingness to cut costs, and steady growth.

The idea in investing is, of course, to make money. However, the goals behind the obvious goal help shape investors' attitudes, their financial latitude, and their willingness to take on risk (exhibit 2-20). Younger affluents focus on retirement savings and education costs. Middle-aged affluents are predominantly concerned with providing for their future years, while older affluents—presumably having completed much of their retirement planning—are less concerned about retirement and more concerned with current cash flow.

Exhibit 2-19. Profit distribution fairness: investors' views

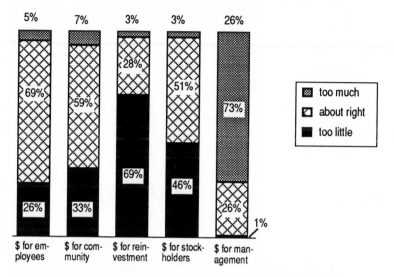

5%	7%	3%	3%	26%

	69%	59%	28%	51%	73%

too much
about right
too little

69%
46%
26%
1%

| 26% | 33% | | | |

$ for em-
ployees $ for com-
munity $ for rein-
vestment $ for stock-
holders $ for man-
agement

Source: *How the Interests of Key Corporate Constituencies Converge and
Conflict*, Sirota Alper & Pfau

Exhibit 2-20.   Importance of investment goals by age (percent
saying very important)

Goal	<35	35-54	55+
Saving for retirement	55%	68%	49%
Reducing income tax	48%	37%	47%
General savings, investment	53%	50%	39%
Providing current income	35%	15%	35%
Funding college education	50%	31%	16%
Saving to buy 2nd home	10%	5%	4%

Source: *The Affluent Investor*, SIA/Nuveen Research

Publicity changes attitudes, even among media-hip affluents who
usually feel they have a sense of the story behind the story. Several
years of coverage of scandals in stock, bond, and commodities markets, including insider trading convictions, have the affluent losing
faith—more than half (54%) of affluents (household income $50,000+)
feel businesses are not as ethical as they used to be. Upscalers are a
little more cynical than others: slightly less than half (49%) of the total
population has lost faith recently.

Most affluents (53%) rate U.S. businesses as "average" in ethics, and 24% rate them as "low." This middling-to-poor rating is surprisingly low among an affluent sector that has traditionally had a high opinion of the good will and uprightness of business. Affluents perceive the areas most affected by fraud to be: stocks, bonds, and real estate (exhibit 2-21). Affluents are less wary of government securities fraud than the average consumer.

Exhibit 2-21. Areas believed to be affected by fraud

Financial instrument	% affluents	% total
Stocks and bonds	34.4%	29.2%
Real estate	21.4%	19.9%
Commodities	15.8%	11.1%
Precious gold, metals	12.0%	8.1%
Government securities	11.0%	16.3%

Source: *October 1989 Nightly Business Report/Reuters Poll on Business Ethics*, Nightly Business Report

---

Affluents are split as to whether or not government should step further into the marketplace to police dishonesty: 45% think more government is the answer; 47% think government should keep out and let industry solve its own problems.

Despite the S&L debacle, most affluents (HHI $60,000+) think their savings are safe—81% think it's unlikely that their financial institution will fail. If it does, however, and the government takes over, affluents are likely to do a swift transfer to another place of safekeeping.

Three-quarters of affluents would take their money out of a government-run savings operation. In comparison, 71% of the total population would do the same, showing slightly higher levels of trust among non-affluents.

Nearly 90% of affluents have not felt panicked enough to move their money in 1990. Those who did went from a savings and loan to a regular bank; non-affluents who transferred money did so between regular banks (exhibits 2-22, 2-23, 2-24, 2-25).

Exhibit 2-22. Percent of affluents by HHI who own the following

savings bonds

16.5%

16.6%

19.7%

money market funds:

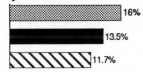

16%

13.5%

11.7%

- ▦ $100,000+
- ■ $75K-$99,999
- ◩ <$75,000

common or preferred stock:

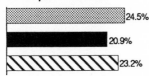

24.5%

20.9%

23.2%

Source: *Upper Deck Report*, Mediamark Research, Inc.

Exhibit 2-23. How likely do you think it is that the institution holding your money will fail?

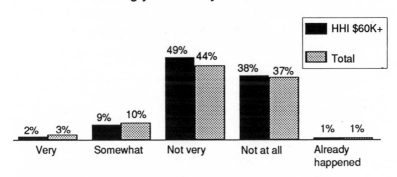

■ HHI $60K+

▦ Total

Very	Somewhat	Not very	Not at all	Already happened
2% 3%	9% 10%	49% 44%	38% 37%	1% 1%

Source: *Confidence in the Safety of Financial Institutions*, The Gallup Organization/Bank Advertising News

Exhibit 2-24. If your financial institution failed and the government took it over, how likely would you be to move your money out?

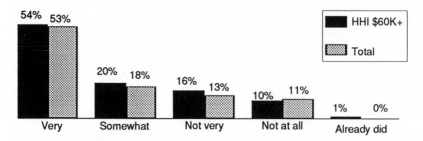

Source: *Confidence in the Safety of Financial Institutions*, The Gallup Organization/Bank Advertising News

Exhibit 2-25. How affluents moved their money

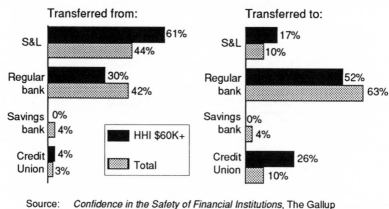

Source: *Confidence in the Safety of Financial Institutions*, The Gallup Organization/Bank Advertising News

However, 51% of affluents checked out their banks' financial records (compared with 47% of the total); 25% of affluents inquired about the health of their banks by talking to someone at the bank (21% for total); 28% of affluents got the input of someone outside the bank like a stockbroker or advisor (20% of total did so).[54]

Equity for debt swap

Affluents (annual household incomes of $60,000+) are the most likely income group to have equity in a home but the least likely to apply for bank credit based on that home equity. An overwhelming 85% of them own, or will soon own, a house, condo, or co-op (compared with only 58% of the total population). Of these potential borrowers, only 10% of the affluents indicate they are "likely" or "somewhat likely" to apply for a home equity line of credit within the year. Those in other income groups are slightly more likely to head to the bank, ownership papers in hand as collateral: $40,000-$59,999 (15%); $20,000-39,999 (14%); under $20,000 (12%).

It's not for lack of knowledge that affluents aren't interested in equity lines of credit. About 70% of them (71% in November 1988, 68% in April 1989, and 65% in September 1989) have been aware of advertising for such bank credit (exhibit 2-26). During those same survey waves, 64%, 54% and 57% of the total population indicated familiarity with "equity line of credit " ads. Despite some statistical fluctuations over time, newspapers seem to be more effective than television in getting ads to the affluent.[55]

Exhibit 2-26. Source of advertising awareness by household income (Sept. '89; caution small cell sizes)

	$40,000-$59,999	$60,000+
TV	27%	32%
Newspaper	24%	24%
Direct mail	10%	22%
Radio	13%	4%
Magazine	7%	2%
Other	13%	12%
Don't know	6%	4%

Source: *Home Equity Study, September 1989*, The Gallup Organization

---

Inheritance

According to the Urban Institute, intergenerational transfers account for approximately four-fifths of the nation's wealth. But Baby Boomers may not be able to count on an inheritance for a windfall.

Children of elderly affluents may find themselves hit with increasing levels of inheritance tax. The Federal government is keeping a watchful eye on the wealthiest elderly generation in history to see what will happen to their money when they die. Chances are, their children will see a good portion of it. A Cornell study finds that today's 64 million Baby Boomers stand to inherit about $6.8 trillion between 1987 and 2011. Equality will not be the reigning doctrine: the richest 1% of the population will divide one-third of inherited wealth, with each receiving an average inheritance of approximately $3.6 million; the next richest 9% will divide another third, each receiving an average of $396,000; and the remaining 90% will divide the rest, each pulling in an average of $40,000.

The prospect of inheritance will help upscale Baby Boomers maintain their leveraged, spendthrift ways. However, because age-consistent patterns will appear as Boomers mature, a considerable amount of inherited money will likely to be used for charities and college tuition as well. Baby Boomers stand to become the wealthiest generation of elderly in the nation's history: smaller families and dual earnings, coupled with inheritance, spell rich retirement for many.

A Gallup Poll reminds us that Americans are apt to congratulate an individual if he is rich but blame society if he is poor. Half of all Americans think "strong effort" is the seed which bears riches; only a third (33%) attribute wealth to "luck or circumstances beyond one's control."[56]

Chapter

III

Values

Value is a key word for understanding the affluent consumer. Find out what the affluent consumer values—and what all consumers value as symbols of affluence—and you will find out when consumers are likely to put their money where their mouths (and their ideas of affluence) are. Find out how you can communicate a certain value, and you will discover how to speak the language that motivates an affluent consumer. Affluent consumers are more likely to practice what they preach in the coming decade, as we see the resurgence of some new old-fashioned values—spending money on certain products and services will actually become a statement. Knowing where affluents' hearts and minds are has never been as valuable as it is now, particularly because we are in a period of transition. The decade of affluence expansion has evolved into a decade of retrenchment and maturation.

The main thing to remember as we face a new age of affluence: *affluent consumers value "value" itself.* In the following chapters, we will see how highly affluents value the perceived quality of a product or service, as well as which products and services they think of as high end or quality offerings. We will also examine the ever-changing lines between luxury and necessity; knowing where affluents draw the lines on these concepts can lead to a better understanding of how to present your goods to them. And we'll take a look at one of the most recent developments in the affluent market, an attitude shift that promises to become a full-blown trend among affluent and affluent-minded consumers alike: a return to the romance, security, and well-worn patina of Old Money—often offered in brand-new packages.

The motivating forces behind new ideas of value are evident in some basic shifts in the more traditional sense of the word values. Families are in; we've seen that affluents have larger households than average. And the smaller families of younger affluents are getting more attention (both from affluents and from marketers) than ever before— the importance of these units doing well enough to keep success all in the family has increased as their size has decreased. Older affluents will work hard to keep their position and their wealth, and younger affluents—who feel that they may not enjoy the unprecedented economic gains of their elders—will work even harder to make their own money. Many of them have been raised in affluence, and they expect the fruits of labor; they also feel that they *deserve* to buy things for themselves. They seek ways to make up for the time they spend in busy careers by seeking goods and services that sell the hottest affluent commodity of the 1990s: time. During the morning after the conspicuous consumption of the 1980s, we will see more concern for the rest of the world—expressed in affluents' stated concerns about the ills of society and of the environment (as well as what factors they consider as they make their purchases and their charitable donations). As you read the following chapters, keep in mind how one shift in values (more concern for the environment, for example) changes the value of an affluent purchase (desirable packaging that is not harmful to the environment). This chain of values will be the key to understanding the value mindstyle of the 1990s affluent consumer.

Quality

Say quality and novelty to the affluent, and mean it, and you'll get their attention. But keep in mind that while experimentation is important, those affluents who are time-squeezed will stick to what they know *really* works, getting the most value for their money. Price isn't as important as the value perceived. And the affluent consumer demands to perceive the quality of your products and services alike. Affluents like novelty and they gather reliable information before making significant purchases. However, because so many affluents are time-pressured, they will selectively apply their info-gathering impulse. They will gather data on a novel product the same day that they will select another brand name product they associate with value because time does not permit further thought. A brand name that says quality will be a bankable image in the time-pressured 1990s.

Earlier we discussed the mixed reviews affluents give to banking, but it's not just banks that have trouble getting high marks from affluent consumers. Among the six industries included in a Gallup/*Bank Advertising News* poll (exhibit 3-1), insurance companies and airlines get the least praise from affluents: among those earning $75,000 or more, only 5% think airlines give "excellent" service and only 11% think insurance companies do. Compare these figures to the 14% and 23% of the total population who give "excellent" ratings to airlines and insurance companies, respectively.

Exhibit 3-1.   Percent of affluents ($75,000+) compared to the total population who say the following industries provide an excellent quality of service to their customers

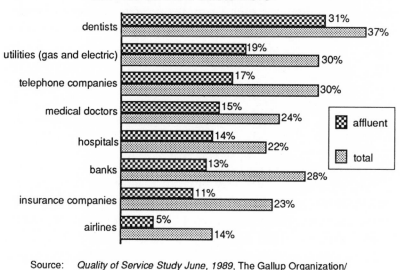

Source: *Quality of Service Study June, 1989*, The Gallup Organization/ *Bank Advertising News*

Banks, third-to-last on the list, rate excellent with only 13% of affluents, compared to 28% of the total. Utilities, telephone companies, doctors, and hospitals are a little more likely than banks to elicit an excellent from affluents, but that isn't saying very much. Even these industries don't have the well-to-do kicking up their heels in praise. Affluents just don't seem to dole out top ratings quite so easily as the rest of the population. Of all the categories, dentists get the highest praise from affluents and non-affluents alike.[57]

The affluent are among the first to try new products, especially if they answer time needs. Concomitantly, they have traditionally been low in brand loyalty, while the mass market has been far more brand loyal. However, recent research from the Roper Organization[58] has seen a reversal in this trend—affluents are actually becoming *more* brand loyal. Possibly because they are too busy to gather information about new products (they have always been info-junkies on products), or because they are besieged with too many product messages, they are sticking with what works for them.

The upper affluent look for quality first, status second, and for many, foreign products have very high appeal. They're in the market for products they can count on, and reliability is key in choosing a store.[59]

One of the best monitors of the emerging affluent mindstyle—the "Era of the Influents" from *Town & Country* magazine—offers a gentle (and genteel) reminder of what qualities the affluent will value:

- Disdain for the mediocre;
- Education;
- Elevated levels of taste;
- "Good name"—honesty;
- Character, integrity.

Old Money over New Money

New money can't buy old money, but it sure can try. One of the biggest trends you will see in the coming decade is the indiscreet love affair between people with the means (cold cash) pursuing the objects and services with the ways of old money about them. It's the aura of aristocracy, the beautiful romance between money and social position that will leave many consumers breathless with the desire to acquire. This is no fairy tale; it is one of the most important waves of the monied future, especially for advertisers. And even if you're not a romantic you better learn to think like one—if only for as long as it takes for you to come up for the extra marketing air you will need.

Perhaps the mystique that old money has for even the newest of affluents is best explained by Nelson W. Aldrich, Jr., in his book *Old Money, The Mythology of America's Upper Class*. In it, he recognizes the very powerful allure of what has come to be known as Old Money— sometimes less a reference to any hard currency and more of an encompassing reference to the currency of "culture" and "class." America dreams of the ways of Old Money—the ease, the lack of struggle, the freedom, the sense of arrival, the social presence, the luxury of enough time.

Yet, money mindstyles do battle within each of us; those with Old Money, those with New Money, even those with No Money, shift between the ease of the Old and the drive of the New. The New World invented New Money values—boldness, individualism, single-mindedness, tenacity, change, energy, motion, efficiency. This is the entrepreneurial ethic. We don't discover ourselves; we invent ourselves. King Lear said "Nothing comes from nothing," but Americans' greatest legends of success tell about creating *something* out of *nothing*.

Sometimes thought of as a wrinkle in America's egalitarianism, or a holdover from our English monarchy heritage, inherited fortunes link two powerful concepts: money and time. It is time that contributes to the social presence of Old Money, for the lineage so necessary to Old Money implies adherence to history, tradition, and continuity. Old Money, in fact, transcends money. The key element is family, not the individual. The Old Monied individual literally feeds off a past of which he was not a part. (Yet, as a sign of our national mentality, the law recognizes only individuals as owners of wealth, never families).

Riding a wave created by their ancestors, inheritors of Old Money start out where New Money would like to end up. Old Money is somehow allowed a reprieve from the responsibilities and choices made by New Money. Old Money is dictated a curriculum which demands attendance at certain schools and clubs (prep schools, then Harvard or any substitute Ivy League), the development of particular customs, patterns, demeanors, (sportsmanship, teamwork, grace), and an education in, and appreciation of, the fine arts. Offering predetermined life directions (and even personality characteristics, and recognizable names and nicknames), Old Money is a haven from existentialism. It provides physical and metaphysical absolutes in a world otherwise immersed in uncertainty. It is confident, fearless, formal and gallant; New Money is careless, nonchalant, insouciant, unstudied, natural, and energetic.

The Old is a system of abundance, not of scarcity. Those in it pay prices, but not costs. They don't buy; they discover or find, and in so doing, they influence national tastes. Removed from the explicit flows of money, Old Money concentrates instead on the long-term accumulation and protection of a legacy so large it can't be contained in a single generation. This extended-time outlook is the very characteristic of Old Money that makes change and flux painful. The best example of this is the fashion industry. While on the one hand, fashion offers wonderful expression of talent and beauty, fashion's unpredictability makes following fashion stressful for Old Money, whose members tend to ignore fashion novelties. It is because fashion, more than almost any other industry, acts as a reminder of the fluidity and flexibility of the market that Old Money shies away from it.

New Money rules are those of evolution, and its practitioners make their way according to a doctrine of scarcity, competition, and survival of the fittest. Costs are real because risks are real. To New Money minds, wealth is a measure and a tool of usefulness, of potential energy—a step in turning possibility into actuality. Wealth is not efficient when it is stored over long periods of time, it becomes like sedimentary deposits of financial flow. Underlying the basic structure of New Money is a fear—fear of ending up on the wrong side of the success equation. The balance in the jungle is between physical life and death; in the marketplace, and in New Money minds, the balance is between psychological life and death, between security and insecurity, success or personal oblivion.

Struggle and uncertainty plague, yet motivate, the New Money mentality. New Money people identify themselves with what they produce, how we act within and against external boundaries. "What do you do?" Americans ask of strangers, judging them by their arenas of action. Based on possibility rather than history, the New Money outlook is zealously open—open to change, open to opportunity, open to the manhandling of fresh chaos. Such a view would seem to have little patience or respect for inherited wealth which carries with it a social place, a fixed and perhaps predetermined destiny of ready-made identity. Indeed, New Money slaps the face of Old Money, but only with one hand. The other is held in firm salute.

Whether the entrepreneurial personality will admit it or not, it uses Old Money as a guidepost for success. Meanwhile, the social imagination of Old verifies itself by the dynamic standards of New Money. Seemingly at odds, the two are linked by a very strong force: mutual envy.

Envy requires selective blindness, a blocking out of self in favor of others. A form of self-hate, envy creates a hyper-awareness of others' actions, possessions, feelings, and philosophies. Those filled with envy walk the line between love and hate, wanting and despising. The basic germ of envy is insecurity, which can flourish in a stifling and critical environment. The tension between Old and New resonates within the envious, forcing the Old to justify themselves separate from their fortunes, and forcing the New to justify themselves by way of their fortunes.

Already successful, the Old Monied are denied the process of success. They look upon New Money as extraordinary, almost illogical. With New Money, creator and possessor are one in the same. A man born with a financial legacy, however, cannot enjoy the stark necessity of creating himself. He must console himself with validations. Despite formally accepted rationalizations for Old Money, some of its ranks work very hard to distance themselves from their last names and their fortunes, feeling they have committed an egregious offense by being born into wealth.

Ultimately, Old would not be Old without New—and vice versa. Well-protected and often inertial stashes of Old Money wealth sometimes need swift injections of New Money cash. Conversely, were it not for the dynamics of New Money markets, long-held fortunes would dwindle. The interdependence is not just for pragmatic survival but also for social survival. The reciprocity of envy affirms yet challenges both.

Aldrich's book offers the following opinions:

> Inherited concentrations of wealth can pose a very special problem for a democracy. The primal nightmare of a democracy is the emergence of an oligarchy that would, through the power associated with wealth, perpetuate

itself and eventually constitute a kind of aristocracy. The United States is the country where it's not supposed to matter who your father is ... at the same time, of course, it does matter who one's father is.

It is the pride and glory of old wealth that irks the self-image of New Money, no matter how self-made. Under all the action is a desire to be idle, to play instead of work, to address wants rather than needs. Old Money inspires envy in New Money, and the greatest offense is the feeling "We were here first." Despite this country's unabiding respect for the individual hero—a symbol extended into the entrepreneurial marketplace during Reagonomics—our mythology and fantasy emulate the order and security of family money.

The newly rich suffer attacks on their taste, grace, culture, and habits. Old Money grants that New Money has money, but lacks breeding, something they can never acquire. Ostentation is a ubiquitous sign of New Money, perhaps a scramble to show their arrival, but modesty is the Old's way. Humility and control are hallmarks of Old Money as evidenced in their concern for social graces, sportsmanship, and the control of aggression. Similarly, hype is not important to an Old Money player — whether on the field or in the stock market. Charity is a central old money theme, altruism being one of the class' strongly-held notions of itself. [60]

Happily sitting in the shadows behind the glare of the Trumped up visibility of New Money and greed-mongers in the 1980s, Old Money will move into a leadership role in the 1990s. Not only does their very nature say preservation, but their values are traditional and enduring. They shop for quality but consider value right along with it, and shun an overpriced product. They enjoy the ability to discern quality; they respect the value of an old name, be it family or brand.

These will become leading social and consumer values in the 1990s. Conspicuous consumption will remind affluents (and the rest of the population who turns progressively more to them for market leadership) of the uncertainty that can result from affluence—"enlightened consumption" will be the admired priority. As Laurel Cutler, vice chairman of FCB/Leber Katz Partners and "Era of the Influents" study supervisor puts it, "Nancy Reagan's real pearls and fake values will be replaced by Barbara Bush's fake pearls and real values."[61]

For affluents worried about getting the most out of their money in terms of social benefits, the money itself will not be as valuable as the old commodities of history, tradition, and family that Old Money (even when there's none left) represents. As author Vance Packard says in his book, The *Ultra Rich: How Much Is too Much*, "People today who are rich enough to buy anything they want do not necessarily constitute any kind of social elite." They do, however, constitute a consumer segment that is often eager to purchase the objects associated with Old Money—and the old social elite.

In fact, although everyone in the *Social Register* is wealthy, the exclusive guide is less about income than it is about values. Old Money makes the grade and perpetuates its presence because only members can nominate potential members. For the most part, the 32,500 names listed by the Social Register Association all correspond to the same ethnicity—white Anglo-Saxon. Blacks, Jews, Asians, and Hispanics are notably absent. However, race isn't the only discriminating factor: the wrong job, the wrong marriage, or the wrong public scandal can get you tossed off the list. (In general, actors don't make the grade—Jane Wyatt is an exception.)

New York is the seat of social clout, with 23% of Registry blue-blood there. Philadelphia is home to 13%; Boston, 8%. Stephen Higley, of Oklahoma State University, suggests George Bush to be the classic registry type: born in Greenwich, Connecticut, son of a U.S. Senator, summered in Maine, captain of Yale's baseball team, member of Skull and Bones, married to a plucky Wellesley woman. Higley also suggests, however, that as American money goes global and as now-under-represented cities like Detroit, Los Angeles, Houston, and Dallas develop, the Social Register will wane in importance as a benchmark for affluence and influence. Until then, however, inertial forces in our culture keep the phrases "Social Register" and "rich and powerful" inextricably linked.[62]

Luxury vs. Necessity

Luxury is changing. It's becoming more about doing and less about having. Sure, the old standbys are still there—jewels, resort hotels, fine food and drink—but a new dimension of luxury is emerging, one that values free time, personal fulfillment, doing the right thing, and enjoying life. *What the neighbors think* is less the basis of luxury than it once was. *What the consumer thinks* is becoming the focus of luxury. This trend isn't a replacement of the luxury concept; it's an expansion of it. It is, in fact, the luxury of pleasing yourself—even if your greatest pleasure is not breakfast at Tiffany's, but lunch hour at the used book store.

Conspicuous consumption will turn to experiential enlightenment—so finds *Luxury In The Nineties*, a Nissan study. Impressing friends and the Joneses will still motivate the quest for luxury to some degree (basic elements of human nature never change), but pleasing the self is becoming the goal. The new age of luxury means there will be more satisfaction in what affluents do and less in what they have. This transition fosters a new intangible measure of luxury—feelings. The rules of the game are no longer "Whoever has the most, wins" but "Whoever feels the best, wins." You may even see such philosophies on T-shirts in the 1990s.

The Nissan study measures the attitudes of 1000 opinion leaders, consumers who adopt new products easily and are very up-to-date on new developments in the marketplace (aged 21-65 years old and earning at least $30,000, average household income is $51,000). They know about technology, spend more than most on new products, know a lot about the products they buy (sometimes more than the salespeople), and show an interest in civic and community leadership.

Traditional standards of luxury are now merely one kind of the new three-dimensional idea of luxury. Conventional, Intemperate, and Instrumental luxuries make up the whole picture. The conventional standards are those we normally associate with financial arrival, material wealth, and upward mobility. According to the Conventional definition, luxury is all about visible signs of financial health; and that definition still holds true (exhibit 3-2).

The objective signs of Conventional luxury rest on prestige—possessions which are out-of-reach for most consumers are symbols of luxurious living. The second form of luxury is Intemperate. Such luxuries emphasize personal experience as an end in itself rather than as a performance for others. In fact, the privately enjoyed Intemperate forms of luxury are almost the antithesis of Conventional luxuries, which advertise themselves heavily.

Exhibit 3-2. A "conventional" luxurious lifestyle is: (percent who agree with description)

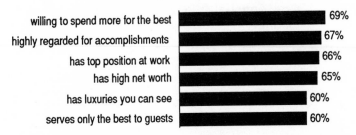

willing to spend more for the best	69%
highly regarded for accomplishments	67%
has top position at work	66%
has high net worth	65%
has luxuries you can see	60%
serves only the best to guests	60%

Source: *Luxury in the Nineties: A Study Assessing the Meaning of Luxury Among Opinion Leaders*, Infiniti Division Nissan Motor Corporation USA

The thought of Instrumental luxuries may seem to be oxymoronic—if they're instrumental, how can they be luxuries? These luxuries are instrumental in fortifying happiness and freedom. Instrumental luxuries are those that relieve stress, streamline time usage, and just plain add to the fun of life. That these functions are seen as Instrumental indicates an increasing belief in an entitlement to enjoyment and pleasure, as well as confidence in the continuance of the affluent lifestyle. Most Instrumental luxuries focus on entertainment (to pass leisure time) and help (to gain security in an increasingly uncertain world). Exhibit 3-3 shows a breakdown of some of the different types of luxuries and how they score in the survey.

Of course, a single endeavor can fulfill more than one motivation for luxury—owning an art collection can be a show for friends, a source of deep personal aesthetic pleasure, and a healthy investment, all at the same time.

Luxury isn't easy. The image of *striving* for luxuries still exists; what is just outside one's reach is a luxury. For a low-income family, an occasional night out to dinner may be luxurious, while an affluent couple may dine out every night and consider that a necessity. It's the relativity principle applied to marketing: *an item's luxury value depends on how far one is from being able to obtain it.* And what happens once you've got it? Why, you want something else, of course—a luxury in hand for more than a short time is no longer a luxury, reaching is central to the concept of luxury. Luxuries pertaining to relief from time and money pressures are desired the most but acquired the least.

Exhibit 3-3.   Conventional, intemperate, and instrumental luxuries

Conventional luxuries	Diff. score*	Intemperate luxuries	Diff. score
Owning expensive jewelry	+88%	Staying at resort or luxury hotels	+75%
Owning a "prestigious" credit card	+75%	Drinking high quality wine or liquor	+71%
Shopping at "prestigious" stores	+55%	Eating out 3+ times per week	+53%
Owning a car with all the extras	+46%	Belonging to a health club	+46%

Instrumental luxuries	Diff. score
Owning a CD player	+75%
Having hired help at home	+55%
Having a personal secretary	+47%
Owning a personal computer at home	+38%
Having a financial advisor	+38%
Owning home video equipment	+38%

*Difference score: the difference between luxury and necessity. The higher the score, the greater the luxury.

Source: *Luxury in the Nineties: A Study Assessing the Meaning of Luxury Among Opinion Leaders*, Infiniti Division Nissan Motor Corporation USA

Exhibit 3-4 lists the luxuries held in high esteem and which are the most difficult to obtain. They are related in the sense that a healthy investment strategy can enable early retirement, which in turn can free up time for traveling. "Owning a jacuzzi" seems an anomaly on a list of otherwise heavy-hitting plans and desires, and reminds us that

Exhibit 3-4.   Most desired/least acquired and percent who desire

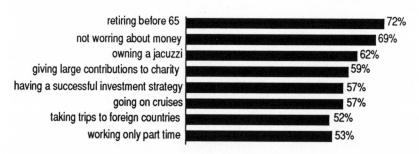

retiring before 65	72%
not worrying about money	69%
owning a jacuzzi	62%
giving large contributions to charity	59%
having a successful investment strategy	57%
going on cruises	57%
taking trips to foreign countries	52%
working only part time	53%

Source: *Luxury in the Nineties: A Study Assessing the Meaning of Luxury Among Opinion Leaders*, Infiniti Division Nissan Motor Corporation USA

Exhibit 3-5.   The top 20 luxuries

(All three types of luxuries make it on the Top Twenty list—conventional, intemperate, and instrumental. Unlike the most desired/least acquired list, the following list is not weighted by likelihood of acquiring the luxury.)

Luxuries	Diff. score*
Owning expensive jewelry	+88%
Owning a second home	+86%
Eating at fine restaurants	+77%
Staying at resort and luxury hotels	+75%
Owning a compact disc player	+75%
Drinking high quality wine/liquor	+71%
Owning a prestige "gold" credit card	+70%
Owning a cordless telephone	+57%
Shopping at "prestige stores"	+55%
Having hired help at home	+55%
Eating out more than 3 times per week	+53%
Having a personal secretary	+47%
Owning a car with all the extras	+46%
Belonging to a health club	+46%
Owning a personal computer at home	+39%
Having a financial advisor	+38%
Owning home video equipment	+38%
Having cable television	+27%
Only working part-time	+26%
Owning a garage door opener	+25%

*Difference score: the difference between luxury and necessity. The higher the score, the greater the luxury.

Source: *Luxury in the Nineties: A Study Assessing the Meaning of Luxury Among Opinion Leaders*, Infiniti Division Nissan Motor Corporation USA

the urge for physical pleasure will always have a priority, as it has since before the Romans.

Accessibility is clearly a factor in determining luxury. But so too is the power to have other people help in a consumer's life, whether day-to-day (as with a maid or a nanny) or year-to-year (financial advisor). *This service element of luxury is marketing news.* Consumers want to reshape their use of time, and services that help to do that are part of the new experiential luxury wave.[63]

The Roper Organization's Premium Class (PC) (households bringing in $100,000+/year) have not let money go to their heads—they know that many of the goods and services they enjoy regularly are, indeed, luxuries, even though they are requisite to the lifestyle they enjoy. For example, 75% see a financial advisor as a luxury, yet most require them; over 80% deem a deluxe hotel to be a luxury, but you probably won't find them checking in at the Motel 6. Regular use of goods and services deemed as luxuries is one of the privileges enjoyed by the PC.

The PC is busy. Two-thirds of PC women are employed (vs. 55% in the nation as a whole), and only 21% of the entire PC is retired (vs. 36% of the nation). Dual-income PC households are the busiest, and rely on certain "necessary" convenience items more than other PCers— 51% find a phone answering machine to be a necessity (vs. 38% of one-income PCers), and 35% find a maid or housekeeper to be a necessity (vs. 23% of other PCers). Self-employed PCers are much more likely to live by their car phones—over a quarter find it a necessity, more than double the rest of the PC (exhibit 3-6).

If everyone has a luxury, it's not a luxury anymore. Television used to be a luxury; now every household has one (or two or three). The same is true for washing machines, dryers, cars, and air conditioning. The luxury-necessity spectrum is constantly reshaping itself according to changing times, changing technologies, and changing mores.

Exhibit 3-6. **The Premium Class evaluates its luxuries and necessities**

	Luxury	Necessity
A second car	26%	73%
Microwave oven	42%	57%
Answering machine	50%	49%
Home computer	57%	42%
VCR	62%	36%
Maid/housekeeper	79%	30%
Elite colleges	67%	30%
Pay cable	72%	27%
Private schools	73%	25%
Financial advisor	73%	25%
Deluxe hotels	83%	16%
Car phone	85%	14%
Vacation home	87%	12%
Swimming pool	91%	98%
Flying first class	94%	6%
Fur coat	93%	6%
Custom made clothing	95%	5%

*Note: figures don't add to 100 because of DK, multiple answers, and rounding.

Source: *The Public Pulse*, February 1990 issue, The Roper Organization, Inc.

Free time is perceived as a necessity but is a luxury when it is very hard to come by (e.g., the two-wage-earner couple with children). Similarly, an annual vacation is considered a necessity, but where one takes it and how one spends it are luxury options. Owning a car is crucial, but extras are luxuries. One of the handiest measures of the affluence of any historical era are the objects that pass from the luxury to necessity status. In exhibit 3-7, consumers assessed threshold necessities, affirming their sense of entitlement to relieve stress, manage time, and protect their valuables.

Exhibit 3-7. Luxuries becoming necessities (positive score=luxury; negative=necessity)

	Diff. score
Owning a home security system	+5%
Owning a car radio/cassette deck	+2%
Owning a telephone answering machine	+2%
Living within 15 miles of work	-2%
Taking a yearly vacation trip	-6%

*Difference score: the difference between luxury and necessity. The higher the score the greater the luxury.

Source: *Luxury in the Nineties: A Study Assessing the Meaning of Luxury Among Opinion Leaders*, Infiniti Division Nissan Motor Corporation USA

A higher income shifts the ground floor of luxury, leaving a "luxury perception gap" between those of low and high affluence. For example, those earning $30,000-$40,000 are more than twice as likely as those earning over $60,000 to say personal computers and home video equipment are luxuries; to the upscale, these are the refrigerators of everyday life (exhibit 3-8).

The chart shows that $60,000+ affluents rank "shopping at prestigious stores" on a higher luxury scale than other affluents. For all other luxuries, however, scores from ultra-affluents are lower than from the other income groups. That's because they have more of what it takes to acquire luxuries, and the just out-of-my-reach line is not as forbidding for them. As an example of how income relates to luxury perception, the luxury index for "having a personal secretary" is 133 among those earning over $60,000. The same item has a significantly higher luxury index (155) among those earning $30,000-$40,000. Technology and self-help items are most likely to fall towards "neces-

Exhibit 3-8.   Luxury vs. necessity by household income

	$60,000+	*$40,000-$60,000*	*$30,000-$40,000*
Owning expensive jewelry	+87*	+89	+87
Staying at a resort or luxury hotel	+67	+77	+78
Owning a CD player	+66	+80	+77
Shopping at "prestigious" stores	+64	+51	+54
Drinking high quality wine/liquor	+64	+71	+74
Owning a prestige gold card	+62	+68	+77
Having hired help at home	+51	+53	+61
Eating out more than 3 times per week	+43	+55	+57
Having a personal secretary	+33	+50	+55
Belonging to a health club	+32	+50	+50
Having a financial advisor	+21	+41	+50
Having a personal computer	+20	+39	+50
Owning home video equipment	+17	+44	+44

*Scores represent difference between "luxury" and "necessity"; a highly positive score implies a high luxury quotient

Source: *Luxury in the Nineties: A Study Assessing the Meaning of Luxury Among Opinion Leaders*, Infiniti Division Nissan Motor Corporation USA

sity" for the upper-affluents, while tangible possessions (shopping spree goodies, jewels) remain luxury items for all, regardless of affluence level.

The evolution of a luxury into a necessity can often be a matter of time as exhibit 3-9 indicates. It all depends, of course, on what you consider

Exhibit 3-9.   Evolution of luxury into necessity

Necessities	*Diff. score**
Owning central air conditioning	-10%
Owning a color television	-16%
Owning a dishwasher	-20%
Owning auto air-conditioning	-29%
Owning a microwave oven	-32%
Having free time to enjoy things	-38%
Exercising	-46%
Having time to oneself	-66%
Furthering one's education	-75%
Spending time with one's children	-75%
Owning a clothes dryer	-83%
Owning a clothes washer	-85%
Owning an automobile	-89%

*Difference score: the difference between luxury and necessity. The more negative the score, the more necessary the item is perceived to be.

Source: *Luxury in the Nineties: A Study Assessing the Meaning of Luxury Among Opinion Leaders*, Infiniti Division Nissan Motor Corporation USA waste. Having more money changes one's perspective of what is wasteful or unnecessary spending. One's taste for waste follows one's ability (or lack thereof) to spend.

Lower incomes (household income under $40,000/year) correlate to harsher standards, a greater tendency to classify certain expenditures as wasteful; higher incomes (household income $40,000+) correlate to looser standards, a greater waste tolerance (see exhibit 3-10). The items on which attitudes are most widely split are "foreign vacations" (38% of under-$40,000/year earners see it as a waste; only 19% of affluents do—a percentage spread of 19), "Broadway shows" (38% of the under-$40,000, vs. 22% of affluents, a spread of 16 percentage points), "expensive jewelry" (70% vs. 55%, a spread of 15 points), and "a second home" (42% vs. 27%, a spread of 15 points). Only in the skies do perceptions reverse: 69% of those in the under-$40,000 sample consider flying first class instead of coach a waste. A slightly higher percentage of affluents, 72%, agree.

Since affluents make a habit of psychologically transforming wants into needs, they are less likely to perceive consumption of luxuries as wasteful—that is, as beyond need. Perhaps for the lesser earners, the rationale at work is: I can't afford it, but I don't want it anyway because it's wasteful. The big spenders may be thinking: I'm buying it. I'm not wasteful; therefore, it's not a waste. The only way to test if such self-preservation tactics contribute to perceptions about spending would be to keep tabs on waste attitudes as a household shoots up (or falls down) the earnings ladder. Whatever the internal emotional dynamics, though, the empirical data bear out that waste is—like most things—a relative concept.[64]

Jim Buck, senior vice president, Payment Systems, Inc., offers important guidelines:[65]

> The most important thing to remember is that the affluent market is not homogenous. A $100,000 a year senior corporate executive and $100,000 a year small business owner have very different ideas in terms of product usage. In some cases, occupation and source of wealth become very important considerations. In the lower-to-middle affluent selects where income range is $50,000 to $100,000, the presence and number of children is important.

Exhibit 3-10. "It's a waste of money": percentage (by income) who agree

	Total	<$40,000	$40,000+
Luxury car costing $40,000+	80%	82%	75%
Casino gambling	77%	80%	72%
Having car phone	74%	77%	70%
Flying first class	69%	69%	72%
Buying designer clothes	68%	71%	66%
Buying imported beer	66%	71%	59%
Buying expensive jewelry	65%	70%	55%
Using credit	49%	51%	45%
Having second home	36%	42%	27%
Seeing Broadway shows	32%	38%	22%
Taking foreign vacations	31%	38%	19%
Stock market investing	27%	30%	21%
Dining at expensive restaurants with family or friends	23%	28%	15%

Source: *The Bruskin Report,* August 1989, R. H. Bruskin Associates

Working and Earning

Here are some observations by affluents about themselves that tell the whole affluent work-earn-spend story. Measuring the percent of affluents (household income $50,000+) who agree with the following statements, a study from the National Sporting Goods Association reports that affluents do not see themselves "living for today " (index 78), TV-watching (index 80), and staying at home (index 91). On the other hand, while affluents agree (66%) that they should try to relax more (index 108), 44% agree that work is more satisfying than leisure (at an index of 104), and 37% agree that they are not too careful about spending (index 101). The percentage ranking defines total *numbers* of affluents with particular attitudes, while the index ranking defines the *frequencies* of a given attitude within the affluent population.

In other words: affluents live hard, play hard, think that they should relax more, but also think that work is actually more enjoyable than leisure. (We'll go further into that in chapter 4.) Perhaps that's because to the vast majority of affluents, work is a career (index 169) rather than just a job (index 75).[66] Affluents work hard for what they have, but they also work hard because they enjoy the work itself. They believe in what they are doing.

Futility is not a characteristic of the affluent temperament—the monied believe in cause and effect. On the other side of the spectrum are the poor and despairing who see little connection between actions and accolades (see exhibit 3-11).

Exhibit 3-11.   Hard work offers little guarantee of success
(percent who completely or mostly agree)

■ 1987 ☐ vs. 1990

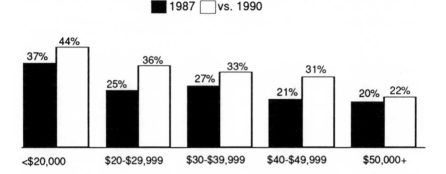

37% / 44%	25% / 36%	27% / 33%	21% / 31%	20% / 22%
<$20,000	$20-$29,999	$30-$39,999	$40-$49,999	$50,000+

Source: *The People, the Press, & Politics 1990: A Times Mirror Political Typology*, the Times Mirror Center for People & the Press

Every income range has curtailed its faith in hard work somewhat since 1987, but the highest range still exhibits the classic capitalist ideal of remuneration in keeping with effort. Since they speak from a position of wealth, affluents are not surprisingly supportive of the philosophical underpinnings of the system which helped them get that way.[67]

The accomplishment values for Influents of the 1990s:

- Hard work;
- Satisfaction in earning and contributing;
- Innovation;
- Productivity.[68]

The affluent work ethic has a variety of ramifications for the affluent market—and the affluent marketer. Affluents feel that they earn what they buy. This is especially true when they buy a product or service that saves them time. They spend a lot of time on their careers, so they have the money to spend on *more* time for themselves. This is a cyclical, self-perpetuating market, because the affluent mindstyle makes time a commodity (in the beginning of this book, we told you that the affluents were redefining themselves and the affluent market).

Affluents do not spend a lot of time in front of the tube; as you will see in chapters 4 and 5. The affluent mindstyle is set to take leisure very seriously; leisure—like lunch in Los Angeles—is something to be done. Affluents have often paid a lot of money for their leisure time, and nothing is going to stand in the way of them spending more money doing exactly what they want to do. They've earned it; they've paid for it; and they will enjoy it anyway they choose.

Career-oriented affluents are business-savvy, and their experience in the workplace only enhances their professional treatment of personal finances. They diversify their own financial portfolios as deftly and as professionally as they attack the fiscal-oriented challenges of their careers. Affluents are out in the world; they are action-oriented, work-oriented, and cause-and-effect-oriented; they literally won't have the time for marketers and advertisers who do not learn to address them and their needs directly. They have the money to buy, but you have to work hard for their money. Perhaps more than in any other market segment, working affluents are going to evaluate how well you do your job, how professional you can be in approaching another professional.

Family and Social Values
Some trend-watchers like to overstate the facts. Trends take time to develop. The changes in social values that we will address here are long, slow evolutions, not the catchy headline-labeled fads that the media make them out to be. We have many years to go before we can judge whether this will indeed be a *decade of decency*, or a *decade of home*. Such trend hypers have suggested that by flipping over one letter of the alphabet, public sentiment is going to turn a decade upside down, reforming the "me" in all of us into a "we" for all of us. We feel the following trends will emerge, but slowly, incrementally, inexorably—not with media speed.

Researchers predict that as the Baby Boomers age, these "sustaining" values:

- Judging for yourself;
- Questioning authority;

- Social consciousness;
- Self-protection; and
- Attacking problems head-on,

will be enhanced by these values as the Boomers mature:

- "Me" becoming "we;"
- Realizing that they can't make it alone;
- Family;
- Longer-term orientation;
- Less superficial values;
- Reaching out: community, nature, etc.; and,
- Preservation.[69]

Boomers may grow into a more caring group; but to announce it with trumpets blaring at this stage in development may be to send out a fad in trend clothing. (Have you seen the bell-bottoms and peace signs that are slowly coming out of hiding?) It is already stylish for everyone from the White House ("the caring thing") to rock star managers ("he won't perform there because of the country's record on human rights") to issue what amount to publicity statements on caring. Another word for this kind of caring might be realignment—realigning ourselves to causes, to ideas, to each other. Having blasted out of a decade like the 1980s, its no wonder everything old—like caring and sharing—is new again. Boomers are going to have to learn to live in what is, in more ways than one, a postboom world.

On the other hand, Boomers are likely to be a vocal bunch—after all, they've made sonic booms in demographic charts ever since their collective arrival—and the generation that spawned the yuppies will probably be capable of sending people who are just as driven out into the world fighting for more than one cause. But a genuine trend is beginning to take root and appear in research data. Expect to see some very real but gradual shifts in opinions and attitudes—shifts that will continue and reverberate in the research data you see over the next few years.

If we take a wait-and-see attitude with yuppies, what are the people who've already made it to the top concerned about? Exhibit 3-12 shows that on a personal front, manufacturing CEOs are concerned with their health and their children. They are *least* concerned about that which they are said (and encouraged) to worry about most: personal image and appearance (9%). A new personal worry appears in the '89 survey—"aging parents," ranked seventh. Here comes the age wave, sweeping more than one generation at a time. Income level ranks eighth behind a list of far-reaching concerns, suggesting that CEOs feel adequately compensated. Anxiety over job changes fell in importance since the last survey was taken, most likely a result of after-Crash reshuffling and successful readjustment.

Exhibit 3-12.   What are people who've already made it to the top concerned about?

	Ranked in top 5 by	'89 rank	'87 rank
Your health and fitness	79%	1	1
Your children	64%	2	3
Estate planning	42%	3	6
Lack of leisure time	42%	3 (tie)	2
Personal investments	40%	5	5
Aging	33%	6	8
Aging parents	25%	7	n/a
Income level	22%	8	9
Career changes/ job stress	21%	9	3
Your marriage	16%	10	10

Source: "18th Annual CEO Survey: Views From the Corner Office," *Industry Week*

Affluents put their two cents in. About a quarter of those with household incomes of $60,000 or more spoke up at a public meeting during 1989, while a fifth got embroiled in a social issue or wrote a public official (exhibit 3-13). There is no data here to directly compare these affluent activities to the rest of the nation's, but the image of affluents as motivated, action-oriented attitude leaders is consistent with them picking up the civic ball and running with it.[70]

Environment

If you don't turn green with the environmental consumerism movement as it transforms the nation (and the world), you're going to turn green with envy at the marketers who capture your affluence market with their environmental posture. The growing trend towards environmental responsibility—if not yet a formal, unified movement—is, on its own steam, one of the few issues soliciting agreement and hearty approval from people of all walks of life. And it is lead by the affluent.

Exhibit 3-13. Percent of affluents who

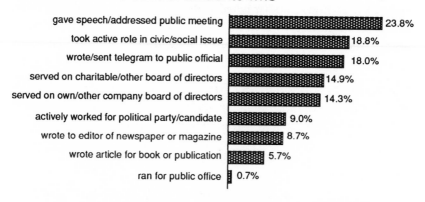

gave speech/addressed public meeting	23.8%
took active role in civic/social issue	18.8%
wrote/sent telegram to public official	18.0%
served on charitable/other board of directors	14.9%
served on own/other company board of directors	14.3%
actively worked for political party/candidate	9.0%
wrote to editor of newspaper or magazine	8.7%
wrote article for book or publication	5.7%
ran for public office	0.7%

Source: *1989 Survey of Adults and Markets of Affluence,* Mendelsohn Media Research, Inc.

No longer the sole domain of those committed few, who wouldn't be caught dead without a copy of *Walden* in their backpacks, environmental issues have become a significant and growing concern on Main Street, USA. Americans who think the overall quality of the environment is deteriorating outnumber those who think it is improving. Concern about the environment has already gone past the limited boundaries of a fad. Cambridge Reports indicates that two out of three consumers support stricter air pollution standards even if they result in such economic costs as the loss of jobs. Bouncing back from last year's decline, a majority of Americans are advocating more regulation of the environment overall.

The greatest concern about environmentalism lives on the upscale end of Main Street. A 1990 study from Scott Paper Company[71] found that 72% of affluents (household income $50,000+) have taken environmental actions, compared to 60% of middle-class and 41% of those below the income middle. Again this mindstyle correlates to education levels—60% of those with college degrees and 67% of those with graduate degrees are environmental consumers.[72] The greenest greens, the hard-core environmental consumers, are firmly upscale. This hard-core 14% of the population is twice as likely to live in an affluent household and twice as likely to have a college diploma.[73]

A look at the psychographics of environmentalism confirms that the upscale side of society is also the most eco-conscious. The Roper Organization finds that the two greenest segments (True-Blue Green and Greenback Greens) each comprise 11% of the U.S. population and are located on the upper end of the education and economic spectrums.

The Roper Organization's 1990 report, *The Environment: Public Attitudes and Individual Behavior,* commissioned by S.C. Johnson & Son, shows that compared to the average U.S. citizen, True-Blues are:

- two and a half times more likely to read labels (64% vs. 26% U.S. average);
- twice as likely to avoid aerosols (55% vs. 23%), buy biodegradable trash bags (52% vs. 25%) and soaps/detergents (58% vs. 24%);
- more than three times as likely to buy recycled products/ packages (52% vs. 14%), refillable products (45% vs. 14%), and to avoid restaurants which use styrofoam containers (33% vs. 7%);
- much more likely to recycle/return newspapers (59% vs. 26%), bottles and cans (76% vs. 46%), and sort the trash (55% vs. 24%);
- four times as likely to give money to environmental groups (32% vs. 8%), to cut down on car use (29% vs. 8%), and write to politicians about the concerns (24% vs. 4%).

The green consumer will become a driving force in the 1990s. Pin this reminder above your desk—the green consumer is most likely an affluent-minded consumer.

Deep concern about the environment reaches from the traditional avenues of action among political and environmental activists all the way to the CEO's agenda of top priorities. Environmental degradation is ranked ninth on the following table of CEOs' concerns for the nation, showing that, in keeping with their career worry of environmental control, executives are sensitive to the national, and presumably global, dimension of the problem. Also worth noting is that commitment to the environment has become stronger over the past two years. Buried in the depths on '87 priority lists, the planet makes headway into the Top 10 in '89—a far more dramatic rise than for any other national problem. Note the increased concern for the environment as both a national and a workplace problem (exhibits 3-14 and 3-15).

Exhibit 3-14.   CEOs' national worries

	Ranked in top 5 by	'89 rank	'87 rank
Federal budget deficit	77%	1	1
Drug abuse	68%	2	8
Trade deficit	52%	3	3
Loss of basic industries	43%	4	5
Government regulation	41%	5	4
Taxes and tax policy	39%	6	2
Inflation	33%	7	7
U.S. political leadership	26%	8	6
Environmental degradation	25%	9	15
Crime	23%	10	13

Source: "18th Annual CEO Survey: Views From the Corner Office,"
Industry Week

Exhibit 3-15.   CEOs' career/workplace worries

	Ranked in top 5 by	'89 rank	'87 rank
Product quality	61%	1	2
Cutting labor/production costs	55%	2	4
Company's future	53%	3	1
Keeping up with technology	35%	4	2
Product development	34%	5	13
Compliance with regulations	28%	6	5
Product liability	25%	7	7
Environmental control	23%	8	23
Competition from imports	22%	9	8
Employee drug use	20%	10	19

Source: "18th Annual CEO Survey: Views From the Corner Office,"
Industry Week

Environmental policy—money where the mouth is?

Environmental activism increases with income. In fact, the wealthiest Americans demonstrate more willingness to sacrifice the economy for environmental protection (62%) than do those in the lower income brackets (exhibits 3-16 and 3-17). In addition, more than half (57%) of those respondents with graduate/professional school on their resumes agree that an economic sacrifice must be made when it comes to securing environmental protection (vs. 16% with the same educational credits). When asked if existing air pollution regulations are effective, 64% in the affluent range say no (vs. 27% in the same upscale household incomes who believe existing regulations are indeed doing the necessary job).[74]

Exhibit 3-16. Affluents' opinions on economic growth vs. environment (by income)

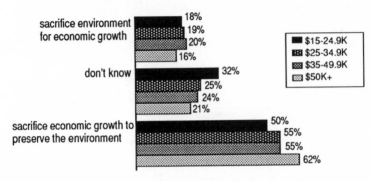

Source: *The Environment: New Concerns, New Choices*, Cambridge Reports' Trends and Forecasts

In the affluent range of $50,000+ household income, 62% of the respondents—the highest percentage in any of the income

Exhibit 3-17. In the past year, have you or has anyone in your household donated to or been active in a group or organization working to protect the environment? (by income)

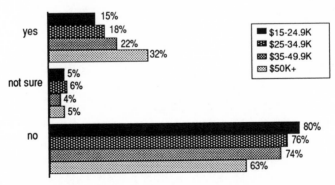

Source: *The Environment: New Concerns, New Choices*, Cambridge Reports' Trends and Forecasts

categories—think there is too little government regulation and involvement in the area of environmental protection.

Other environmental nightmares

The Cambridge Reports' research also tackles the topics of water pollution, depletion of the ozone layer, and the greenhouse effect. Overall, Americans are increasingly concerned about their drinking water; yet, those earning more than $50,000 a year are a bit more optimistic—15% of affluents, vs. 22% of the general population think most underground water sources are contaminated. On the other hand, the affluent are the most likely to say that the depletion of the ozone layer is a very serious problem (53% vs. 39% overall). The same holds true in the education category—the more education, the more grave the ozone problem appears to be.

In turning to the greenhouse effect, credit the high visibility given the topic in the media to the seriousness with which the plurality of Americans treat it. Thirty-nine percent of the population rates the gradual warming of the earth's atmosphere as "very serious." This represents a fifteen-point increase over the past two years. Of the reported income groups, the greatest percentage of concerned respondents falls in the most affluent $50,000+ category (47%).[75]

For quick reference, we offer guidelines we developed in another publication devoted to marketing green products. These strictures will insure that you make a strong and positive impact on the upscale sector that drives the green movement. These leaders are also consumers who will reward your efforts with strong and lucrative brand loyalty.

Exhibit 3-18. Resources that might be depleted in 20-25 years

	Influentials	Total public
Clean air	66%	61%
Drinking water	53%	47%
Wild animal life	49%	41%
Wilderness areas	45%	38%
Farmland	44%	38%
Oil	42%	31%

Source: *The Influential Americans: Who They Are, How To Reach Them,* The Roper Organization, Inc.

Making green your competitive edge

Start today
- Work toward a vision of your company and its products in a green future.
- Discover what is green about each product and make it known—to every one.
- Set an example—for the industry and the nation.

Be pro-active
- Anticipate consumers' concerns and address them.
- Educate your customers about the green issues that affect your product.

Take the high road
- Avoid short-term, quick-fix solutions.
- Build coalitions with environmental and regulatory bodies.
- Incorporate a cradle-to-grave approach that handles the full life cycle of your product.

Empower the consumer with solutions
- Provide interchangeable alternatives to current products.
- Show consumers how to make a difference by using your products.

Source: J. Ottman Consulting, in *Environmental Consumerism: What Every Marketer Needs to Know*, Alert Publishing Inc., 1991

Charitable Contributions

On the face of it, affluent charitable contributions are impressive: 94% of affluents gave donations in the past year, and the average amount was $1,010, over one-and-a-half times the $640 given by those in the household income group just below them ($35,000–$49,999). The affluent spread their donations among a variety of organizations (religious, church, civic, community, education, etc.). However, the *percent* of income donated was the lowest of all income groups, 1.4%, and is dramatically low when compared to the 2.1% of income donated by those with household income of $15,000. It seems those who can least afford it give the most, while those who could most afford it give the least.[76]

Also, it should be noted that the majority of affluent contributions do not go to share-the-wealth causes. Over half of the dollars given by affluents to philanthropic causes, and claimed as tax deductions, go to institutions that serve affluents' interests and values—private education and medical institutions and cultural organizations. This is not to proclaim that the affluents dodge taxes by funneling their wealth into self-serving causes, but it does attest that the affluent are not altogether altruistic with the points of light they wish to offer back to the society that has served them. (See chapter 7 for more on this subject.)

Wealthy households give smaller percentages of their incomes to charity than do others. In real dollars, though, their generosity is greater (exhibit 3-19). The wealthiest of the wealthy give 2.9% of their total income. The national norm is 2.5%, but it's the middle-income folks who keep their fists tight: the lowest income group gives the highest percentage—5.5%. The average $379 annual gift from lowest-income givers doesn't hold a candle, though, to the $2,893 from the rich.

Exhibit 3-19. How much people give

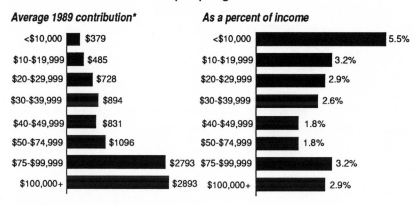

Average 1989 contribution*

Income	Amount
<$10,000	$379
$10-$19,999	$485
$20-$29,999	$728
$30-$39,999	$894
$40-$49,999	$831
$50-$74,999	$1096
$75-$99,999	$2793
$100,000+	$2893

As a percent of income

Income	Percent
<$10,000	5.5%
$10-$19,999	3.2%
$20-$29,999	2.9%
$30-$39,999	2.6%
$40-$49,999	1.8%
$50-$74,999	1.8%
$75-$99,999	3.2%
$100,000+	2.9%

*average for givers only

Source: *Giving and Volunteering in the U.S. 1990*, Independent Sector

The statistics are deceiving here, because the affluent are much, much more likely to give than are others. When compared on a total-household basis rather than a per-giver basis, the percentage disparity virtually disappears. In other words, the affluent's tendency to give a smaller portion of their income is compensated by their increased likelihood to give anything at all (exhibit 3-20).

Exhibit 3-20. Giving by income groups, 1989: average contribution, percent of income, and percent of group who give

Income level	Average 1989 contribution*	As % of income	% who give
<$10,000	$186	2.5%	49.0%
$10-$19,999	$316	1.9%	65.1%
$20-$29,999	$560	2.1%	76.9%
$30-$39,999	$732	2.0%	81.9%
$40-$49,999	$702	1.5%	84.5%
$50-$74,999	$936	1.5%	85.5%
$75-$99,999	$2575	2.9%	92.1%
$100,000+	$2512	2.4%	86.8%

* average for all households

Source: *Giving and Volunteering in the U.S. 1990*, Independent Sector

Affluents are the most likely of income groups to blame the new tax laws for cutting back on charitable donations (13%). However, it still allows full deductions for charities for those who itemize, i.e., high-income earners. Still, to claim the deduction, they have to open the wallet, and affluents like to stay close to their money. Similarly, they keep their hands out of their pockets when confronted with street beggars. Affluents are more likely to see homeless people than are other income groups, are approached the most frequently for handouts, and give very rarely.[77]

Almost half of all Americans plan to itemize their deductions (41%), and 74% of these itemizers intend to claim a deduction based on charitable donations. Affluents are more likely than other income groups to claim a deduction based on a charitable gift (exhibit 3-21). This fact—combined with affluents' seeming reluctance to give on the spur of the moment—point to the fact that the care affluents seem to take in keeping a watchful eye on their charitable financial dealings mirrors the more careful attention they give to the general handling (banking, investments) of their finances.

Exhibit 3-21. Percent of itemizers who say yes they intend to claim charitable deductions or no they don't

	Yes	No
Total	73.6%	22.5%
Income level:		
<$20,000	51.4%	47.2%
$20-$29,999	69.9%	23.6%
$30-$39,999	74.6%	21.7%
$40-$49,999	72.0%	22.7%
$50-$59,999	79.7%	16.5%
$60-$74,999	80.3%	15.7%
$75-$99,999	91.6%	7.2%
$100,000+	84.9%	10.7%

Source: *Giving and Volunteering in the U.S. 1990*, Independent Sector

Time is just as good as money when it comes to sharing wealth; this is perhaps especially true for affluents, who so closely connect time and money in all aspects of their lives. Here, the stereotypical connection between riches and charities is borne out by the data: high-income volunteers give more time (exhibit 3-22).

Since the impediment to volunteering for most people is a scheduling or time constraint, those working the hardest chalk up the least hours.

Exhibit 3-22. Average hours volunteered per week (by income level)

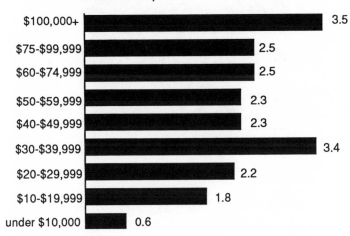

Source: *Giving and Volunteering in the U.S. 1990*, Independent Sector

Without indulging in second guessing the affluent impulse towards giving time to volunteer work, it is important to remember that many affluents have more money (and therefore more time) to give as they may choose.

Affluents also may feel more comfortable thinking about others from the context of their more familiar social and professional circles. As we have noted, affluents are not likely to appreciate being approached directly for giving by the people or organizations most likely to benefit directly from their help. In most cases, the affluent volunteer is recruited by a friend or finds out by way of an organizational tie—60% of the time, it's a religious group (see exhibit 3-23).

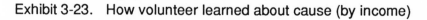

Exhibit 3-23. How volunteer learned about cause (by income)

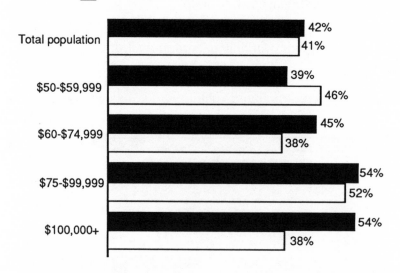

☐ Was asked by someone

■ Through participation in an organization

Total population	42%	41%
$50-$59,999	39%	46%
$60-$74,999	45%	38%
$75-$99,999	54%	52%
$100,000+	54%	38%

Source: *Giving and Volunteering in the U.S. 1990*, Independent Sector

Public service messages on TV reach a surprising number of affluents: 71% of those with incomes of $100,000 or more say they saw a cause advertised recently, as compared to only 58% of the total population. When affluents do take the step of giving up time and energy, it's because they "want to do something useful" (exhibit 3-24). About 60% cite this as the reason, though 40% say they also do it for enjoyment. Over half of all Americans volunteered in 1990.[78]

Exhibit 3-24.   Reasons Americans give for volunteering (by household income)

	Total	$50,000-$59,999	$60,000-$74,999	$75,000-$100,000
Wanted to do something useful	62%	63%	59%	73%
Thought I would enjoy the work	34%	37%	40%	41%
Family member or friend would benefit	29%	37%	32%	32%
Religious concerns	26%	29%	25%	35%
Had a lot of free time	10%	4%	10%	6%
Previously benefited from the activity	9%	12%	7%	16%

Source: *Giving and Volunteering in the U.S. 1990*, Independent Sector

---

On Being and Feeling Wealthy

A recent poll by the Gallup Organization suggests that many affluent Americans can wipe that apologetic look off their faces; they're not bad guys anymore. Most of the nation think it's OK to be rich and, given the choice, would choose rich over not-rich. But even those Americans who are sure they'll never see buckets of green, harbor little resentment for the wealthy; in fact, a majority of the country perceive rich people as a benefit to society (exhibit 3-25).

Exhibit 3-25.   Does the country benefit from having rich people in tis midst?

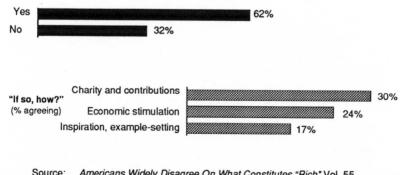

Source: *Americans Widely Disagree On What Constitutes "Rich"* Vol. 55., No. 9, The Gallup Poll

Free-speaking Americans love to express their opinions. However, angry people probably won't be gathering outside of the halls of prosperity in this country: a whopping 82% of Americans do not feel jealousy towards the wealthy, and 52% feel respect and admiration. This charitable attitude towards the wealthy is due in part, no doubt, to the ever-present possibility that most Americans treasure— you *can* get there from here—no matter how low on the economic totem pole "here" happens to be. But perhaps prefacing a growing feeling that the doors of upward mobility are frequently slamming in the hopeful faces of an increasing number of Americans, two-thirds of us do think that the distribution of wealth in this country should be more even.

Even during the continuing polarization of wealth in the nation, more than half of Americans (55%) say there is just about the right number of rich people. As discussed earlier, we're apt to congratulate an individual if he is rich, but blame society if he is poor. On the other hand, 45% think poverty stems from outside factors, while 35% think being poor is a sign of deflated effort. That's somewhat of a compassionate twist from dominant opinion six years ago, when only 34% were willing to blame poverty on circumstances.

Exhibit 3-26.   Do you think rich people in America today are happier than you, less happy, or about the same?

Source: *Americans Widely Disagree On What Constitutes "Rich"* Vol. 55, No. 9, The Gallup Poll

---

Given the option, most Americans would add at least one to the roll call of the rich in this country: 59% of Americans say they want to be rich, while 38% say no, thanks. But if the road to riches is full of compromises (well-documented in 1980s cultural vernacular, especially in films like *Wall Street*—with "Greed is Good" as the eleventh commandment), some sacrifices are *not* worth making (exhibit 3-27).

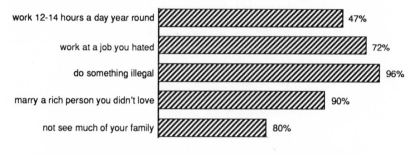

Exhibit 3-27.　If it were guaranteed to make you rich, would you . . . (percent saying "not very willing to")

work 12-14 hours a day year round — 47%
work at a job you hated — 72%
do something illegal — 96%
marry a rich person you didn't love — 90%
not see much of your family — 80%

Source:　*Americans Widely Disagree On What Constitutes "Rich"* Vol. 55, No. 9 The Gallup Poll

Reflecting what we've seen as a growing trend towards the mindstyle of old money, the poll finds that we long not for lavish parties, spiffy clothes, or speedy cars, but rather for security, freedom, and the financial latitude to be generous.

The most popular reason for wanting to be rich derives from two of the most profound trends in society: the rising cost of health care and the aging of the population. Clearly, worries about affording medical care for aging parents and oneself is becoming an underlying theme in most Americans' thinking (exhibit 3-28). As a result, "not having to worry in the event of illness or emergency" (81% agree) is the number one reason Americans would like to be rich. Almost as many Americans cite "sending children through college without financial strain" (79%). Wanting to contribute—both to charity and to children—is a strong motivation, too.

Of course, the driving push of affluence does not rest on its laurels of past achievements; rather, it rests on a fundamental aspect of human nature—the desire to do better, and the drive to have more than you have now.

Exhibit 3-28. How important is each of the following as a reason for wanting to be rich? (percent saying "very important")

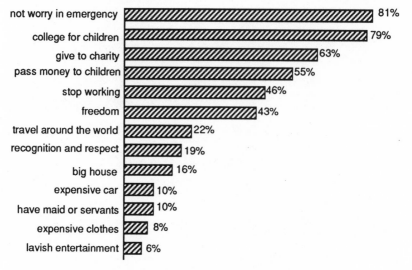

not worry in emergency	81%
college for children	79%
give to charity	63%
pass money to children	55%
stop working	46%
freedom	43%
travel around the world	22%
recognition and respect	19%
big house	16%
expensive car	10%
have maid or servants	10%
expensive clothes	8%
lavish entertainment	6%

Source: *Americans Widely Disagree On What Constitutes "Rich" Vol. 55, No. 9, The Gallup Poll*

Exhibit 3-29. Satisfied with personal finances (percent who completely or mostly agree)

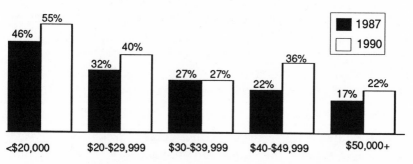

	<$20,000	$20-$29,999	$30-$39,999	$40-$49,999	$50,000+
1987	46%	32%	27%	22%	17%
1990	55%	40%	27%	36%	22%

Source: *The People, the Press, & Politics 1990: A Times Mirror Political Typology*, Times Mirror Center for the People & The Press

Across the board, each income range is more satisfied than it was three years ago, but in comparison to one another, the income ranges are vastly different. Affluents are about half as likely as average to feel settled financially. Hunger for more seems to be a pillar of the affluent mindstyle, particularly among New Money affluents.

This dynamic is a practical and psychological fallout from the affluence explosion of the 1980s. As we moved into the tighter-money 1990s, this infusion of new affluents felt threatened. In many cases they *should* feel threatened—the recession is hitting the ranks of the barely affluent. Many dual-income couples eked their way into affluence on the strength of boomtime bonuses, second jobs and real estate investment. Recession is squeezing all three to some degree: bonuses are down (as much as 50% by some reports); "extra" jobs are one of the first things to be eliminated in corporate trimming; real estate is flat or falling. So, nouveau- or barely-affluents find their new-found status under siege. Any time substantial layoffs among upscale professions are publicized there is an immediate gasp among the barely-affluent. Some reports estimate that 35% of Wall Street jobs have been eliminated in the past four years. Fear will drive many affluents for the next few years, particularly younger affluents, now under age 45.

Hunger will keep the affluents affluent; hunger will keep others doing what they can to become affluent. But consider for a moment one of the reasons given for wanting to be wealthy: the desire to be financially able (to be and *feel* secure enough) to contribute to others. This reason—traditionally defined by the term largesse—also puts a curious financial spin to the old idea of the white knight in fairy tales. In the 1980s, corporate raiding led to the term white knight being applied to the individual or corporation who could save a business from a hostile takeover. In the 1990s, growing social and economic problems will contribute to the fantasy of a wealthy white knight who—by benefit of good will *and* wealth—can save others from the harsh realities of bifurcation and recession. And in many cases, the basic desire for financial security will make heroes of those who can just manage to keep their heads (and those of their families) above water. Hanging on securely to what you already have (among affluents, this will translate as preservation; among others, this will translate as something closer to survival) will never seem more like a heroic deed than it will in the coming decade.

Chapter

IV

Lifestyle

To see how the upper half spends, look at how the upper half lives—not to mention how they *want* to live, or how the lower half wants to live *like* them. We know that it is difficult to get a quantitative measurement on discretionary income; we also know that discretionary income— as vague as that term is — is the best way we have to describe the money available for extra expenditures that we so often associate with the affluent consumer. Of all the categories analyzing the affluent consumer, lifestyle probably comes closest in encompassing and measuring the *qualitative* aspects of discretionary income. This section includes the gray areas of affluence that require the most gray matter activity from marketers.

If the best way to get to know someone is by living with them, consider this chapter your invitation to get to know affluent consumers up close and personal, without Robin Leach. You'll see what they do over the weekend with their leisure time—and find out that affluents stay *busy* almost all of the time. Accompany them on trips—both for business and for pleasure—and note how often they travel, how they like to get where they're going, and what they expect when they get there. Follow them when they go out to eat, and let them order dinner for you. Their choices will tell you a lot about what foods they prefer, what treats they demand, what kind of service they want, and whether or not they are as conscious of good health as they say they are.

On the drive back to their home, make sure you recognize the make and model of their car. Affluents often spend a lot of time *in* their cars, and they often spend a lot of money *on* their cars. Is the garage connected to a home they own, a house they rent, or an apartment building? Once inside, a quick glance around the affluent household should tell you quite a bit about your host: scan the array of electronic equipment and appliances. See if there is any gear to tell you what kind of exercise and sports the affluent prefers. Also note whether or not your particular affluent consumer is—like many of his or her fellow affluents—involved in remodeling a room (especially the kitchen).

Very important to your investigation will be to see how what the products the affluent buys measures up to how the affluent lives. Does everything you see point to affluence, until you check your host's bank book? Or do things look curiously spartan and grim, until you find out that the house is sitting on an oil field? Is the immediate environment a pretty accurate stage setting for the active affluents who live there? No detail is too small. If you get close enough, you will be able to see indications of how affluents want to live, compared to how different affluents really spend their time—*and* their money. You will also see products that become upscale image icons to the rest of the consuming public—these will trickle down into mass popularity as less expensive, approximate versions. For every $2,500 stationary bicycle you find in an affluent fitness room, you'll find three $69.95 bikes in middle-class bedrooms.

Leisure

Despite the stereotypes which promulgate an image of scads of leisure hours, affluents are busy, very busy. They *like* to be active in their long-houred work lives and in their leisure. They spend a lot for services that would be a luxury to most, but are necessities to them in order to manage their time efficiently and enjoyably. Their higher discretionary income levels permit them to do so.

Leisure is an ambiguous term to use when you are talking about affluent consumers. Affluents may consider swinging in a hammock on a Sunday afternoon a leisure activity; they are, however, likely to have busily traveled somewhere other than their own back yard to swing. And it is just as likely with this group that they have leisurely enjoyed any number of activities—from three sets of tennis and an aerobic workdown afterwards to a few decisive car phone meetings on the way back to the resort—before they've hit that hammock. Remember that affluents may have ambivalent feelings about leisure. A recent survey by the National Sporting Goods Association finds that while 66% of affluents say that they "should try to relax more," a full 44% agree that "work is more satisfying than leisure."

Satisfying leisure for the affluent, therefore, can include a lot of activities and pursuits that aren't stereotypically restful or playful. Look to other areas of the affluent lifestyle—such as travel, sports, hobbies, health, home, and even media—to see more specifically how affluents often do something with their leisure time. Relate factors such as education, for instance, to the affluent idea of reading as a pleasurable leisure activity. Keep the affluent mindstyle in mind as an especially important factor, both for deciphering affluent leisure in particular and affluent lifestyle in general. Mindstyle will explain some of the constantly shifting lines between affluent work and play, between affluent obligation and enjoyment.

The Lifestyle Market Analyst examines the activities of households, rather than individuals, by many demographic criteria.[79] The list in exhibit 4-1 includes just some of the activities passionately pursued by households with $50,000+ and $75,000+ annual household income.

Although affluents can often be found in the office and on the road, perhaps the biggest news about affluent leisure is how many of the elements of affluent mindstyle and lifestyle can converge in the affluent home. Affluents are *not* likely to be glued to the television screen, and although they may be in the kitchen, or working out in the exercise room, it is very likely that they are planning or having a party or a dinner. And—true to the busy affluent leisure style—they are likely to be doing more than one thing at a time; in the case of entertaining at home, they will probably be taking care of business and pleasure.

Everyone likes a party, but affluents *really* like a party. When asked if they like entertaining, 61% of affluents (household income $75,000+) said "very much." About 44% of those with household incomes of

Exhibit 4-1.   Most popular affluent household lifestyle activities/interests by age category within affluent income segments (average U.S. household index=100)

$50,000 + HHs	Index	$75,000+ HHs	Index
18-34 years			
Snow skiing frequently	256	Snow skiing frequently	365
Real estate investments	232	Real estate investments	349
Racquetball	221	Tennis frequently	310
Tennis frequently	199	Racquetball	266
Wines	188	Wines	260
Stock/bond investments	181	Stock/bond investments	235
Personal/home computers	181	Foreign travel	229
Golf	180	Career-oriented activities	225
Running/jogging	177	Running/jogging	225
Science/new technology	172	Fashion clothing	201
Boating/sailing	157	Personal/home computers	198
35-44 years			
Real estate investments	234	Real estate investments	325
Personal/home computers	225	Tennis frequently	276
Stock/bond investments	187	Snow skiing frequently	265
Tennis frequently	184	Wines	237
Wines	175	Personal/home computers	233
Snow skiing frequently	175	Stock/bond investments	222
Golf	165	Foreign travel	215
Running/jogging	161	Career-oriented activities	212
Foreign travel	154	Running/jogging	201
Science/new technology	154	Fine arts/antiques	185
Racquetball	148	Racquetball	182
45-64 years			
Real estate investments	273	Real estate investments	356
Stock/bond investments	244	Foreign travel	285
Foreign travel	219	Stock/bond investments	276
Wines	178	Tennis frequently	239
Golf	178	Wines	227
Attend cultural/arts events	171	Attend cultural/arts events	200
Personal/home computers	167	Fine arts/antiques	197
Community/civic activities	163	Golf	185
Fine arts/antiques	156	Personal/home computers	183
Tennis frequently	153	Gourmet cooking/fine foods	176
Gourmet cooking/fine foods	143	Current affairs/politics	175
65+ years			
Stock/bond investments	357	Stock/bond investments	384
Foreign travel	305	Foreign travel	358
Real estate investments	252	Real estate investments	331
Golf	218	Current affairs/politics	227
Community/civic activities	194	Golf	222
Attend cultural/arts events	184	Grandchildren	210
Fine art/antiques	153	Attend cultural/arts events	204

(cont.)

(Ex. 4-1 cont.)

Wines	135	Community/civic activities	194
Avid book reading	130	Fine arts/antiques	192
Gardening	127	Wines	171
Coin/stamp collecting	125	Tennis frequently	171

> Source: *The Lifestyle Market Analyst,* National Demographics and Lifestyles/SRDS

$50,000–$75,000 agreed. That percentage drops to only 39% of those with household incomes between $25,000–$40,000. The affluent are more inclined than others to view a party as a chance to score business points, whether by talking shop (69% of affluents do this at parties) or by handing out business cards (18% do).[80]

Exhibit 4-2. If you had to choose one of the following couples whose style of entertaining you identify with, who would it be?

	$25,000-$40,000	$40,000-$50,000	$50,000-$75,000	$75,000+
The couples from "thirtysomething"	26%	30%	29%	28%
The Cosbys	20%	21%	21%	13%
Roseanne and John from "Roseanne"	21%	16%	12%	14%
Rob and Laura from "The Dick Van Dyke Show"	7%	5%	10%	3%
The Bushes	3%	5%	6%	16%
The Reagans	4%	3%	2%	4%
Blake and Krystal from "Dynasty"	2%	2%	3%	3%
None	9%	7%	8%	10%

> Source: *The Crown Royal Report on American Entertaining,* Research & Forecasts, Inc.

Affluents are nearly three times more likely to have a party or social get-together at home than elsewhere. A median 1.2 times a month, affluents host some kind of social shindig. Compare this to a median .5 times per month for celebrations outside the home.[81]

No matter where the party is, if affluents are present, there's likely to be wine. The majority of affluents (household income $60,000+) say they are users of American table wine. No other alcoholic beverage gets a majority vote, though vodka and imported table wine are not too far behind in popularity among the affluent (exhibit 4-3).

Exhibit 4-3.   Popularity of particular alcoholic beverages

% of affluents who use

American table wine	70%
Vodka	49%
Imported table wine	46%
American champagne/sparkling wine	42%
Scotch	39%
Cordials or liqueurs	40%
Gin	37%
Rum	34%
Bourbon	34%
Wine coolers	33%
Imported champagne/sparkling wine	31%
Brandy or cognac	31%
Canadian whiskey	29%
Before/after dinner wine	28%
Tequila	24%
Blended or rye whiskey	23%
Irish whiskey	15%

Source: *1989 Survey of Adults and Markets of Affluence*, Mendelsohn Media Research, Inc.

As the Mendelsohn research points out, the most popular hard liquor is vodka, followed by scotch, gin, rum, and bourbon. Whiskey's not their first choice; but among the various whiskey forms, Canadian is affluents' favorite. The stereotypical affluent drink—champagne—makes a splash, with two-fifths of affluents sipping American brands and nearly a third toasting with imported bubbly.

Affluents like home entertaining despite the fact that it's costing them more now than it did five years ago. Among $75,000+ affluents, 63% agree they're spending more on home parties, compared with 60% of those in the $50,000–$75,000 income range, 47% of those in the $40,000–$50,000 range, and 46% of those in the $25,000–$40,000 range. The higher costs aren't just because of higher prices, either; nearly half (48%) of affluents believe their increased entertainment spending reflects that they're having more parties—and making more expensive choices when they do (exhibit 4-4).

When they don't have friends and business associates over, affluents turn to other members of the family for some joint entertainment ventures of their own. For the group of affluents characterized as Influentials, for instance, the family is a vehicle through which they enhance their experiences of leisure at home (exhibit 4-5).

Exhibit 4-4.   Percent of affluents (HHI $75K+) who agree,
                that aside from a general rise in prices, the
                following have made their entertaining more
                expensive

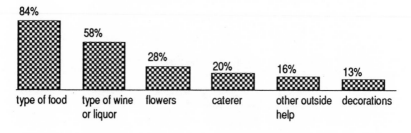

type of food	type of wine or liquor	flowers	caterer	other outside help	decorations
84%	58%	28%	20%	16%	13%

Source: *The Crown Royal Report on American Entertaining*, Research &
           Forecasts, Inc.

Exhibit 4-5.   Activities frequently done as a family unit

	Influentials	Total public
Have family meal together	72%	63%
Sit and talk as family	68%	51%
Visit friends together	60%	48%
Watch TV together	60%	58%
Take vacation together	59%	44%
Attend religious services together	55%	39%

Source: *The Influential Americans: Who They Are, How To Reach Them*,
           The Roper Organization, Inc.,

For the active (and actively socializing) affluents, one community
mainstay is "the Club." More than half belong to some sort of private
group—ranging from athletic to alumni—with golf and tennis leading the list (exhibit 4-6).

Travel

Judging by how, when, where, and why they go, travel appears to be
one of the major rewards—and obligations—of the affluent lifestyle.
Whether it's for business, pleasure, or a little bit of both, affluents are
often on the road or in the air. Affluent travel affects a wide variety of
consumer markets. The travel industry encompasses airlines, car
rental agencies, hotel and resort facilities, and, of course, travel
agencies. A considerable number of travel-related affluent consumer
activities, including dining and shopping, have a marked impact on

affluent consumer activity in general. Perhaps because travel is such an important part of the affluent lifestyle and mindstyle, a large body of research data is available on affluent travel patterns, habits, and preferences.

Exhibit 4-6.   Percent of affluents (HHI $60K+) who:

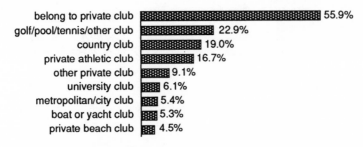

belong to private club	55.9%
golf/pool/tennis/other club	22.9%
country club	19.0%
private athletic club	16.7%
other private club	9.1%
university club	6.1%
metropolitan/city club	5.4%
boat or yacht club	5.3%
private beach club	4.5%

Source: *1989 Survey of Adults and Markets of Affluence*, Mendelsohn Media Research, Inc.

According to *Affluent Travelers*, a study by Reed Travel Market Reports, affluents make up nearly two-fifths of the entire travel market—travelers earning $40,000+ account for 37%, or 242.8 million of the 656.2 million trips taken by all Americans in 1988 (exhibit 4-7). The trend among the wealthy has been one of increasing travel. The number of trips taken by affluents increased 64% from 1984 to 1988, far outpacing the 24% figure for the total population.

Exhibit 4-7.   Trips by upscalers (HHI $40,000+) as percent of total trips

1984	28%
1985	28%
1986	31%
1987	36%
1988	37%

Source: *Affluent Travelers*, Reed Travel Market Reports

The U.S. Travel Data Center finds affluent travelers to be a special breed—older, better educated, and more likely than others to be on business rather than on vacation (exhibit 4-8).

Airlines and rental cars are used by a significantly higher percentage of affluent travelers than the average. Airlines are used by 34% of affluents, vs. 24% of total; rental cars, 13% of affluents, vs. 8% of total. The South is the favored destination of affluents; 30% of them go there. Also, they show a slightly higher preference for the West and the East than do total travelers. Travel outside the U.S. is on the agenda for 8% of affluents, and 6% of the total. Summer is the season of choice for $40,000+ travelers: 30% get going during the hot months (compare this to fall 26%, spring 22%, and winter 21%). Affluents indeed take more trips, but the trips are getting shorter—the average stay is down to 4.0 nights from 5.1 in 1984.[82]

Exhibit 4-8.   Demographics of affluent travelers

	Affluent travelers	Total travelers
Men	60%	53%
Women	40%	47%
18-24 years	10%	15%
25-34	24%	26%
35-44	30%	22%
45-54	21%	15%
55+	15%	22%
Median age	40 years	39 years
Less than college education	55%	70%
College graduate or more	45%	30%
Professional or managerial	27%	16%
Lower level technical or managerial occupations	25%	19%
Clerical or sales	13%	14%
Blue collar	14%	17%
Retired	6%	14%
Live in East	22%	18%
South	31%	36%
Midwest	23%	25%
West	24%	21%
Trip Characteristics*		
Vacation	51%	60%
Weekend	37%	41%
Business	27%	17%
Visit friends or relatives	26%	33%
Entertainment	19%	23%
Outdoor recreation	15%	14%
Personal/family	5%	7%

*doesn't add to 100 due to multiple answers

Source: *Affluent Travelers*, Reed Travel Market Reports

Another study measuring those affluents who obviously enjoy traveling (and traveling often) is the *Frequent Leisure Travelers—A Study of Markets and Media*, by Marketing Projects Group, Inc. In their vacation travel fantasies, affluents fly first class to Hawaii for about two weeks, stay in a deluxe hotel, and tour all the sites. In reality, the study notes that while affluents' leisure travel is far from this ideal vacation, they do their best to come close.

The upper-affluent are more likely to reach the ideal vacation paradise described above. Upper-affluents (household income $100,000+) take more leisure trips than do other affluents (household income $50,000-$99,999)—7.41 vacation trips in the past 12 months, versus 6.01—and they go farther when they do travel. Also, they are more likely to seek sophistication and luxury in their trips. When the upper-affluent say "leisure," they mean it, especially if leisure encompasses the freedom to devote time and energy more to the *manner* in which things are done and less to (the practical) *how* they get done.

By an overwhelming margin, affluents want control over their own plans while they are on vacation—plans which are much more likely to include a day-walk than a late-night dance. Though the majority of both affluent groups want to vacation in a casual atmosphere, the upper-affluent are more likely than others to opt for a sophisticated one. They are a little less likely than others to want seclusion, and, as exhibit 4-9 displays, their favorite vacation activity is cultural touring.

The upper-affluent rank sports-related travel relatively higher than do other affluents. The $100,000+ group prefers ski extravaganzas and diving expeditions over scenic encounters and theme park excitement (exhibit 4-10). Both groups predominantly opt for cultural sites in major cities and rustic weekends at country inns. In comparison to the moderately-affluent, the upper-affluent enjoy adventure trips, spa visits, and Club Med. In real numbers, none of these trip themes are very popular among the affluent.[83]

A study of upscale frequent leisure travelers (HHI $100K+, and having taken at least five leisure trips or more in the past three years) finds the affluent leisure traveler has sea legs (exhibit 4-11).

Of the slim majority of affluents who are either somewhat likely or very likely to take a cruise in the next three years, 68.4% of moderate affluents and 59% of upper-affluents want to go to the Caribbean. The locations next in popularity for cruise destinations are Alaska (37% and 44%), the Bahamas (34% and 22%), Bermuda (26% and 23%).

Exhibit 4-9. Affluent leisure trip characteristics

	HHI $50, 000-$99,999	HHI $100,000+
Mean number of leisure trips taken past 12 months	6.01	7.41
Mean number of leisure trips taken past 3 years	16.24	18.95
Types of trips likely:		
Frequent short trips (2 to 4 days)	48%	46%
Fewer trips with longer stays	38%	42%
Many budget trips	43%	25%
Few expensive trips	37%	55%
Close to home (<100 miles)	19%	11%
Farther from home	65%	72%
In U.S.	76%	65%
Foreign	14%	25%
Auto travel	58%	31%
Airline travel	32%	58%
Fly economy class	77%	69%
Fly first class	5%	18%
Use economy hotels	51%	25%
Use first class hotels	33%	60%
Sophisticated atmosphere	10%	23%
Casual atmosphere	75%	63%
Visit cities, being around people	43%	46%
More secluded	39%	35%
Night life	16%	16%
Daytime activities	66%	65%
Organized tours	11%	9%
Make own plans	76%	77%
Spontaneous travel	28%	24%
Planned travel	57%	60%

*sub-columns do not add to 100% due to respondents who had "no opinion"

Source: *Frequent Leisure Travelers—A Study of Markets and Media 1990*,
Erdos and Morgan/Marketing Projects Group, Inc.

Other places on the affluent cruise-to list include Hawaii, Mexico, Greece, and the South Pacific.

Exhibit 4-10. Types of leisure trips expected over next 12 months (numbers rounded)

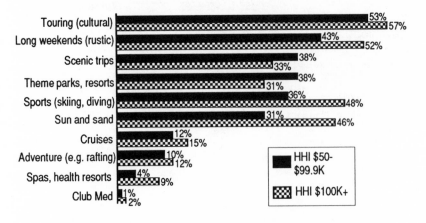

Source: Frequent Leisure Travelers—A Study of Markets and Media 1990,
           Erdos and Morgan/Marketing Projects Groups, Inc.

Exhibit 4-11. Affluents' likelihood of cruising in the next three years

	HHI $50,000-$99,999	HHI $100,000+
Not at all	46%	46%
Somewhat	31%	30%
Very	22%	23%

Source: Frequent Leisure Travelers—A Study of Markets and Media 1990,
           Erdos and Morgan/Marketing Projects Group, Inc.

The ideal cruise length is about a week: a mean of 7.68 days for the $50,000-$99,999 group and 8.02 days for the $100,000 and over group. During their cruise week, affluents want mostly to enjoy fine dining (86% of moderate affluents agree and 87% of upper-affluents agree), to rest and relax (73% and 70%), to go on land expeditions (68% and 67%), to watch live entertainment (62% and 54%), and to shop duty-free (46% and 34%). Other cruise activities mentioned include: couple-oriented activities, gambling, meeting people, exercising, movies, lectures, and totally free, unplanned time.[84]

Leisure travelers come in all shapes and sizes, but The American Express Global Travel Survey finds there are basically five types of leisure travelers: Adventurers, Worriers, Dreamers, Economizers, and Indulgers, with Adventurers and Indulgers tending to be the more affluent. Moreover, the members of these groups tend to have similar likes, dislikes and desires in the regions that have the most travel-ready populations—the United States, the United Kingdom, Japan and West Germany, all of which boast the highest tourism expenditures and largest number of international travelers (see exhibit 4-12). (Traveler is defined as those who had spent at least one night away from home in paid lodging during the past year. Roughly six in ten adults met this definition.)

Exhibit 4-12.   Percentages of Adventurers and Indulgers by country

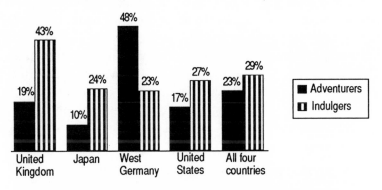

Source: *American Express Global Travel Survey: A Typology of the Traveling Public conducted in The U.S., West Germany, United Kingdom, and Japan*, American Express Travel Related Service, Co.

Adventurers

Members of this group are motivated to seek new experiences, and value diversity in their travels. They are independent, in control, and confident about their ability to make travel decisions and master diverse travel situations. They don't need to be pampered. Travel plays a central role in the lives of adventurers. It helps to shape their sense of themselves and add richness to their lives. They are generally better educated and more affluent than fellow travelers in their own country. The group is predominately male (57%), and unlike all other groups, tends to be made up of younger travelers, with 44% of its members between the ages of 18 and 34. They are the most frequent travelers of the five groups, with an average of 3.8 trips taken in the 12 months preceding the interview. Adventurers tend to agree with the following statements:

- "I feel confident that I could find my way around a city that I'd never visited before."
- "I really hate traveling with a group of people, even if they're people I know."

Indulgers

This group likes to be pampered. Travel itself is not a central or important experience for the Indulgers. Rather, travel is a way that they indulge themselves. Indulgers are generally willing to pay for a higher level of service when they travel, and they are not intimidated by the process of travel. Neither do they find travel to be a stressful experience. Indulgers are better off financially relative to other travelers in their own country and they are equally divided between men and women. They are second only to Adventurers in the number of trips taken during the previous year, with an average of 3.4 trips. The total amount of money spent on their last trip is higher for the Indulgers compared to other travelers, except among Americans. However, Indulgers feel differently about how their money is spent. Indulgers tend to agree with the following statements:

- "I don't worry about how much things cost when I travel."

- "It's worth paying extra to get the special attention I want when I travel."

Exhibit 4-13.   Median amount* budgeted for next pleasure trip

	Total travelers	Adventurers	Indulgers
United Kingdom	$516	$516	$688
Japan	$387	$540	$464
West Germany	$807	$807	$807
U.S.	$600	$700	$600

*exchange rate calculated at time of study, 3/10/89

Source: *American Express Global Travel Survey: A Typology of the Traveling Public conducted in The U.S., West Germany, United Kingdom, and Japan*, American Express Travel Related Service, Co.

To everything there is a season. For leisure travel among the affluent, the season is summer. Both income groups prefer the dog days for vacations, but in keeping with their love of skiing, the upper-affluent are also likely to pack up and head out in the winter (exhibit 4-14).

Exhibit 4-14. Season to travel

	HHI $50,000-$99,000	HHI $100,000+
Summer	61%	58%
Fall	47%	47%
Winter	36%	53%
Spring	41%	45%

Source: *Frequent Leisure Travelers—A Study of Markets and Media 1990,* Erdos and Morgan/Marketing Projects Group, Inc.

To get where they're going, upper-affluents are more likely than moderate-affluents to fly first-class (18% vs. 5%) and to sleep in deluxe or first class hotels (60% vs. 33%). In fact, only 32% of affluents in the $50,000-$99,999 income range fly to their vacation destinations; the majority (58%) drive. Compare these statistics to the analogous figures for the upper-affluent: only 31% drive to their vacation spots; 58% fly. The percentages for flying and driving are almost exactly reversed between the two affluent subgroups, with the moderately-affluent more closely aligned with the general population's travel attitudes.[85] Rounding up the total number of roundtrip airline flights taken within the last year (estimated average times) for consumers with household incomes over $75,000, the total number is 5.1; compare this to the U.S. average for adults of 3.3 roundtrip flights.[86]

Price is the affluents' primary concern when choosing an airline and, despite their financial resources, upper-affluents are nearly as likely as other affluents to choose based on price. Moreover, the more wealthy affluents actually care a great deal more than their less-wealthy counterparts about amassing penny-saving frequent flier miles. On a relative scale, the upper-affluent are less concerned about an airline's safety record, reputation, and baggage handling service. Airline clubs, not regarded by the moderate affluents, are important to almost 10% of upper-affluents (exhibit 4-15).

Exhibit 4-15.   Percent of affluents who say these are
                important factors in airline selection (numbers
                rounded)

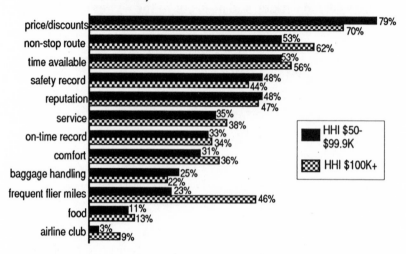

Source: *Frequent Leisure Travelers—A Study of Markets and Media 1990,*
          Erdos and Margan/Marketing Projects

The same rules which are said to apply in real estate apply to hotel selection: location, location, location. Nearly 80% of all affluents rank location the most important factor in choosing accommodations while on leisure travel. Price is the next-ranked factor for the $50,000-$99,999 group: 66% make a selection based on room prices or discounts. For the upper-affluent, the dominant value after location is reliability, which 58% rank as important. The percentage gap shows clearly the degree to which upper-affluents focus their decision-making on location (exhibit 4-16).

Upper-affluents don't care as much as others about price, efficiency, or hotel orientation (family or tourist). They do care more about reputation, management, atmosphere, restaurants, room size, exercise facilities, and—given their concern for frequent flier miles—airline tie-ins (exhibit 4-17). The hotel chains rated as having the best reputations are: Marriott (which also ranks on top as "first choice to stay"), Hyatt, and Hilton. Affluents consider Holiday Inn to be both family-oriented and tourist-oriented.

Exhibit 4-16.   Influences in choosing lodging for Family Circle
panelists with HHI <$35,000 and those with
$35,000+

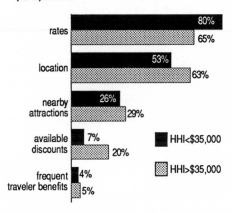

rates — 80% / 65%
location — 53% / 63%
nearby attractions — 26% / 29%
available discounts — 7% / 20%
frequent traveler benefits — 4% / 5%

■ HHI<$35,000
▨ HHI>$35,000

Source: *Family Circle* Consumer Panel

Exhibit 4-17.   Hotel selection factors—percent who say they
are important (numbers rounded)

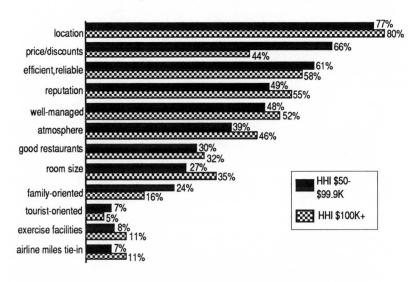

location — 77% / 80%
price/discounts — 66% / 44%
efficient,reliable — 61% / 58%
reputation — 49% / 55%
well-managed — 48% / 52%
atmosphere — 39% / 46%
good restaurants — 30% / 32%
room size — 27% / 35%
family-oriented — 24% / 16%
tourist-oriented — 7% / 5%
exercise facilities — 8% / 11%
airline miles tie-in — 7% / 11%

■ HHI $50-$99.9K
▨ HHI $100K+

Source: *Frequent Leisure Travelers—A Study of Markets and Media 1990*,
Erdos and Morgan/Marketing Projects Group, Inc.

Like airlines, rental cars are selected by affluents largely on the basis of price: nearly three-quarters of affluent leisure travelers use car prices or discounts as an important decision factor. Another bargain-based criteria—free mileage—ranks second behind price. Although upper-affluents are slightly more concerned than others about car types available, the clear message is that affluent leisure travelers want to go for a ride without feeling like they're being taken for a ride. Even the upper-affluent keep their eyes on their wallets when they make travel plans. Airline tie-ins are, again, relatively more popular among the upper-affluent than among the moderately affluent. Also ranking higher in relative importance are: location, reputation, express service, and—by a very small margin—firm size (exhibit 4-18).

Exhibit 4-18. Rental car selection factors—percent who say they are important (numbers rounded)

	HHI $50,000-$99,999	HHI $100,000+
Price/discounts	74%	72%
Free road mileage	58%	55%
Car types available	34%	40%
Location	34%	38%
Reputation	28%	31%
Express service	15%	28%
Airline miles tie-in	13%	18%
Size of firm	4%	5%

Source: Frequent Leisure Travelers—A Study of Markets and Media 1990, Erdos and Morgan/Marketing Projects Group, Inc.

Trains are making a comeback as a great way to hide away and get a taste of nostalgia at the same time, especially among older, more affluent consumers who want luxury and comfort that they can't find on airlines. Decorated with the finesse of the finest houses, posh Pullmans offer affluents a chance to mix business travel with pleasure. And the words so far are: on a roll. One ritzy train is currently gallivanting around the Midwest, and in the next four months, two more luxury lines will pick up steam.

Business travel means big business among affluent consumers. Groups of business travelers with high median incomes include frequent travelers, international travelers, car renters, and airline customers. Demographic determinants are also significant; the highest likelihoods of affluence among business travelers are for males and for those over age 34 (exhibit 4-19).

Exhibit 4-19. Likelihood of affluence among business travelers

	% with HHI $50,000+	Index	Median HHI
All business travelers	30%	100	$38,570
Business travel segments			
Male	33	110	$40,555
Female	28	93	$36,500
Age 18-34	21	70	$33,636
Age 35-44	38	127	$43,684
Age 45+	38	127	$43,333
Frequent	48	160	$48,333
International	44	147	$46,111
Meeting attendees	32	107	$39,545
Airline customers	41	137	$45,263
Car renters	43	143	$46,111
Hotel guests	33	110	$40,556

*Index base is "all business travelers with a household income of $50,000 or more."

Source: *1988 Survey of Business Travelers*, Reed International

According to the U.S. Travel Data Center, the quintessential business traveler is likely to be 25 to 44 years old, college educated, high wage earning, and employed in the professional, managerial, or technical profession. The majority of those who subscribe to *Fortune* magazine also fit this profile, making *Fortune* readers an excellent proxy for studying the $75 billion-a-year business travel market. *Fortune* subscribers are the travel market's dream:

- Almost all (94%) subscribers take an overnight trip (either for business or pleasure) in a year.
- On average, each traveler takes 14.6 trips and spends $5,800 a year.
- The majority of trips (12.3) are exclusively for business reasons, a figure three times the national average of 4.5 business trips per year.
- Forty percent of the Fortune business travelers surveyed are frequent travelers—10 or more overnight business trips per year.
- This frequent group averages 25.1 trips a year.

Business travelers fly in vast numbers—85% take at least one round-trip flight, and 73% take three or more in a year. The average number of plane trips each year is 11.3, 10.2 of those for business. Given leaner corporate travel policies reflecting increased cost-consciousness, business fliers are less likely to fly first class (9%) than they are to fly full-fare economy (35%), business class (31%), and discount economy (27%). The most important factors ("very important" or "fairly important" on a four-point rating scale) in selecting an airline are convenient schedules (92%) and convenient destinations (90%). Also of high importance: good on-time performance (84%), good safety record (83%), comfortable seats (82%), fast check-in (82%), and friendly, efficient personnel (81%). Of less importance are preassigned seats (78%), efficient reservations (77%), efficient baggage handling (74%), good in-flight service (72%), low fares (62%), and catering to business travelers (52%).

Fortune surveyers find that frequent business fliers are less concerned than the total group about baggage handling (they are more likely to carry their bags on board) and, not surprisingly, are more concerned about the availability of a Frequent Flier program.

Leading the list of most frequently *used* domestic airlines for business travel are Delta/Western (55%), United (52%), and Eastern (45%); this research was taken when there still *was* an Eastern. The most *preferred* domestic airlines are American/Air Cal (22%), Delta/Western (18%), and United (15%). Among internationally-based airlines, the most widely flown are British Airways (8%) and Lufthansa (6%), while the most preferred are British Airways, Singapore Airlines, and Lufthansa (all at 3%).

Though not an important factor in choosing an airline, frequent flier programs apparently are important for *something*: 62% of the *Fortune* business travelers surveyed participate in at least one program. Of those who take an airline trip for business reasons, 87% of those who fly frequently (10+ trips per year) currently participate in a frequent flier program, vs. 62% of average fliers. Frequent fliers belong to an average of 3.8 different plans, the most popular being those offered by Delta/Western (56%), American/Air Cal (54%), and United (49%).

Less than a quarter (24%) of the business fliers say they belong to an airline club or lounge; however, for frequent fliers the percentage is considerably higher (46%). The most popular airline clubs: United (32%), American/Air Cal (25%), Delta/Western (20%), Eastern (19%), and TWA (17%).

Almost every *Fortune* respondent (93%) stays overnight in a hotel or motel at least once a year. Nearly eight out of ten (77%) stay in hotels or motels for business purposes; the average number of nights away on business: 26.3. Almost a quarter of the business travelers (23%) stay in a hotel/motel 35 nights or more. By industry standards, the frequent hotel/motel business guest is one who stays five or more nights in a 12 month period, and 82% of business travelers fall into this category. Respondents who stay in a hotel/motel for leisure do so an average of 11.9 nights.

The average amount spent by business travelers on an overnight stay in a hotel or motel is $88.70 per night; 6% spend $150 or more per night; 11% spend less than $50. The average hotel/motel tab for leisure travelers is $84.60.

The most important factors in selecting a place to stay are location (90%), friendly and efficient staff (87%), good reputation (85%), attractive rooms (85%), and reasonable rates (84%). Other significant determinants: fast check-in and check-out (82%), positive previous experience (79%), efficient reservations (77%). The least importance is placed on the recommendations of a travel agent (17%) and the availability of golf or tennis (12%).

The most frequented hotels/motels are Holiday Inn (48%), Marriott (47%), Hilton Hotels (46%), Sheraton (36%), and Hyatt (35%). Also used fairly often: Best Western (27%), Ramada Inns (23%), Embassy Suite Hotels (21%), and Westin (20%). The most preferred hotel is Marriott (20%), followed by Holiday Inn (13%) and Hyatt (12%).

A quarter (24%) of hotel/motel business patrons indicate membership in a Frequent Hotel Guest Program. Among that group, 53% belong to Marriott's program, 19% to Hilton's, and 19% to Hyatt's. On average, members belong to 1.4 different programs.

Seven out of ten business travelers rent a car; 60% rent for business purposes only. On average, those who rent for business do so 7.4 times and spend $41.10 per day. A large segment (36%) rent seven or more times and is considered the "frequent renter" group. These renters average 15.5 car rentals per year for business. Leisure renters average 2.6 rentals per year and spend and average of $38.80 per day.

Nearly 90% of car renters for business indicate that the condition of the car is an important factor in choosing a car rental company. Also important to business car renters: proximity to the airport (85%), fast pick up/drop off (85%), convenient location (83%), efficient counter personnel (82%), and efficient reservations (80%). Lowest on the list of importance is that the car rental company is owned by its employees (9%).

The most frequently used company is Hertz (60%), followed by Avis (42%), Budget (35%), and National (33%). These are followed by Alamo (12%), Dollar (8%), Thrifty (4%), General (2%), and Econo-Car (1%). More than a third (38%) choose Hertz as the best; 21% choose Avis. Frequent Car Renter programs are used by 20% of the business car renters, with Hertz the most popular (44%).

Leading the list of U.S. cities visited for business are New York City (48%), Chicago (45%), Atlanta (42%), Los Angeles (41%), Dallas/Fort Worth (40%), and Washington, DC (39%). These are followed by Boston (35%), San Francisco (35%), Denver (29%), San Diego (28%), Orlando (27%), Miami (27%), and Philadelphia (26%).

The business traveler is the one who controlled booking and payment decisions. Though actual reservations may have been made by someone else, generally, the traveler him/herself—and not an assistant, a secretary, or a travel agent—chooses the airline carrier, car rental company, and hotel. The sources most often relied upon for information are previous personal experience (making the first experience a critical one in determining repeat business), recommendations from friends and colleagues, and advice from corporate travel departments (exhibit 4-20).

With all of this travel experience, you might think that affluents could be amateur but knowledgeable travel agents. Affluents are slightly more travel-savvy than the rest of the population, but they still can be

Exhibit 4-20. Sources of information used most often for business travel by those who took a business trip in the past year

	Took an airline trip	Stayed in hotel/motel	Rented car
Previous experience	59%	65%	57%
Personal travel agent	32%	25%	16%
Corporate travel dept. or company designated travel agent	30%	27%	33%
Official airline guide	22%	2%	2%
Recommendations of friends/colleagues	17%	44%	12%
Word-of-mouth	14%	30%	13%
Newspaper/magazine advertising	11%	14%	13%
Television advertising	10%	10%	8%
Telephone book	6%	9%	7%
Travel books/brochures	6%	20%	6%
Promotional advertising (mailers)	5%	7%	6%
Radio advertising	4%	3%	3%
No answer	4%	3%	6%

Source: "The Business Traveler—A Study of Fortune Subscribers," *Fortune*

misinformed about travel laws, customs, and definitions. For example, fewer than a quarter of affluents (24%) know that a direct airline flight is not the same as a non-stop flight, and only slightly more (25%) know the U.S. spans six time zones, not four (Eastern through Aleutian Hawaii). Also, only a paltry 26% of affluents know that European Plan or EP in a hotel doesn't mean "with meals included" (exhibit 4-21).

Of the 18 questions asked, affluents got an average of 9.0 correct, while the lowest income group ($15,000-$19,999) got an average of 7.8 right, and the total survey group scored 8.2.

A higher percentage of affluents failed the question on hotel tipping ($1 per night for the maid is the custom). The biggest knowledge gaps between affluents and others are in these areas: hotel weekend savings (more likely than others to know about same-room-lower-rate policies on weekends), travel agent commissions (more likely to know that there's no charge to consumers), and airline economy class status (more likely to know it's not a specific section of the plane but a price coding).

Exhibit 4-21. Here's how affluent travel smarts compare to
the average (correct answer in parentheses):

	% of affluents who answered correctly	% of total U.S. who answered correctly
A federal law prohibits smoking on domestic flights of less than two hours (TRUE)	88%	83%
Many hotel chains offer frequent traveller programs (TRUE)	80%	75%
A hotel can charge guests for unused rooms if the guests have not called to cancel their guaranteed reservations (TRUE)	78%	75%
You can determine whether you're driving east/west or north/south by the number of the interstate route (TRUE)	71%	68%
Airlines have the legal right to give your seat away if you check in at the gate after the designated time (TRUE)	71%	67%
You are not entitled to any compensation if an airline bumps you from a flight but is able to get you to your destination within a hour of your original arrival time (TRUE)	71%	64%
If you have no collision insurance coverage when renting a car, you are liable for the total cost of repairs in the event of an accident (TRUE)	66%	65%
On weekends, many hotels offer the same rooms at much lower rates (TRUE)	59%	46%
The national speed limit is 55 m.p.h. (FALSE)	50%	43%
Travel agents charge a 10% commission to consumers (FALSE)	48%	35%
The per mile cost of driving is cheaper than flying (FALSE)	42%	39%
A super saver airline fare will not allow you to stay overnight in a connecting city (TRUE)	40%	32%
When staying at a hotel, it is customary to leave a $1 per night tip for the room maid (TRUE)	33%	39%
The economy class section is located at the rear of the plane behind full fare coach (FALSE)	27%	17%
A concierge is a manager of a European hotel (FALSE)	27%	24%
The term "European Plan" or "EP" means that meals are included in the hotel room rate (FALSE)	26%	23%
The United States spans four time zones (FALSE)	25%	22%
In airline travel, a "direct" flight does not make any stops enroute from one destination to another (FALSE)	24%	24%

Source: *Omni Hotel's America's Travel IQ*

The Omni Hotel study also finds that the majority of affluents do know:

- Rhode Island is not, in fact, an island (89% of affluents, vs. 76% total).
- Yellowstone National Park is not located in Washington state (84% vs. 75%).
- The Continental Divide is not a border between the U.S. and Canada (75% vs. 63%).
- The Adirondacks are located in New York (68% vs. 54%).

Most, though, have yet to learn that:

- Mount Rushmore is not located in North Dakota (38% vs 40%).
- The Grand Canyon is entirely within Arizona (36% vs. 36%).

Affluents are more likely than others to know cities' major attractions, and one reason may be that they get out of the neighborhood more: the mean number of over-100-mile trips taken in the past year by affluents is 9.1. For others, it's 5.7.

Sports

Images of cricket, a pastoral game of lawn tennis, fox hunting, and even gentlemen discreetly playing cards are mainstays of old money affluent sports. But the national boom in physical fitness, awareness, and practice, has muscled into the affluent sports arena. Active affluents get sweaty like the rest of the nation. They have incorporated a large variety of sports into the affluent lifestyle, and they often approach their athletic regimen with the same discipline they apply to their careers.

Also like the rest of the nation, enthusiasm for sports and concern for physical fitness seem to go hand in hand—the terms exercise and sports are often used interchangeably, both by researchers and by consumers who closely connect the two activities. And if their actions speak as loudly as their words, they exercise a lot—60% of affluents say that they perform some kind of regular physical exercise in order to keep physically fit, compared to 52% of the general public.[87] (We'll go into more detail about physical activity specifically related to fitness later in this chapter).

Affluents ($50,000+ household income) substantially exceed national averages for participation in seven of eight outdoor activities. The only exception is camping/fishing/hiking/hunting, in which they are just a fishline below the national averages. For instance, affluents snow ski 58% more than the average American (18% of affluents participate), go boating 38% more than average (23%), travel 26% more (62%), and go to sporting events 23% more (40%).[88]

Exhibit 4-22.   Percentage of people who participate at least three times a month in sports (by income)

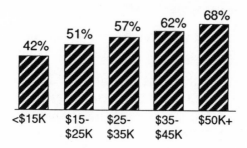

Source: National Sporting Goods Association

A snapshot view of what sports affluents prefer (or at least what sports they prefer to gear up for) is provided in a look at affluent sporting goods equipment purchases. *Lifestyle Characteristics of Sporting Goods Consumers* integrates the PRIZM market segmentation system with the National Sporting Goods Association's consumer survey of sporting goods purchases during 1987. For a narrower focus, however, we have based the following results only on $50,000+ household income consumers. Consumers in this group purchase about one-third of all sporting goods. Almost half of all golf, ski, and tennis implements end up in their hands (and on their feet); less than 10% of such equipment is bought by those earning under $15,000 (28% of the population).

When it comes to buying sporting equipment, mass merchants have mass appeal while specialty stores and sporting outlets have class appeal. Buyers with household income over $50,000 are much more likely to make purchases at sports stores than are other buyers— specifically for tennis, exercise, and team sports equipment, sports clothing, and hiking gear. Some equipment, like cleats and skis, is

---

Exhibit 4-23. Percent buying equipment, by household income

HHI	Golf	Tennis	Ski
<$15,000	7%	6%	7%
$15,000-24,999	11%	12%	7%
$25,000-34,999	12%	15%	22%
$35,000-49,999	24%	20%	25%
$50,000+	47%	47%	40%

Source: *Lifestyle Characteristics of Sporting Goods Consumers*, National Sporting Goods Association

---

purchased almost exclusively from sporting goods outlets, regardless of the buyer's income bracket. In every category of sporting goods, the affluent catch a disproportionate share of the market. Topping the list are golf and tennis equipment, of which they buy 47% (exhibit 4-24).

Exhibit 4-24. Affluents' role in the sporting goods market

Equipment	Percentage purchased by affluents ($50,000+)	Median income
Golf	47%	$47,800
Tennis	47%	$47,700
Sports Clothing*	41%	$43,500
Ski	40%	$43,600
Downhill	45%	$46,600
Cross-country	21%	$34,100
Exercise	36%	$39,800
Treadmills	51%	$50,400
Weight Benches	24%	$32,300
Cleated Shoes	32%	$39,600
For Soccer	42%	$45,800
For Baseball	25%	$34,600
Athletic Clothing*	31%	$36,600
Footwear	30%	$36,600
Running	34%	$39,500
Team Sports	28%	$35,500
Hockey Skates	42%	$44,000
Basketballs	27%	$34,800
Outdoor equipment	23%	$33,300
Hunting	23%	$30,500
Fishing Tackle	20%	$31,200

*Athletic clothing includes sweat shirts, sweat pants, and elastic-waistband shorts; sports clothing includes bathing suits, golf clothing, and ski wear.

Source: *Lifestyle Characteristics of Sporting Goods Consumers*, National Sporting Goods Association

Getting dressed for fishing, running, tennis, and camping costs remarkably more for affluents than for others. The average consumer with an income of $50,000 or more spends $118.91 per year for salt-water fishing attire, while the average consumer spends $86.44 (index of 138, meaning that affluents spend 38% more on these clothes). The affluent runner also spends more than the average runner ($103 vs. $76, Index=136), as does the affluent tennis player ($130 vs. $97, Index=134) and camper ($131 vs. $99, Index=133). Clothing categories in which affluents spend less than the average person are calisthenics ($45 vs. $75, Index=60, affluents spend 40% less than the total), bowling ($101 vs. $115, Index=86), and hunting ($52 vs. $61, Index=88). Absolute dollars show that as with average consumers, skiing and golf take the lead in affluent sport-clothing expenditures: $211.01 and $168.78, respectively (exhibit 4-25).

Exhibit 4-25. Affluent vs. total population spending for sports attire in 1989 (Index of 100=total)

Average dollar expenditure per buyer	Affluent	Total U.S.	Affluents' spending index
Aerobic	$ 81.46	$ 71.12	115
Backpacking/wilderness	$ 98.41	$ 78.92	125
Baseball	$ 48.92	$ 49.17	100
Basketball	$ 66.95	$ 61.72	109
Bicycle riding	$ 97.37	$ 88.63	110
Bowling	$ 52.27	$ 60.96	86
Calisthenics	$ 45.15	$ 75.48	60
Camping	$131.14	$ 98.94	133
Exercise equipment	$ 93.45	$ 89.44	105
Exercise walking	$ 78.01	$ 62.91	124
Fishing—fresh water	$ 89.66	$ 67.58	133
Fishing—salt water	$118.91	$ 86.44	138
Football	$ 77.98	$ 64.16	122
Golf	$168.78	$141.11	120
Hiking	$ 69.20	$ 61.30	113
Hunting with firearms	$101.19	$115.53	88
Racquetball	$ 52.11	$ 50.03	104
Running/jogging	$103.15	$ 75.77	136
Skiing-alpine/downhill	$211.01	$188.77	112
Skiing-cross country	$101.25	$ 92.73	109
Soccer	$ 73.65	$ 54.80	134
Softball	$ 62.64	$ 49.28	127
Swimming	$ 60.02	$ 45.93	131
Target shooting	$109.81	$ 93.61	117
Tennis	$129.69	$ 97.16	134
Volleyball	$ 45.05	$ 40.78	111

Source: *Sports Clothing Expenditures in 1989*, National Sporting Goods Association

No snapshot of affluents at sport would be complete, however, without notice of a growing and rather surprising movement: a revolution of new greenbacks on the green. Making something of a comeback is one of the quietest (and most old money style) sports around: golf. Today there are more golfers than ever (24% more in 1987 than in 1985), and these new golfers seem to be following in their fathers' footsteps (they're male, young, make more money, are more educated, and work at professional/management/administration jobs).[89]

In fact, according to Dr. Gordon Benson, author of *Golf Participation in the United States: 1988*, 21.7 million Americans play golf (9.7% of the U.S. population over age five). Golfers are male (77%), young (50% between ages 20 and 39) and have a median household income of $42,100 (32% above the national average). The more educated you are, the higher your income, the more high-status your profession, the more likely you are to play golf.

Golf is an upscale game, but dismiss any vision of duffers strolling manicured private club greens. The overwhelming majority of golfers (77%) use public courses. Private course players include more females (26% vs. 22% of public golfers), older players (average age is 41 vs. 37), and those with higher household incomes (16% have household income of $75,000+, vs. 7% of public golfers). Private golfers also play more rounds annually than do public golfers and tend to live in the South, the traditional stronghold of private golfers. Golfers in the Northeastern (30%) and Western (31%) states average higher household incomes than golfers in the North Central (25%) and Southern (25%) states. The same relationship between regions exists for the percentage of golfers with household incomes of at least $50,000.

Golfers tend to be loyal to the game. Nearly 30% have played for at least 20 years. But there are golf drop-outs: quitters include proportionally more women (36% quit vs. 23% who play), those with lower annual household income ($36,300 vs. $42,100 of current golfers) and those with lower educational attainment (exhibit 4-26).

The clash between old and new has begun, but this time it has a small twist. As it happens—though golf has long been associated with a certain country club kind of crowd—it seems that the links have also traditionally been associated with some pretty interesting color and plaid pattern combinations. Ordinarily pin-striped captains of indus-

Exhibit 4-26. Demographic profile of all golfers (percent of
U.S. population, age 5+)

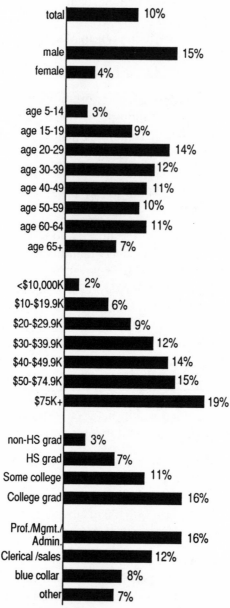

Source: *Golf Participation in the United States: 1988*, Dr. Gordon Benson,
National Golf Foundation

try have been known to wear kelly green trousers, bright yellow shirts, white belts, and matching shoes, cutting themselves some fashion slack when out on the greens. But the *Wall Street Journal* reports that the traditional colors of old money—Ralph Lauren-style khakis and beiges—have hit the golf courses, mostly on the backs of Boomers discovering the game. Dapper inveterates have been none too pleased. The evolution from kinetic colors to subdued styles has brought an element of fashion to golf, and some of the old-time flashy dressers such as Doug Sanders bristle at the idea. He says he can't distinguish the khaki-and-beige "whippersnappers" from their caddies.

Health

Action and exercise are vital parts of affluents' daily lives. Active affluents make strong connections between health, sports, exercise, and nutrition. And though they are more passionate than others about fitness and health—they are 30% more likely to exercise frequently and to lead active lives—the majority of them (51%) believe that they still don't exercise enough (exhibit 4-27).

Half the nation is afflicted with chronic inertia, exercising less than 24 days a year; however, only 37% of affluents flop into this category. To the contrary, 40% of affluents (compared to 31% of the total) are highly kinetic, exercising more than 150 days per year.[90]

Exercise trends in this country are moving in both directions, widening the gap between the fit and the unfit. The affluent exercise more or about the same as they did a few years ago. In comparison, the general population is more likely to have cut back on exercise—implying a connection between fiscal and physical health. Affluents are not overwhelmed by the plethora of exercise information available. Those in lower income groups, however, are more skeptical and less involved with fitness than are affluents.

In short: affluents can't seem to get too much of what they perceive to be a good thing for their health. Furthermore, affluents believe, as a rule, that exercise can enhance and lengthen life as well as improve appearance. But only 38% of affluents are satisfied with the amount of exercise they get, compared to 43% of the total. The vast majority of affluents (80%) are convinced of the importance of exercise. Such attitudes can vary with income, as exhibit 4-28 shows.

Exhibit 4-27. Affluent exercise behavior and attitudes

Exercise frequency	*$50,000+*	*$25,000-$50,000*	*<$25,000*	*All groups*
Inactive (0-24 of 365 days)	37%	51%	61%	50%
Moderate (25-149 days)	24%	19%	16%	19%
Active (150+ days)	40%	31%	23%	31%
Present vs. past exercise (3-4 years ago)				
More	29%	25%	23%	26%
About the same	38%	36%	29%	34%
Less	28%	30%	33%	30%
Perceived exercise sufficiency				
More than enough	5%	6%	5%	5%
Enough	38%	44%	46%	43%
Not enough	51%	44%	40%	44%
Not at all	6%	6%	8%	7%

Note: sub-columns may not add to 100% due to unreported answers.

Source: *The National Fitness Study 1989: A Demographic, Behavioral, and Psychographic Profile of Active and Inactive Americans*, National Sporting Goods Association

Exhibit 4-28. Fitness consciousness (by income level)

	$50,000+	*$25,000-$50,000*	*<$25,000*	*All groups*
Exercise is very important to me, and I am a frequent participant in fitness activities.	24%	17%	11%	17%
I know exercise is important, and I'd like to participate in fitness activities more than I do.	56%	53%	49%	53%
Exercise may be important, but I just don't feel the need to get involved in fitness activities.	18%	27%	34%	27%
I just don't think that exercise is all that important.	1%	2%	5%	3%
There are so many conflicting reports, I don't really know if exercise is good or bad for me.				
Agree	13%	20%	27%	20%
Indifferent	20%	25%	33%	26%
Disagree	67%	55%	39%	53%
Exercise is dangerous. It does more harm than good.				
Agree	2%	3%	6%	4%
Indifferent	7%	13%	19%	14%
Disagree	90%	83%	74%	82%

Note: sub-columns may not add to 100% due to unreported answers.

Source: *The National Fitness Study 1989: A Demographic, Behavioral, and Psychographic Profile of Active and Inactive Americans*, National Sporting Goods Association

Affluents may be driven towards perfection of mind and body, but they place more emphasis on their desire to do better than on their failure to do enough. Even if affluents are mad at themselves for not doing more exercise, they still basically like what stares back in the mirror (exhibit 4-29).

Exhibit 4-29. Perceptions of body image (by income group)

Perceived body weight	$50,000+	$25,000-$50,000	<$25,000	All groups
Underweight	7%	8%	9%	8%
About right	36%	34%	32%	34%
Overweight	58%	59%	59%	58%
"I'm more physically fit than most people my age"				
Agree	58%	50%	46%	51%
Indifferent	24%	29%	29%	27%
Disagree	18%	22%	24%	21%
"Compared to other people my age, I look pretty good in a bathing suit"				
Agree	42%	40%	35%	39%
Indifferent	26%	25%	24%	25%
Disagree	32%	35%	40%	35%

Note: sub-columns may not add to 100% due to unreported answers.

Source: *The National Fitness Study 1989: A Demographic, Behavioral, and Psychographic Profile of Active and Inactive Americans,* National Sporting Goods Association

More likely than other income groups to see themselves as "about right" in weight and "pretty good" in a bathing suit, affluents are thus motivated towards exercise by positive body psychology, not negative self-recrimination. In other words, the fact that they don't exercise as much as they ideally want to isn't manifest in the form of harshly skewed body images. The affluent don't feel guilty when they don't exercise enough, but they might like to do more in the future.[91]

Does wealth make health? Forty-five percent of affluents ($40,000+) pop vitamins daily; only about 30% of those with annual household incomes of less than $15,000 do so. Two factors are probably at play in this statistic: 1) affluents find it easier to afford dietary supplements; and 2) they are likely to be better educated about nutrition. Indeed, the same study finds affluents and the highly educated most likely to indulge in bottled food chemistry (45% of those educated 13 or more years take vitamins). No accompanying cross-correlation tells us exactly what portion of those two groups intersect, but we know education and affluence are usually interdependent variables.

Within the affluent household groups, those in the 45-64 and 2-6 age ranges are most likely to rely on vitamin supplements—51% and 50% of each age group, respectively. By comparison, consider that only 23% of kids 2-6 in homes with household incomes less than $7,000 and 39% of 2-6 year-olds in homes with household incomes between $7,000 and $14,999 take their Flintstones (exhibit 4-30).

Exhibit 4-30.   Vitamin intake (by income)

HHI	Total	Adults 18-44	45-64	65+	Kids 2-6
<$7,000	27.8%	26.6%	27.8%	30.2%	22.8%
$7,000-$14,999	32.5%	30.6%	30.4%	37.0%	38.6%
$15,000 -$24,999	34.8%	32.2%	35.1%	43.1%	44.2%
$25,000-$39,999	38.8%	36.6%	43.2%	42.6%	51.2%
$40,000+	44.8%	41.7%	50.6%	44.3%	50.3%

Source: "Use of Vitamin and Mineral Supplements in the U.S. Current Users, Types of Products, and Nutrients," *Advance Data Number 174*, National Center for Health Statistics

It's little wonder, then, that affluents—who believe in action—are likely to believe in action before it is necessary as a reaction to a problem. Not only do they prefer to pop vitamins; they also believe an act of prevention is preferable to a pound of cure. They are more careful than lower income groups about what they eat, and they are leading the anti-smoking trend, thinking hard about what they're not doing (exhibit 4-31).

Exhibit 4-31.   Eating habits and smoking trends (by income groups)

Eating habits	$50,000+	$25,000-$50,000	<$25,000	All groups
Diet regularly	10%	9%	8%	9%
Careful but does not diet	57%	51%	49%	52%
Eat anything	34%	41%	43%	39%
Smoking				
Yes	23%	28%	35%	28%
No	77%	72%	65%	72%

Source: National Sporting Goods Association

Since it is highly unlikely that you will be able to grab a glass of lemonade, sit out on the porch, and invite the affluents to talk about what ails them, exhibit 4-32 is a very useful substitution for a chat about health—a laundry list of a year full of affluent ailments. The researchers should be congratulated for getting this information from a notoriously closed-mouthed group of survey subjects—the Exclusive Set ($75,000+)—who don't usually enjoy even answering questions about such private things as dishwashing detergent and lawn fertilizer.

Exhibit 4-32. Exclusive Set ailments in the past year, and index of ailments by sex and age (index of 100 = Exclusive Set total)

| | % of Exclusives who suffered from ailment within past 12 months | Exclusive Set subgroup indexes** | | | | |
| | | Sex | | Age groups | | |
		Men	Women	18-34	35-49	50+
Acne	18%	71	131	154	98	39
Arthritis	14%	89	112	76	86	145
Asthma *	4%	126	72	102	136	54
Athlete's foot	14%	153	43	100	98	103
Backache	23%	92	108	89	121	88
Cold	45%	96	104	102	116	79
Cold sores	15%	81	120	117	111	66
Constipation	12%	75	127	107	114	73
Cough	26%	97	103	95	104	101
Denture pain *	1%	17	189	43	165	89
Diarrhea	14%	79	122	87	126	84
Fever	13%	90	110	121	101	74
Groin irritation *	3%	146	50	102	138	51
Gum disorder	4%	92	109	58	95	157
Hayfever	13%	89	112	120	113	60
Headache	64%	88	112	101	112	84
Heartburn	16%	99	101	88	109	104
Hemorrhoids	12%	97	103	83	114	104
Indigestion	20%	94	106	102	83	119
Motion sickness	6%	64	139	104	123	67
Muscle ache	22%	99	101	101	114	81
Nervous tension	12%	76	125	118	101	77
Osteoporosis *	1%	11	196	3	29	303
Poison ivy	8%	90	111	119	79	103
Post-nasal drip	14%	71	131	103	105	90
Psoriasis *	3%	56	147	52	162	80
Rectal itch *	4%	120	78	100	100	101
Sinus congestion	26%	98	102	91	110	99
Skin itch/rash	7%	65	137	110	117	67
Sleeplessness	9%	91	109	122	87	89
Sore throat	26%	98	102	106	118	72
Sunburn	18%	83	118	133	99	62

(cont.)

(Ex. 4-32 cont.)						
Tired/run-down	13%	76	126	106	105	88
Toothache	5%	89	111	84	133	79
Tooth sensitivity	8%	61	142	112	110	74
Upset stomach	16%	94	106	105	115	76
Warts *	2%	54	148	82	136	77

* Caution: small cell size. Results unstable. **Note: the index is not a comparison between Exclusives and others; it is a gender and age break-down of Exclusives.

Source: *1989 Simmons Exclusive Set*, Simmons Market Research Bureau

Stress

With all of their pressures (often self-imposed) to do well, to do better, to do the right thing with their money, their image, and even the pressure to maintain and improve their health—you might think that affluents would be carrying the extra burden of the stress of success. But the wealthy and the powerful carry less stress than the rest. Of course, stress is all about perceptions which means affluents feel more secure about their coping mechanisms. One of the benefits of relative stresslessness: better health and lower risk of disease.

By asking a battery of questions designed to assess, "How unpredictable, uncontrollable, and overloaded is your life?", researchers from Carnegie-Mellon University [92] found low perceived stress levels among those with high incomes, high education levels, and professional employment.

On a "stress scale" of 0-45, the total sample population scores a 19.6. Compare this to 23.1 for those earning $5,000-$10,000 annually and 18.4 for those earning over $50,000 annually. Perceptions of stress decline linearly as household income increases up to $30,000. After that, the trend is less clear, but, still consistent; the $45,000-$50,000 range ranks at 16.1. Exhibit 4-33 details results for income, education, and profession.

As shown, an advanced degree correlates with significantly lower stress levels than do other educational categories. Despite this marked difference across the education spectrum, income proves to be the statistically more powerful stress determinant. By way of illustration, consider that the stress differential between income groups is 7.0 (i.e. 23.1 minus 16.1) while that for education is only 3.9.

Conclusions with respect to profession are less predictable than those for income and education, however, the Carnegie study finds that

service, clerical, and sales workers—but especially unskilled labor-
ers—suffer lots of stress in their lives.

Exhibit 4-33. Mean perceived stress score by income, education, and profession (range=0-45) mean score
for total population=19.6

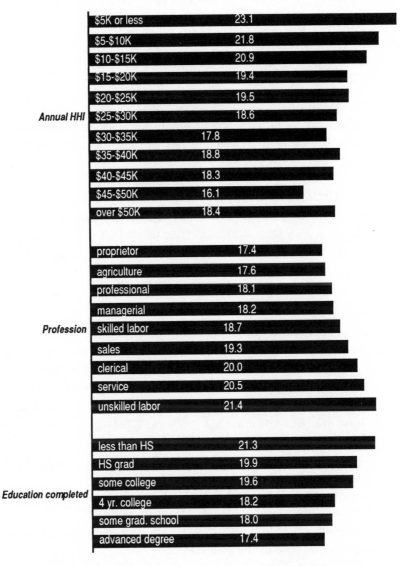

Annual HHI	$5K or less	23.1
	$5-$10K	21.8
	$10-$15K	20.9
	$15-$20K	19.4
	$20-$25K	19.5
	$25-$30K	18.6
	$30-$35K	17.8
	$35-$40K	18.8
	$40-$45K	18.3
	$45-$50K	16.1
	over $50K	18.4
Profession	proprietor	17.4
	agriculture	17.6
	professional	18.1
	managerial	18.2
	skilled labor	18.7
	sales	19.3
	clerical	20.0
	service	20.5
	unskilled labor	21.4
Education completed	less than HS	21.3
	HS grad	19.9
	some college	19.6
	4 yr. college	18.2
	some grad. school	18.0
	advanced degree	17.4

Source: *Perceived Stress in a Probability Sample of the United States*, by
Canegie Mellon University psychologist Sheldon Cohen

Constant feelings of stress may be symptomatic of deeper psychological disorder—the distinction is that pathological stress is accompanied by hostility, diminished self-esteem, anxiety, and psychosomatic complaints. The data presented here derive from localized stress—focusing on events and feelings within the last month—rather than long-standing and enveloping sensations of stress.

Both types of stress, however, are shown to lead to increased risk of disease. High stress levels are associated with insufficient sleep, skipping breakfast, smoking, decreased frequency but increased quantity of alcohol consumption, and lack of exercise.

It seems that affluents' success stress is not of the pernicious, disease-inviting ilk. Instead, affluents traditionally overpower external factors on their way toward their goals, a posture that actually enhances confidence and bolsters coping skills.

Food, Nutrition, and Eating Out

Affluents are eating more cautiously, paying as much attention to what they put into their bodies as they do to how much of it they manage to burn off in exercise. Although they don't fit the picture of the lord of the manner at a table full of rich foods, they are willing to put their money where their mouths are. *Trends and Forecasts*[93] finds that the affluent ($50,000+ annual household) work at their health:

- Eighty percent of the affluent, compared to 73% of the general public, say that they are eating healthier foods like whole grains, fruits and vegetables, and less fat, salt, and high-cholesterol foods. They are also more likely than the average citizen to think that food products available today are generally healthier than those available ten years ago (59% vs. 47%).
- They'll pay for natural foods. Affluents are more willing than average Americans to pay more for products without additives (62% vs. 55%).
- They're weight-watchers. Forty-five percent of the affluent admit to being weight watchers although only 12% say they are currently on a diet; still more than 40% say they are doing neither, vs. 50% of the general public.

Nutrition counts with affluents, and they carry their health-consciousness into restaurants. Those with incomes over $40,000 feel they are well-informed about food and diet—95% say they've got nutritional knowledge. The National Heart Association would be pleased with affluents: they restrict their intake of fat, cholesterol, salt, additives, and sugar; they eat high fiber, calcium; and they exercise (exhibit 4-34).

Exhibit 4-34.   Conscious eating

	% of $40,000+	% of total
Make an effort to eat		
High fiber	74%	68%
High calcium	48%	52%
Starchy food (i.e. rice, pasta, whole grain bread)	73%	70%
Tried in past year to		
Lose weight	50%	44%
Control high blood pressure	24%	25%
Food restrictions within past year		
Salt	76%	70%
Additives	60%	53%
Sugar	71%	63%
Cholesterol	71%	66%
Fat	74%	70%

Source: *Attitudes Toward Nutrition in Restaurants: Assessing the Market,* National Restaurant Association

Affluents eat out more than others, but dining out doesn't mean ditching diets. In an average two weeks, affluents get fast food or take-out 3.8 times (total population does this average of 3.2 times), go to a family-style restaurant 2.2 times (compare with 1.7 for total), and dine at a fine restaurant .7 times (.5 for total). They would probably dine out even more if they could find restaurants that meet their specific dietary needs: they want low salt, low fat choices. (For special occasions and celebrations, though, affluents tend to suspend their nutritional vigil.)

Affluents look for menu items that match their nutrition standards: overall, they are less likely to order fried foods and rich desserts than the average consumer. They opt, instead, for broiled and baked entrees of lean meat, poultry, or fish and are more likely to order fruit-based rather than cream-based desserts (exhibit 4-35).

Affluent dollars will follow the majority of them out the door as their ideas about nutrition will lead them to their favorite restaurant; more than half (52%) of affluents have been to a restaurant offering light, healthy, or special menu items—compared to 45% of the total population.[94]

Exhibit 4-35.   Likelihood of ordering in restaurant

	% of $40,000+	% of total
Breakfast		
Whole grain muffins	71%	67%
Cereal with lowfat skim milk	58%	53%
Bagel or bread with lowfat cream cheese	50%	45%
Appetizers		
Raw vegetable appetizer	71%	61%
Raw fish or shellfish appetizer	20%	15%
Entrees		
Lean meats	83%	81%
Broiled, baked fish or seafood	83%	78%
Steak or roast beef	75%	75%
Poultry without skin	75%	74%
Fried fish or seafood	52%	57%
Fried chicken	45%	43%
Calorie controlled entree	50%	45%
Desserts		
Fresh fruit	93%	88%
Premium ice cream	44%	50%
Lowfat, low calorie fruit-based dessert	47%	49%
Fruit ices or sorbet	51%	46%
Rich, gooey or chocolate desserts	40%	41%
Beverages		
Regular soft drink	47%	56%
Diet soft drink	47%	42%
Caffeine-free soft drink	42%	42%
Caffeine-free coffee	31%	32%
Other items		
Vegetables with herbs or lemon juice	69%	64%
Reduced calorie salad dressing	61%	58%
Food cooked without salt	59%	57%
Low fat frozen yogurt	58%	50%
Low fat cottage cheese	47%	44%
Sugar substitutes	39%	42%

Source: *Attitudes Toward Nutrition in Restaurants: Assessing the Market,*
National Restaurant Association

In nixing fat, cholesterol, and salt from their diets, the upscale tend toward simply seasoned foods prepared without oil. They are watching calories as well as nutrition and are more likely than average to order diet over regular sodas. Lowfat is a powerful catchword for affluents: from frozen yogurt to cottage cheese to salad dressing to wherever food science may lead in the future.

Exhibit 4-36.   Food attitudes

(based on 5 point scale where 5=strongly agree, 1=strongly disagree)

	$40,000+	Total
Good diet and nutrition play role in preventing illness	4.6	4.5
Eating fruits and vegetables is important	4.4	4.4
Prefer broiled to fried foods	4.3	4.0
Important to eat three well-balanced meals a day	3.8	3.9
Tired of hearing about what's good and bad to eat	2.9	3.0

(based on 5 point scale where 5="describes your behavior completely," 1="does not describe behavior at all")

	$40,000+	Total
Often skip at least one meal per day	3.4	3.4
Pay attention to nutrition content of foods	3.7	3.5
Eat whatever, whenever you want	3.1	3.4
Family affects what you eat	3.2	3.1
You're a "meat and potatoes" person	2.7	3.1
Pay attention to the calorie content of foods	3.1	3.0

Source: *Attitudes Toward Nutrition in Restaurants: Assessing the Market*,
National Restaurant Association

Hobbies

As a general rule, all kinds of sports and hobbies are more popular among Influentials than others—if only because they represent an outlet, a connection, a venue of constant learning. Consider the average number of hobbies among Influentials, 4.7, compared to that of the total population, 3.4.

Exhibit 4-37.   Influentials and their hobbies

Hobbies	Influentials	Total public
Reading	65%	42%
Music	47%	37%
Travel	44%	23%
Cooking	41%	34%
Gardening	34%	24%

Source:*The Influential Americans: Who They Are, How To Reach Them*, The Roper Organization, Inc.

Intellectual hobbies capture the Influential interest: reading is profoundly popular among this plugged-in consumer group. They like to think, and often direct their mental energies to the mysteries, achievements, and problems of the planet.

Exhibit 4-38. What interests Influentials

Interests	Influentials	Total public
Developments in national government	85%	58%
Medical breakthroughs	75%	57%
Local government	73%	52%
Foreign relations	68%	46%
Business/industry developments	65%	37%

Source: *The Influential Americans: Who They Are, How To Reach Them*, The Roper Organization, Inc.

The Homestead

In absolute dollars, affluents spend about twice as much for housing as the average consumer does, but as a percent of income, they spend much, much less. The recently compiled Department of Housing and Urban Development *1987 American Housing Survey* reveals that affluent households paid between $650 and $900 per month for housing, while the average American household paid a mere $388. However, there is a bigger picture: for the average consumer, housing took up 22% of income, while for affluents, housing bit off only about 10% of income (exhibit 4-39).

Exhibit 4-39. Household characteristics—affluents vs. total

	$60,000-$79,999	$80,000-$99,999	$100,000-$119,999	$120,000+	U.S. total
1987 monthly housing costs—median	$689	$762	$846	$879	$388
1987 monthly housing costs as percent of income—median	13%	11%	10%	7%	22%

Source: *American Housing Survey for the U.S. 1987*, Department of Housing and Urban Development

---

According to the study, affluents live in newer, larger, and more valuable living units than average Americans—newer by about six years; larger by about two rooms; and more valuable by about $80,000. However, affluents do pay more real estate tax: an average of $50 more per month than others (exhibit 4-40).

Exhibit 4-40. Household characteristics—affluents vs. total

	$60,000-$79,999	$80,000-$99,999	$100,000-$119,999	$120,000+	U.S. total
Year built—median	1968	1969	1967	1968	1962
Number of rooms—median	6.7	7.1	7.3	7.3	5.3
Number of bedrooms—median	3.2	3.3	3.3	3.3	2.6
Value of housing unit—median for owner occupied	$111,600	$137,400	$161,400	$174,000	$67,900
Purchase price—median for owner occupied	$60,800	$65,800	$76,100	$89,300	$31,400
Persons in household—median	3.2	3.2	3.2	3.0	2.3
Monthly real estate tax cost—median for owner occupied	$101	$117	$132	$125	$55

Source: *American Housing Survey for the U.S. 1987*, Department of
Housing and Urban Development

Affluent households tend to be larger than others, as shown in exhibit 4-40: median household size of 3.2 people for most affluents vs. 2.3 for the rest of the nation. Nearly all affluent households—about 95%— are two-or-more-person arrangements, compared to 75% for the total population. Whereas only 5% of affluent households are comprised of singles living alone, 25% of total households are.

As a rule, if an affluent's home is his or her castle, chances are the affluent is the king or queen of that castle; an overwhelming percentage of affluents (compared to the total U.S. population) own their homes (exhibit 4-41).

In search of the perfect castle, affluent homebuyers are predictably interested in building size, lot size, and proximity to cities. Stylistic wants are a little less formulaic, though. Here, from *Builder* magazine's "1989 Home Buyers Survey," are some recent twists of trend:

Affluent homebuyers want:

- exterior brick siding;
- security system;
- open space;
- ice-dispensing refrigerator;
- walk-in closet;
- library/office.

What's not hot:

- asphalt-composition roof;
- wood-burning stove;
- maid's room.

Exhibit 4-41. Percent of affluents (HHI $50,000+) compared
to the total population who

Category	Total population	Affluent consumers	Index
Status			
own	57.5%	82.0%	143
rent	30.3%	10.6%	35
live w/ parents	9.8%	6.2%	63
Type			
house	62.1%	79.4%	128
condominium	5.1%	6.5%	127
apartment	18.4%	5.6%	30
mobile home	3.0%	0.7%	23
other	2.0%	1.2%	60

Source: *Affluent Consumers: A Special Report,* Deloitte & Touche/Impact
Resources

Examining what makes the homestead go, we find that heat for most
affluent homes comes in the form of a hot-air furnace—about 60% use
this method to keep the homefront toasty, compared to the total
average of 55%. With a use index of about 112, affluents are about 10%
more likely than others to use a furnace. When it comes to steam,
though, the index difference heats up—to as high as 140 for those with
a $100,000-$119,999 income. Although the actual percentages for
affluent use of steam heat are lower than those for furnace heat (only
in the 15-20% range as compared to 60%), frequencies with respect to
the total population are very high. Other heat sources—room heaters,
portables, stoves, and fireplaces—are not common in affluent households.

Fuel for the fire comes in the form of piped gas for most affluents—
about 55%, vs. 51% for the total population. This represents an index
of about 110 in comparison to the total population. Electricity is used
about half as often and is less frequent in comparison to non-affluent
households. The most affluent households are an exception to this
rule; they are more likely than average to use electricity. All house-

holds are most likely to catch water flow from public or private systems as opposed to wells, but affluents are even more likely. Well water indexes tread around 91 (exhibit 4-42).

Exhibit 4-42.   Heat and water sources

	$60,000-$79,999	$80,000-$99,999	$100,000-$119,999	$120,000+	Total U.S.
Warm-air furnace					
heating equipment	63.8%	62.9%	59.9%	62.0%	54.9%
Index	116.2	114.6	109.1	112.9	100.0
Steam, hot water system					
heating equipment	15.5%	18.6%	21.3%	16.9%	15.2%
Index	101.9	122.4	140.1	111.2	100.0
Electricity as heating					
fuel	22.0%	21.7%	19.4%	25.3%	22.7%
Index	96.9	95.6	85.5	111.5	100.0
Piped gas as heating					
fuel	57.1%	55.4%	55.4%	53.8%	50.6%
Index	112.8	109.5	109.5	106.3	100.0
On public water or					
private system	87.3%	87.4%	86.7%	87.6%	85.6%
Index	102.0	102.1	101.3	102.3	100.0
Well water	12.4%	12.2%	12.7%	11.7%	13.4%
Index	92.5	91.0	94.8	87.3	100.0

Source: *American Housing Survey for the U.S. 1987*, Department of Housing and Urban Development

With so many affluents as homeowners, it probably makes sense that one of the hottest new housing trends among affluents is the desire to improve their home by some kind of remodeling project.

Let the sun shine in. That's the rule affluents are using in making their home-remodeling decisions. With a statistically pronounced inclination towards windows, skylights, greenhouses, sun rooms, and vaulted ceilings, affluent households with income over $100,000—and to a lesser degree affluents in $50,000-$99,999 households—want their remodeled homes to blend in with the outdoors, according to the "Remodeling Consumer Study 1990," from *Professional Builder*.

The study notes that free-flowing open spaces and lots of sunlight are the keys to a happy affluent home. This contradicts a more general consumer trend of well-defined rooms walled off from one another. In both the kitchen and bath—as well as in new rooms they plan to add on—affluents want the simple elements of the great outdoors: space and light.

Half of upper-affluents ($100,000+ household income) who plan to remodel within the year will include cathedral, vaulted-type ceilings, or some kind of dramatic window treatment in their new rooms. For affluents in $50,000-$99,999 households, the new-room emphasis is on family entertainment (i.e. a den or TV room), but 25% of them also want cathedral ceilings and window treatments. Exhibit 4-43 shows that the "greening" of society includes affluent homes as well—a third want to design plant-friendly niches in their remodeled rooms.

Exhibit 4-43.   What will you include in your room addition?

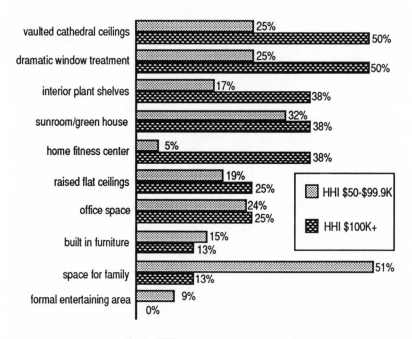

Source: "Remodeling Consumer Study 1990," *Professional Builder*

More than half of upper-affluents (60%) and about two-fifths of other affluents (42%) plan to touch up the kitchen this year. Upgrading present cabinetry—including making it more spacious—ranks top on their list of priorities; 90% of $50,000-$99,999 households and 89% of $100,000+ households agree that the cabinets are the most important kitchen remodeling job.

Also, more than 70% of both groups plan to upgrade their kitchen appliances. New lighting and windows will make new cabinetry and new appliances look better: 81% of upper-affluents want new kitchen lights and 42% want windows. Among other affluents, the percentages are 76% and 32%, respectively.

Add water to space and mix in some light, and you get the formula for affluent bath remodeling. While upgrading cabinetry is most important (86% of $50,000-$99,999 households and 60% of $100,000+ households agree), and increasing storage space also ranks high (with more than 50% of both groups), knocking down walls and adding skylights are decidedly upper-affluent. A third of $100,000+ households compared to 22% of $50,000-$99,999 households will remove at least one wall somewhere in the bathroom, while 54% will add windows and 46% will put in a skylight. Only 32% of $50,000-$99,999 households are adding windows and only 27% a skylight. The affluent bath—like the kitchen and add-on rooms—will flow with space and be drenched with rays.

Upper-affluents are so space-conscious that they even go for the illusion of more space created by mirrored walls—29% of those in $100,000+ households want them. This is in sharp contrast to other affluents (only 8% of $50,000-$99,999 households want mirrored walls) and to the total population (7%).

Whether its spiffing up the kitchen or bath, adding a room, or major redesign, upper-affluents plan to spend about twice as much as other affluents on their remodeling jobs. Exceptions to that are adding a sun room, expanding the attic, and adding a garage. For those jobs, upper-affluents budget less than the amount budgeted by $50,000-$99,000 affluents.

Exhibit 4-44. Remodeling plans and expected costs

	HHI $50,000-$99,999		HHI $100,000+	
	% who plan	mean estimated cost	%who plan	mean estimated cost
Remodel kitchen	42.1%	$ 9,697	60.4%	$17,255
Remodel bath	38.6%	$ 3,939	35.4%	$ 6,779
Enclose porch	9.0%	$ 4,045	20.8%	$ 7,400
Add room	22.4%	$20,418	18.8%	$47,750
Finish basement	9.3%	$ 5,295	14.6%	$11,333
Exterior facelift	10.3%	$ 5,344	14.6%	$13,933
Add sunroom	6.9%	$ 8,917	6.3%	$ 6,533
Add bathroom	4.1%	$ 4,667	4.2%	$15,000
Expand attic	1.7%	$ 4,700	4.2%	$ 800
Redesign > 1/2 house	5.9%	$32,250	4.2%	$60,000
Add garage	8.3%	$ 8,756	2.1%	$ 3,000
Mean estimated amount will spend on remodeling jobs over next 12 months:		$13,981		$29,442

Source: "Remodeling Consumer Study 1990," *Professional Builder*

Besides revealing cost data, exhibit 4-44 shows what jobs are popular with each affluent segment. Porch enclosures and attic expansions are disproportionately popular with upper-affluents, while garage add-ons are disproportionately popular with other affluents.

Remodeling ideas for the affluent come mainly from magazines—about three-quarters of them cite periodicals as their primary source. Friends' houses also have an impact on their ideas. Having the least effect on affluent's remodeling choices: newspaper articles and, believe it or not, interior decorators. The vast majority of affluents looking to remodel call in a builder/remodeler to do the job. For upper-affluents, a subcontractor is also on the scene (exhibit 4-45).

Exhibit 4-45.   Which professionals will you employ to accomplish your remodeling project?

	HHI $50,000-$99,999	HHI $100,000+
Builder/remodeler	73.7%	62%
Subcontractor	39%	62%
Architect	18%	23%
Other	8%	8%

Note: columns sum to greater than 100% due to multiple answers.

Source: "Remodeling Consumer Study 1990," *Professional Builder*

Affluents find remodelers the way they find doctors and lawyers: referrals from friends and family. The *Professional Builder* study says that far and away, this is the method of shopping for their professional remodelers. Flyers at their doors, ads in the Yellow Pages, and newspaper blurbs just don't catch their attention.

Now we know how much they'll spend, but how will they pay? According to the same *Remodeling Consumer Study 1990*, the majority of affluents will rely on cash: 67% of $50,000-$99,999 households and 79% of $100,000+ households pay with cold currency. But some affluents can't take the cash shock of a $20,000 job. For them, a home equity loan will be the answer—25% of $50,000-$99,999 households and 21% of upper-affluent households will take out a loan to tide them through the short-term payout crunch. One way for affluents to ease some of the cost burden is to do the work themselves—about 80% plan on doing their own painting, and about 75% will do their own general clean-up.

The time and effort affluents put into the structure of their house beautiful is matched only by the care with which they furnish their interior home environment. Exhibit 4-46 is a list of some of the most common extras that make their way into affluent homes:

Exhibit 4-46.   Affluent purchases in the last year

	Percent of affluents who purchased item in last 12 months	Estimated median spent
Home furnishings	85%	$2000
Furniture	67%	$1000
Floor coverings	41%	$1000
Wall coverings	40%	$ 250
China	20%	$ 250
Sterling silver	12%	$ 250
Crystal	22%	$ 250
Other home furnishings	53%	$ 500
Home improvement materials	74%	$ 750
Entertainment appliances	61%	$1000
Color TV	31%	$ 500
VCR	26%	$ 500
Video camera	10%	$1000
CD player	15%	$ 500
Other hi-fi	14%	$ 500
Personal computer	18%	$2000
Software	29%	$ 200

(cont.)

(Ex. 4-46 cont.)

Household or kitchen appliances	58%	$ 500
Kitchen appliances	39%	$ 250
Other household appliances	40%	$ 250
Watches	43%	$ 200
Fine jewelry	57%	$ 500
Costume jewelry	53%	$ 100
Antique furnishings	14%	$ 500
Original artwork	34%	$ 250
Coins	9%	$ 250
Stamps	4%	$ 100
Fine porcelain	10%	$ 250
Photographic equipment	82%	$ 100
Film	80%	$ 50
Books	89%	$ 100
Hardcover	73%	$ 75
Paperback books	83%	$ 50
Luggage (inc. carry-ons)	38%	$ 100
Sports equipment	71%	$ 200
Cosmetics + fragrances	94%	$ 200
Women's apparel	93%	$ 800
Women's shoes	88%	$ 300
Women's evening apparel	58%	$ 250
Women's designer clothes	37%	$ 300
Women's lingerie	84%	$ 75
Men's apparel	91%	$ 750
Children's apparel	60%	$ 300
Men's suits	60%	$ 500

Note: median estimated by spending level containing at least half the buying population.

Source: *The 1989 Survey of Adults and Markets of Affluence*, Mendelsohn Media Research, Inc.

Automobiles

America's love affair with the automobile is alive and well. Getting there is half the fun (and half the fun being seen) especially for affluents. According to a survey, *New Vehicle Financing April 1990*, by the Gallup Organization, nearly a third (31%) of affluents (annual household income $60,000+) purchased a car between April 1989 and April 1990—that's nearly twice the rate for the total population (17%). Of those car purchasers, more than a third (34%) of affluents bought a foreign car as compared to 23% of the total population.

Affluence often implies foreign-car purchase—a relative frequency index of 148 over average consumers. Interesting to note is that Honda is equally popular with both affluents and others, while Acura—made by Honda—has a stronger upscale appeal (exhibit 4-47).

Exhibit 4-47. Of those who bought a car, what is the make?

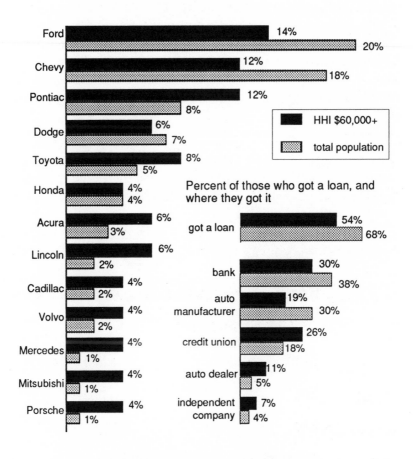

Of those who got a loan, what did they use for collateral?

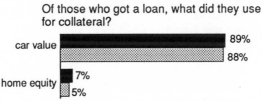

Source: *New Vehicle Financing April 1990*, The Gallup Organization,
           Financial Research Group

Most everyone financed their purchase, though affluents were slightly less likely to do so, 54% vs. 68%. When affluents need new car financing, the bank is the most likely stop: 30% of new-car buyers who finance their purchase do so through a bank. Comparatively speaking, though, the average consumer is a better bank customer for a car loan than an affluent: 38% of total car buyers (i.e. purchasers of 1989 or 1990 car models between April '89 and April '90) went to their bankers. By a large relative margin, affluents look to credit unions for car financing: 26% of affluents vs. 18% of the total. Affluents also got loans more frequently from auto dealers and independent finance companies.

Low rates and convenient service entice affluents to purchase car loans; also, loan programs through work are popular. The average loan shopper can be led by inertia: "bought car there" and "had loans there before" are more likely reasons among non-affluents for choosing a car loan supplier (exhibit 4-48).

Exhibit 4-48.   Reason for loan choice

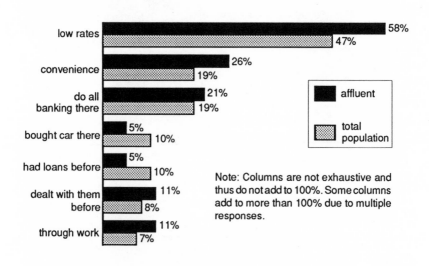

Source: *New Vehicle Financing April 1990*, The Gallup Organization, Financial Research Group

When affluents rate new car dealers, their top concerns are price and availability—the same priorities for car buyers of all income groups. But when buying, affluents are less concerned about the price, vehicle versatility and low-maintenance features; they are interested in the quality, comfort, and style they can afford, and look for roominess, attractive exteriors and favorable product reviews.

Exhibit 4-49. New car buyers by household income

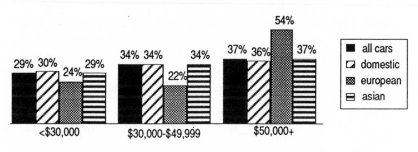

Source: *Newsweek*

It doesn't take a Mercedes test scientist in a lab coat to figure out that affluents are the consumers most likely to buy a luxury car (median price $23,760) or sports model (median $23,018). Those opting for the Lincoln Town Car, Cadillac and Mercedes are predominantly male (although women bought 32% of all luxury cars), married (9% are single), and well-educated. They're also older (80% are at least 45, and 31% are 65+) and (need we say it?) have more money (66% report incomes of $60,000+). Besides roominess and style, they're also interested in size and past experience. Luxury car buyers buy mostly because they want a new car (exhibit 4-50).

Exhibit 4-50. Median household income of selected car owners

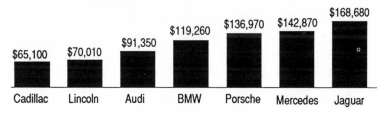

Source: *Esquire*

Those streaking by in a Mazda RX-7 or Porsche are similar to luxury car buyers except that they're younger (76% under age 45) and less likely to be married (31% single). They're also involved with active sports and tune in to Top 40 and Adult Rock radio stations. Almost by definition, the sports car buyer ignores comfort and roominess, maintenance costs or price: the overwhelming appeal is hot style. More than half (61%, compared to 31% of average buyers) said magazine ads were most helpful of all when choosing their wheels.

Nearly all affluents (91%) already own another car, which was almost certainly bought new. Affluents are also more likely to have leased their former car than less-monied groups and to buy their gas with a credit card (exhibit 4-52).

European imports may have allure to all drivers, but affluents are the ones most likely to drive BMWs and Saabs. Because familiarity (especially having one in the garage) is the best indicator of future purchase (according to the Newspaper Advertising Bureau), affluents will continue to be the group with Fiat futures.

Affluents not only spend more than others on their new car, they also spend more time shopping for it. Dealer brochures may seem to be a perfunctory marketing device, but they are the number one ad medium for all buyers, and the higher the income, the more attention is given them. Affluents find magazines significantly more informative and influential than newspapers or television for car information, but they look at newspaper and magazine ads about equally.[95]

The Best! Number One! Consumers have heard too much hype and are skeptical of superlative claims. They rate advertisements in various media as informative, influential, or helpful, but *Newsweek* reports that new car buyers are not particularly convinced by such ads; indeed, the wealthier the consumer, the less he or she is persuaded by "we're the best" type ads. As with almost every category of advertising, the affluent consumer expresses a desire for more informative, practical ads, with less hoopla. Do they get it? They get the superlatives, and they still buy.[96]

Affluent consumers (household income $50,000+) commute by driving much more than the average consumer, and conversely are far less likely to use public transportation (exhibit 4-53). Backing up these findings is a daily total—30% more affluents (73%) drive on a daily basis.[97]

Exhibit 4-51. New vehicle buyer segments

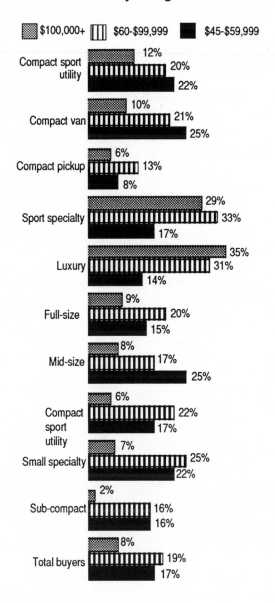

Source: Newspaper Advertising Bureau

For the $60,000+ crowd of big-wheel consumers, cars take the cake; vans and trucks are frosting, even for affluents. Domestics and imports parry for affluent approval (exhibit 4-54).

Exhibit 4-52.   Other vehicles owned: bought or leased (by household income)

	Total	<$30,000	$30,000-$49,999	$50,000+
Bought new	95%	66%	79%	116%
Bought used	50%	65%	56%	41%
Leased	3%	*	2%	4%

Percentages exceed 100% because of multiple vehicle ownership per household.

Source: *Newsweek*

Exhibit 4-53.   How affluents commute

	Total population	Affluent consumers	Index
Drive self	59.6%	70.2%	118
Public transportation	4.6%	2.5%	54
Car pool	2.6%	2.4%	92
Other	2.8%	1.8%	64

Source: *Affluent Consumers: A Special Report*, Deloitte & Touche/Impact Resource

---

Exhibit 4-54.   Cars vs. vans and trucks

	Affluents (HHI $60,000+)
Median #—cars owned or leased	2.4
Median #—cars bought new	1.7
Own or lease domestic car	64.8%
Own or lease domestic truck	14.1%
Own or lease domestic van	13.1%
Own or lease imported car	50.3%
Own or lease imported truck, van	7.1%

Domestic

Buick	10.9%
Cadillac	11.1%
Chevrolet	24.6%
Chrysler	4.8%
Dodge	8.5%
Ford	23.7%

(cont.)

(Ex. 4-54 cont.)

GMC	3.9%
Lincoln	5.3%
Mercury	6.1%
Oldsmobile	13.8%
Plymouth	4.9%
Pontiac	9.1%

Source: *Survey of Adults and Markets of Affluence, 1989,* Mendelsohn
Media Research, Inc.

Chapter

V

Media

In much the same way you might approach an affluent's party (in your best, pressed, evening clothes, invitation in hand), you will need to carefully select your medium (and carry something extra) to reach the affluent consumer with your advertising. The way you market and advertise your goods is the closest you will come to approaching, capturing, and even defining the affluent mindstyle of the affluent market you want to attract and create.

This is an extremely important concept, even in the field of high concept; for media-hip, well-educated affluents, it's going to be harder and harder to separate the medium from the message. They will not only remember what you say in your advertising, but also whether they saw it in the pages of their favorite upscale magazine or on the back of the bench as they drove past the bus stop. When we say media-hip, we mean that affluents know the game. They know what you are trying to do with your ads and are sensitive to the subtle messages you send. Not only do they know the rules of the game, they enjoy it. They like to be surprised and flattered; they appreciate your cleverness and aesthetic values. They know they are a moving target, and dare you to aim for them. And, as you appeal to their mindstyle, you must also appeal to their minds—they want practical information about your product.

We'll focus on a key trend in marketing to affluent consumers—image advertising—in chapter 7. With the warning that it will become increasingly difficult to distinguish what you say from how you say it, the next few pages offer a discussion of the different media you should use to carry your message to affluent consumers. Within this framework, there are very definite differences in effectiveness, depending upon which avenues you choose. Affluent media preferences and usage are well-charted, and they give concrete indicators of how to at least get your message seen and heard among affluent consumers.

In this mass marketing nation, the affluence explosion is revolutionary. Traditional mass marketing approaches are showing their age, and in today's market, they are not aging gracefully. For the affluent market in particular, mass marketing is obsolescent. Because affluents have media patterns that differ from the mass market, advertising strategies will have to change.

Affluents will not sit still for the flow of messages from their televisions. In fact, you are more likely to find them bent over than laid back, concentrating on the small print in front of them. We think that this posture is indicative of the affluents' general approach to media and the message: they are more likely than the average consumer to be *active* in their *pursuit* of what they want from media. Affluents seem, in fact, to have a working relationship with the media available to them. They turn to it for entertainment, yes; but often, they choose the media they can use most effectively to get what they want. And what they want—more, it seems, than entertainment—is information.

Addressing Affluents

Marketing and advertising directly to affluents sounds like a daunting task in the light of much of what we've said: affluents are not a monolithic group, and many different kinds of consumers can be affluent consumers. The basic problem remains: how do you aim at a moving target?

Target-Select tries to address this challenge with a kind of engraved invitation. Launched by Time Warner less than a year ago, the high-tech publishing technique allows marketers to reach very finely sliced segments of the consumer base with laser-jet-printed personalized ads. The idea is to get maximum bang for the advertising buck, and it seems to be catching on. *US News & World Report, Metropolitan Home* and others are joining the trend. In fact, *Metropolitan Home* is coming out with a special February edition—*Ultimate*—targeted to a select 100,000 subscribers with net worths over $300,000.

Time Warner's Target-Select advertising currently appears in *Time, Sports Illustrated,* and *People* with *Entertainment Weekly* and *Money* joining the pack soon. Other publishers—like American Express and the New York Times Co. Magazine Group—have their ears perked up and are exploring the technology.

For a broader approach to a specific target, the Roper Organization offers some general rules-of-thumb to keep in tune with affluent lifestyles and mindstyles. All of these guidelines draw from (as well as support) the variety of data we have gleaned about affluent consumers. They address the mindstyle of affluence, with respect for the affluents' somewhat sensitive reactions to high-pitched pleas. They address the special characteristics of the affluents (and increased appetite for information) that translates into an affluent predilection for information (instead of ads that are long on hyperbole and short on content).

Rules for Reaching Influentials:*

- Articles—as opposed to advertisements—are more effective among Influentials than others.
- Influentials trust the printed word more than other consumers do. Also, they spend more time reading.
- A good way to reach Influentials is through specialty magazines and journals.
- When taking to the airwaves, pay attention to programming. Public affairs and sports programs are good ways to reach Influentials.
- Direct response campaigns—minus any hard-sell—have strong appeal among Influentials.
- Successfully reaching Influentials is tantamount to reaching larger markets—Influentials spread the word.

Messages should:

- emphasize discovery and exploration, not the known;
- appeal to knowledge and judgment, not status;

- challenge, not guarantee;
- show action, not passivity;
- provide news, not hype;
- project decisiveness, not hesitancy;
- reveal a broad-minded sense of cooperation and interdependence, not competition.

*Source: *The Influential Americans: Who They Are, How To Reach Them,* The Roper Organization, Inc.

Media Response

Supporting Roper's findings on direct response marketing to affluents, more than three-quarters (77%) of Simmons' Exclusive Set (educated professionals between 35 and 49 with household income $75,000+) ordered a product or service by phone or mail in the past year, compared to only 51% of lower-income households. Affluents also were more likely to purchase via catalogs, and made more purchases when they did so—an average of five orders, vs. four for other households.

Direct response offers in print, radio, and television media were studied. Affluents most often chose the quickest way to communicate their desire to buy: the telephone. One catalog specialist firm director suggests that since the 35- to 50-year-old affluents grew up with the boom of catalogs and 800 phone numbers, they trust instant buying. Also, upscale buyers aren't squeamish about giving out their credit card numbers over the phone.

Exhibit 5-1.   Who buys direct?

	HHI	
	<$75,000	*$75,000+*
Responded to direct offers (all media)	51%	76%
Responded to catalog offers	40%	62%

Source: *DIRECT* magazine

If there is a credibility gap among affluents, the media, and the rest of the consumer population, that gap can be found in the degree to which affluent householders take what they see and hear on the television screen to heart. For all income groups below the $50,000 mark, TV is a credible source of information; almost half of all these income segments say that television is the most believable medium. While newspapers and radio rank very similarly among all consumer income segments, the affluents' preferences become markedly different when asked about the believability of magazines. Affluents have a decided preference for reading and these results further narrow their preferences to the *format* in which they put the most trust (exhibit 5-2).

Exhibit 5-2.   Which medium is most believable? (by annual household income)

Income	TV	Newspapers	Radio	Magazines
$50,000+	33%	24%	5%	22%
$25-39,999	47%	26%	6%	10%
$15-24,999	48%	24%	4%	11%
$<15,000	48%	24%	4%	7%
National average	46%	24%	5%	11%

Source: *TV Dimensions '89*, Media Dynamics

Once you get your ad in front of the affluents, don't expect them to be impressed by celebrities offering unsolicited advice; the vast majority of affluents are underwhelmed by the credibility of a spokesperson who is famous (but not necessarily and specifically related to the product or service advertised). And don't expect more than a fifth of them to buy the looks of surprise and rapture that a hidden camera catches when an unsuspecting person discovers the virtues of a product. More believable to affluent markets are people (like company representatives) who have something to do with the goods or services offered. Affluents also like to trust their own ability to use gathered evidence (comparative ads and user surveys that get information from more than one source) and make (or at least see) informed decisions based on the facts (exhibit 5-3).

Exhibit 5-3.   Ranking for ad believability among Influentials

1. User surveys—50%
2. Comparative ads—45%
3. Company representatives—35%
4. Hidden camera—20%
5. Celebrity endorsement—15%

Source: *The Influential Americans: Who They Are, How To Reach Them*, The Roper Organization, Inc.

Third class mail gets a rather third-rate response from affluents, especially in the upper reaches of income segments over $50,000. This response, combined with the fact that affluents have responded positively to personalized mailings, suggests that while affluent mailboxes aren't closed to all offers, you'd better use the right kind of address with first class consumers (Exhibit 5-4).

Exhibit 5-4. Response to third-class bulk regular mail (by income, 1988)

HHI	Read pieces immediately		Set pieces aside	
	Percent	Per household	Percent	Per household
<$7,000	37.8%	1.6%	8.9%	0.4%
$7-$9,999	48.5%	2.3%	5.6%	0.3%
$10-$14,999	44.7%	2.7%	7.7%	0.5%
$15-$19,999	47.1%	3.0%	6.0%	0.4%
$20-$24,999	44.7%	3.3%	7.1%	0.5%
$25-$29,999	41.6%	3.2%	8.4%	0.7%
$30-$34,999	40.5%	3.6%	7.4%	0.7%
$35-$49,999	41.3%	4.0%	8.2%	0.8%
$50-$64,999	36.7%	4.3%	8.2%	1.0%
$65-$79,999	38.2%	4.6%	10.1%	1.2%
$80-$99,999	43.6%	6.1%	5.3%	0.7%
$100,000+	33.2%	4.1%	6.0%	0.8%

Source: "USPS Household Diary Survey, 1989," *1989 Statistical Fact Book*, Direct Marketing Association

Media Usage

The affluent don't use media the way the mass market does (precisely because they're not the mass). Their high education levels foster multi-dimensional interests and tastes that require selective feeding. They are variety seekers and discriminatingly choose media stimulation. As affluence becomes progressively more important, advertisers and marketers are going to have to attend to its distinctive tastes more carefully. As mentioned earlier, all the research we've seen confirms that television, except for carefully selected programming, does not hold as much appeal for affluents as it does for the masses (exhibit 5.5). The wealth of options open to them just increases their selectivity. Magazines, newspapers, and news/talk radio are how the wealthy stay informed and entertained.

Television

Affluents seem particularly selective in what they watch on television; their hunger for information affects viewing preferences, and they lean towards documentary formats, news programs, and public television broadcasts. They are willing to pay extra to get a larger variety of viewing options—cable TV is big in affluent households (exhibits 5-6 and 5-7). Aiming for affluent television watchers involves being as selective about programming format as they are; they spend less time in front of the screen than do other market segments, and you must know what kind of show offers even the possibility of affluent viewers tuning in.

Exhibit 5-5.   Average hours of weekly TV viewing (by household income)

	Total U.S.	<$15,000	$40,000+
TV usage by			
Men <18 years	25.9	37.6	20.8
Men 18-34 years	23.8	31.3	19.9
Men 35-54 years	24.4	39.0	20.3
Men 55+ years	32.3	40.7	26.5
Women <18 years	31.4	41.4	24.1
Women 18-34 years	26.7	36.0	20.5
Women 35-54 years	29.0	39.1	24.1
Women 55+ years	38.7	44.7	30.3

Source: *TV Dimensions '89*, Media Dynamics

Exhibit 5-6.   Income distribution of all U.S. households, of pay cable homes, and of non-cable homes

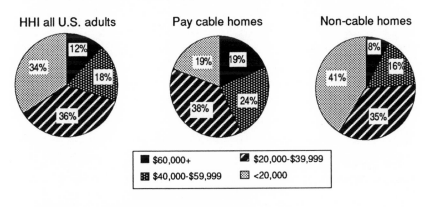

Source: *TV Dimensions '89*, Media Dynamics

Here's more proof that affluent households lean heavily towards cable subscriptions:

Exhibit 5-7. Cable homes among total adults with annual HHI $60,000+

HHI	Percent who are cable subscribers	Percent who are not subscribers
$60,000-$74,999	75.3%	24.7%
$75,000-$99,999	75.7%	24.3%
$100,000-$149,999	76.1%	23.9%
$150,000-$199,999	73.8%	26.2%
$200,000+	80.1%	19.9%

Source: *Cable TV Facts 1990*, Cabletelevision Advertising Bureau, Inc.

According to a Simmons Market Research Bureau 1988 survey, in any week, 65% of those with household income over $60,000 and 57% of those with household income between $40,000 and $59,999 watch cable television.[98]

VCR penetration is near complete among those with annual incomes greater than $50,000 compared with the national average of 61%. "Affluent consumers are less likely to use their VCRs to watch a recorded TV program ... but are more likely than others to be in the market for other video products."[99]

Exhibit 5-8. Media habits of adults (age 18+) with HHI $75,000+, selected categories

	Affluent	U.S. average	Affluent Index
Have cable TV	61%	50%	122
Have VCR	80%	56%	142
Rent videos regularly	26%	20%	132
Have compact disk player	28%	14%	192
Have home computer	48%	24%	203
TV stations regularly viewed			
PBS stations	23%	18%	124
Arts & Entertainment	6%	4%	149
Cable News Network	13%	10%	139
Cinemax	7%	6%	124
ESPN	11%	8%	129
Lifetime	4%	3%	135
The Disney Channel	4%	7%	59
The Movie Channel	7%	6%	129
VH-1	1%	2%	69

(cont.)

(Ex. 5-8 cont.)

TV programs regularly watched

Sports	46%	40%	113
Documentaries/News	60%	51%	116

Radio formats regularly listened to

Easy listening	11%	9%	124
News/talk	15%	10%	148
Classical	9%	3%	268
Sporting events	10%	7%	137

Newspapers (read regularly and occasionally)

USA Today	30%	20%	153
Wall Street Journal	37%	15%	237
Major daily paper	73%	70%	104
Major Sunday paper	69%	64%	107

Buy products by catalog/direct mail

Regularly	15%	10%	153
Occasionally	46%	43%	107
Never	27%	31%	86

Listen to sales solicitations on home phone

Do not listen	56%	46%	121
Est. avg. % solicitations heard	18	22	83

How many mail advertisements read

Just read some	46%	40%	115
Do not read	14%	10%	140

Billboards read from car

Just read some	43%	39%	111
Do not read	10%	8%	124

Source: Impact Resources

Members of affluent ($50,000+) households are more likely to see a feature film on pay cable than through any other film distribution window (exhibit 5-9).

Exhibit 5-9.   Indexes of selectivity of feature film distribution windows (by household income; Index of 100 = U.S. average)

HHI	Movie theater	VCR households	Pay cable	Prime-time TV
Under $25,000	71	58	60	115
$25,000+	118	125	125	91
$35,000+	123	132	133	87
$50,000+	130	140	148	75

Source: *The Media Report*

Sports

When real-affluent men do watch television, tennis, NFL football, college basketball, golf, and college football are the preferred television sport spots. A third (33%) of male television tennis audiences have household incomes of $50,000 or more. Though the largest male audience share for all sports is those with incomes under $30,000, the second largest male audience share, for every sports category, is the affluent man. Below is a chart of television sports audiences (male) broken down by income and sport—in descending order of preference by affluent men (exhibit 5-10).

Exhibit 5-10. Male income percent composition of network sports (regular season; rows add to 100)

	$50,000+	$40,000-$50,000	$30,000-%40,000	<$30,000
Tennis	33%	9%	16%	42%
NFL Football	28%	14%	19%	39%
College Basketball	27%	12%	16%	45%
Golf	26%	12%	17%	45%
College Football	25%	12%	18%	45%
NBA Basketball	24%	11%	17%	48%
Anthology	23%	12%	17%	48%
Baseball	21%	13%	15%	51%
Auto Racing	21%	9%	19%	51%
Bowling	17%	10%	22%	51%
Total U.S. population	28%	13%	17%	42%

Source: *Media Insights: Network Sports Viewing Analysis*, Bozell

Reading

By far the most striking trend in affluent media usage is the affluents' very real preference for the printed word, whether it is in a newspaper or a magazine format. Wealthier affluents are more likely to read for information and advertising than to listen to the radio or watch TV. The trends are striking and unmistakable (exhibit 5-11).

Exhibit 5-11. Affluents prefer to read

HHI	Publications*	Radio**	Television**
$60-$74,999	14.4	11.9	21.4
$75-$99,999	17.2	. 10.9	20.3
$100-$149,999	20.7	9.7	20.0
$150-$199,999	23.7	9.2	18.0
$200,000+	26.6	8.8	18.0

*median number; **median hours per week

Source: *The 1989 Survey of Adults and Markets of Affluence*, Mendelsohn Media Research, Inc.

Affluents not only prefer the printed word as the source of the information and news they so avidly seek, they also are likely to be loyal consumers of printed media, with much higher percentages of frequent usage than the total number of U.S. households (exhibit 5-12).

Exhibit 5-12. Frequent media usage, within the past 24 hours

	Influentials	Total U.S.
Read a newspaper	92%	75%
Watched news on TV	86%	81%
Listened to news on radio	85%	67%
Listened to music on radio	85%	71%
Watched TV for entertainment	70%	70%
Read a magazine	61%	40%
Read a hardcover book	32%	13%
Read a paperback book	27%	16%

Source: *The Influential Americans: Who They Are, How To Reach Them,*
The Roper Organization, Inc.

Affluent consumers (HHI $50,000+) spend an average of 40 minutes a day—Monday through Saturday—reading the daily newspaper, and 50 minutes reading the Sunday paper. Naturally, they have preferences for certain sections (exhibit 5-13). Affluents are also more likely than the total population to read national newspapers (exhibit 5-14).

Exhibit 5-13. Percent of affluents vs. the total population who say they read these sections regularly

Sections read	Total population	Affluent consumers	Index
Local news	62.4%	66.8%	107
Business/finance	36.5%	55.3%	152
National/foreign news	41.3%	54.7%	132
Editorial pages	40.1%	47.7%	119
Entertainment/TV	46.8%	47.6%	102
Sports	37.8%	44.1%	117
Lifestyles	36.6%	43.3%	118
Comics	38.8%	36.8%	95
Food/cooking	30.8%	31.3%	102
Classified ads	29.7%	24.4%	82

Source: *Affluent Consumers: A Special Report,* Deloitte & Touche/Impact
Resources

Exhibit 5-14.   Percent of affluents vs. the total population who say they read these national papers

National papers	Total population	Affluent consumers	Index
USA Today	4.1%	7.2%	176
Wall Street Journal	4.0%	10.2%	255

Source: *Affluent Consumers: A Special Report,* Deloitte & Touche/Impact Resources

The Up Market[100] averages nearly six magazine subscriptions, 88% read a local newspaper every day, and 91% read a local Sunday paper every week. *Fortune* magazine subscribers report that they are exposed to more magazines (53%) and newspapers (42%) now than a few years ago.[101]

Exhibit 5-15.   Newspaper use of the top quintile

Demographic segment	Newspaper index*	Television index*
HHI $60,000+	172	54
Individual wages $35,000+	162	54
College graduate	157	59
Manager, Administrator	155	63
Own home valued at $100,000+	155	59
HHI $50,000-$59,000	145	67
Professional	134	49
Age 45-54 years	133	86

*proportion of total adults in top quintile (20%)=100

Source: Newspaper Advertising Bureau

To get your advertising dollars' worth, you need to know what *type* of affluent consumer reads which publication. The *Affluent Market Research Program*, by Payment Systems Inc., helps you do just that and more. Defining affluence as "households with incomes of $60,000 or more, or a net worth (excluding the home) in excess of $250,000," the study slices the affluent market into eight distinct subsegments:

- **Low End Affluent** (41.6%): household head 35 or younger, not retired, 0-1 child and household income of $60,000-$74,999, *or* more than one child and household income of $75,000-$99,999, *or* net worth of $250,000-$999,999 and income under $50,000;

- **High Income, Full Nest** (11.3%): household head over 35, not retired, more than one child and household income $60,000-$74,999;
- **Young Affluent** (11.4%): household head under 35, household income $60,000 or more, net worth under $1 million, not a senior corporate executive or business owner;
- **Career Affluent** (10.3%): household head 35 or older, not retired, 0-1 child and household income of $75,000-$99,999 or household income of $100,000+ and net worth less than $1 million, not a senior corporate executive or business owner;
- **Retired Affluent** (14.8%): household head retired, household income of $60,000+ or net worth over $250,000;
- **Established Wealth** (6.1%): net worth over $1 million and not a senior executive or business owner or net worth over $5 million;
- **Senior Corporate Executive** (1.1%): not retired, self-defined corporate executive, income of $100,000+, net worth between $250,000 and $5 million;
- **Business Owner** (3.0%): not retired, business owner (half of household income from business), household income of $75,000+, net worth over $250,000.

Not surprisingly, these segments have different appetites and tastes for various reading materials, with the wealthiest being hungriest for information. Among the wealthiest of the wealthy—Career Affluents, Established Wealth, Senior Corporate Executives, and Business Owners—information is boss over entertainment, at least judging by what they read. Newsweeklies and business periodicals are most popular with these ultra affluents; Corporate Executives are by far the heaviest consumers of print media (exhibit 5-16).

A frequency profile of various publications shows that executive affluents just read much more than do others. The trend is marked not just for business publications, either. For example, about 30% of most other ultra-affluents read *Sports Illustrated*, but more than 50% of senior corporate executive affluents do. The big gap exists for magazines like *Fortune, Forbes, Institutional Investor,* and *Money* as well as for more standard reading like *Time* and *Newsweek*. Exhibit 5-17 lists the percentages within each ultra-affluent group who have read a given periodical in the past six months.

Exhibit 5-16.   What the ultra-affluent read

Career Affluents are most likely to read

1. Local business section—84%
2. Wall Street Journal—64%
3. USA Today—60%
4. National Geographic—48%
5. Newsweek—44%

Established Wealth affluents are most likely to read

1. Local business section—82%
2. Wall Street Journal—78%
3. USA Today—55%
4. National Geographic—49%
5. Time—47%

Source: *Affluent Market Research Program*, Payment Systems, Inc.

Exhibit 5-17.   Affluent reading: percent who have read in past 6 months

	Career Affluents	Established Wealth	Senior Corp. Exec.	Business Owners
Architectural Digest	11%	26%	21%	25%
The Atlantic	4%	6%	3%	5%
Barron's	10%	24%	36%	14%
Bon Appetit	17%	15%	13%	19%
Business Month	6%	5%	25%	1%
Business Week	35%	41%	75%	29%
Changing Times	14%	16%	15%	10%
Connoisseur	3%	9%	10%	5%
The Economist	2%	11%	15%	7%
Forbes	16%	41%	54%	24%
Fortune	17%	28%	61%	21%
Golf Digest	13%	22%	36%	18%
Gourmet	12%	15%	21%	11%
Harvard Business Review	9%	10%	30%	8%
HG	3%	8%	13%	8%
INC	9%	12%	36%	21%
Institutional Investor	3%	6%	23%	5%
Investor Newsletter	25%	43%	56%	31%
Investor's Daily	5%	12%	16%	7%
Local business section	84%	82%	92%	84%
Money	34%	33%	48%	32%
National Geographic	48%	49%	44%	40%
Newsweek	44%	40%	54%	35%
New Yorker	14%	24%	31%	13%
NY Magazine	6%	13%	10%	7%
New York Times	30%	45%	61%	30%
NY Times-Sunday	22%	38%	46%	18%
Smithsonian	29%	33%	28%	24%

(cont.)

(Ex. 5-17 cont.)

Sports Illustrated	33%	32%	51%	31%
Tennis	3%	7%	11%	4%
Time	43%	47%	66%	44%
Town & Country	7%	19%	25%	16%
Travel & Leisure	21%	32%	31%	29%
USA Today	60%	55%	70%	56%
U.S. News & World Report	35%	38%	44%	31%
Venture	3%	6%	11%	5%
Wall Street Journal	64%	78%	95%	73%

Source: *Affluent Market Research Program*, Payment Systems, Inc.

The results of the available data on affluent media consumption suggest that when affluents want entertainment, they are not as likely as average households to just turn on the tube; the statistics indicate that they may not see the regular television programming as a preferred form of entertainment. In fact, gathering information seems in itself to be a kind of entertainment to affluents, who will actively use media to get what they want, rather than sit back and let preprogrammed offerings wash over them. Increased numbers of cable subscribers and VCR owners among affluents suggest that while they haven't given up on television, they are eager to maintain some kind of control over what they will see.

Perhaps it's the connection between education and the habit of reading, or perhaps it's the relationship between affluents' desire to know and formats that have traditionally offered more hard information, but one thing is crystal clear: affluents say they enjoy reading, and they will read more, and more often, than any other consumer segment. Information is a key word in discussing affluent media usage. It is the one factor that is continually sought after by affluents in all media outlets available to them.

Part

III

Finding the Affluent Consumer

Chapter
VI

Niches of Riches

Affluence is where you find it—whether it's in a consumer's bank account, lifestyle, or mindstyle. You know where you will not find it: nestled comfortably in the middle of the traditional mass market. *The complex formula of factors that define the affluent consumer will lead you naturally to smaller and more specialized segments of the consumer population.* Slip into the affluent mindstyle, and you will find a group of consumers who do not appreciate being approached as a mass; rather, you will find a group of consumers who value their independence and their individuality—and who are likely to reject you if you create the impression that you are seeing them as a mass. Yet within this group of individuals, there are subgroups that do cohere because of their lifestyle, demographic, or value similarities. These niche markets may not define themselves as groups, but the ties that bind them, however tenuous they seem, make them targetable groups.

Marketers trying to find affluence everywhere may end up like King Midas—when everything you touch turns to gold, you find that you can't *use* anything. On the other hand, marketers who don't put extra effort into finding hidden gold may never come up with that big strike—an open market, untapped by others, because of a vein of affluence that doesn't present itself with bells and whistles as a traditional target group of consumers.

In the introduction of this book, we recommended a general rule of thumb for finding affluent consumers: pick a group of consumers you think is—or could be—your best market; find the available research data on those consumers; and, using that data to estimate the *likelihood* of those consumers continuing their charted spending patterns (as well as their stated values of what they're looking for), back up (or disprove) your initial idea. This formula bears repeating here; coming up with your own hunches—and knowing how to test whether your hunch is a good one—is never more important than when you are trying to find out more about a possible niche market within the larger affluent market.

In this chapter we'll point out some niche groups that we believe exist within the larger affluent market. Some of them have gotten a lot of press (the mature market is a booming focus of research). Some of them may be less familiar (the phenomenon of the "common million-aire," for example). Some of them have been approached as minority markets (the Asian and the gay market, for instance). Others (like the childless affluent households) have been charted, but data about these households has usually been hidden within research about family size in general.

Perhaps the most important thing we've done is point to some niche affluent markets we bet you've never considered as groups before. That's really the most useful thing about this chapter—and the way you think about niche affluent markets in general: know that if the affluent market is somewhat fluid in its definition, the niche affluent markets are doubly so; but they do exist. And even if *they* don't think about themselves as a group, the important thing is that *you* start to think about them that way.

Mature Market
Having reached the point of seeing the kids through college, attaining their peak earnings potential, and having the house decorated, mature Americans currently make up the bulk of the affluent segment. Though they're still worried about having enough of a stash for retirement, they're also quite willing to start enjoying the leisure

experiences that they have put off during their parenting years. They look for life enhancing experiences, like travel, and becoming familiar with healthy activities.

Only 15% of all householders are between 45 and 54, but 31% of affluent ($75,000+ household income), householders fall within that range. This is not to say that the majority of those in that age range are affluent, but rather that the 45 to 54 age range has a higher per capita density than any other range—the corresponding index is 210, so an affluent householder (compared to a non-affluent householder) is more than twice as likely to be a middle-ager.[102]

It's no coincidence that mature consumers, as well as affluent consumers, are the new darlings of the marketing world—their demographics overlap in quite a few areas. Their raw numbers will expand rapidly as the Boomers hit their mid-years, that's a given. While the numbers alone are staggering, even more interesting to marketers *right now* is the mature market's money power; *more than one-third of all U.S. adults—63 million Americans—are over 50, and they control half America's discretionary income and 77% of its assets.* Grey Advertising[103] observes a great many 50+ers radically reorganizing their lives: they "buy second homes, redecorate, buy new cars, travel, dine out, enroll in courses, take up hobbies." That means they're breaking up lifelong habits and trying new things. Eighty-two percent say they're open to new products and experiences that can make their lives more satisfying. Indeed, 84% said they'd switch brands if a new product or service seemed to be more for "people like me."

Grey Advertising segments the mature market (age 50+) into three groups: MasterConsumers, Maintainers, and Simplifiers. MasterConsumers are "both the heart of 50+ opportunity and the key that can unlock the potential for the entire 50+ population"—the most affluent and most active 50+ group in the marketplace. "They are fit, both physically and psychologically, and render the sedentary, isolated stereotypes of the 50+ experience obsolete. Nearly all MasterConsumers (95%) go out of their way to get the best quality at the best price; 92% will spend more for truly exceptional quality; 69% say freedom to travel is one of the most important benefits of being 50+; 94% say they are enjoying their current age."[104]

Exhibit 6-1.   50+: a matter of attitude

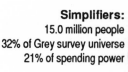

Simplifiers:
15.0 million people
32% of Grey survey universe
21% of spending power

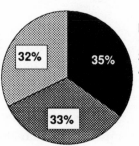

MasterConsumers:
16.4 million people
35% of Grey survey universe
46% of spending power

Maintainers: 15.4 million people, 33% of Grey
survey universe, 33% of spending power

Source: *Grey Matter Alert* 1988, Grey Advertising

As of March 1988, within five-year age groupings, the highest median income for men was for the 6.2 million who were between 45 and 54 years old with income centered at $28,685; 17.3% had incomes of $50,000+. Next in percent in higher income brackets (but greater in total number) were men age 35 to 44. The 17.1 million in this group had a median income of $26,828; with 13.2% earning $50,000+.[105]

Another report flatly states the case: 45- to 64-year-old consumers have "the greatest buying power of any group in America." According to this report, they comprise 22% of the U.S. population, with two-fifths (40%) earning $40,000+ annually. The average spender in this group earns almost $5,000 more a year than the much-courted Baby Boomer.

These Spenders spend, on average, $41.89 per shopping trip ($16.11 per person in their household). Almost half (43%) plan to make a major purchase within the next year. Almost 34% eat at a full-service restaurant at least four times a month, and 46% of them pay more than $30 for a meal in a month's time. As with other affluent groups, print advertising is the most effective way to reach this segment—especially since their favorite leisure activity is reading. [106]

Impact Resources offers its own look at the group they label Spenders (consumers aged 45-64), comparing their demographics, lifestyle, shopping, and media habits with those of consumers 18 years old and older. Chapter 1 gives a more comprehensive look at this market segment.

Women's Market

At least some part of the coming decade will be the era of the woman "who wasn't born yesterday." A *Lear's* magazine survey finds an overwhelmingly secure, happy, vibrant, and pretty gutsy population in age and sex categories heretofore unheralded. Attitudinal in nature, the survey focuses exclusively on college-educated, upscale ($40,000+ household income) women 40 to 65 years of age and, naturally, is not a profile of women in general. The niche these women carve is one that virtually all industries would be happy to share.

Nearly all of the respondents say they enjoy life (95%) and feel it is possible to get what they want (94%). Yet, these generally-satisfied women are not resting on their laurels. They are "in process"—78% see themselves as changing and evolving—leaving behind the old image of the unfulfilled mad housewife and entering into the broader horizon of "very successful" marriages (70%) and "highly satisfied" lives (75%). Coupled with these self-perceptions of continued growth, a series of revealing self-portraits point to women whose currently positive attitudes stand to deepen and develop further. The study finds women describing themselves as: competent 79%, compassionate 75%, productive 70%, useful 67%, purposeful 66%, energetic 57%, and spiritual 51%.

Satisfaction isn't guaranteed. While they are changing and evolving, those who want to change themselves, and are therefore less satisfied with themselves (18%), also see themselves as less energetic, effective, successful, and influential. Self-acceptance is key in terms of satisfaction, and it grows with age—the oldest women (ages 60 to 65, 27%) are more likely than 40- to 44-year-olds (19%) to be extremely satisfied with their lives. Those who are able to utilize and express their creativity (39%) are much more likely to be extremely satisfied than those who do not (14%). Similarly, those who believe they are sexually appealing (23%) report greater satisfaction than those who do not (11%). Of those who want to change themselves (47%) 21% want to improve appearance/lose weight; 17% want to continue to grow/improve as a person; 10% want to be more aggressive/assertive (multiple, unprompted answers).

Exhibit 6-2.   What sacrifices and tough decisions women
would/wouldn't be willing to make in order to do
what they really want to do

Would be willing to make

Financial/lower standard of living	30%
Time/less leisure time	18%
Hard work/longer hours	13%
Family time/less time with family	10%
Move/relocate	9%
More education/go back to school	6%

Would not be willing to make

Family/couldn't sacrifice home life	40%
Financial sacrifices	12%
Relocate/leave country	10%
Compromise my values/beliefs	6%
Leisure/personal time	4%

Source: *The Lear's Report: A Self-Portrait of the Woman Who Wasn't Born
Yesterday*, conducted for *Lear's* by Louis Harris and Associates

Forty-three percent of these women report that having a strong sense
of self is absolutely essential to them (an *additional* 51% find it very
important). Self-awareness influences how positively a woman feels
about herself physically and about her interaction with men (exhibit
6-3).

Exhibit 6-3.   Strong sense of self related to sexuality

Those who say that having a strong sense of self is absolutely essential	43%

Those who say their appearance now is

More important than it was	48%
Less important than it was	33%

Those who say they are sexually appealing

Yes	44%
No	31%

Those who are attracted to men now

More than they were	60%
Same	46%
Less than they were	34%

Source: *The Lear's Report: A Self-Portrait of the Woman Who Wasn't Born
Yesterday*, conducted for *Lear's* by Louis Harris and Associates

Forget the idea of over the hill—75% feel they are as, or *more*, sexually
appealing than they were ten years ago. A solid majority (64%) are

more sexually attracted to men than they were ten years ago, and most (59%) spend more time in bed than they did a decade ago. One-half (54%) find their ideas about the place of sex in their lives has changed—while 43% say the predominant change is that sex is not as important as it used to be, 13% are more open-minded about sex, and 8% find more emotional meaning and depth in sexual encounters. When all is said and done, love is what matters—97% say love is very important in their lives; of these, 53% say it is the most important thing, and all (100%) have people close to them whom they presently love (59% indicate that the family is the most important aspect in their lives. No other category comes close to this level of importance in their lives).

Seventy-five percent of these already-upscale women hold paying jobs and, of these, 96% work outside the home. A day on the job doesn't make these women feel bedraggled—working women feel sexier and are more concerned about their appearance than their nonworking peers. The women who say that they are sexier now than they were ten years ago are more likely to be working (79% vs. 68% whose appearance is less important). Self-worth and physical appeal seem closely related to independence outside the home.

A key driving motivation for these women is creativity, but only one third fully express these creative urges in their lives, while twice as many (62%) are only partially creative; 4% aren't at all creative. Just a job is not enough—they want to be creatively engaged at work, too. The marketer who addresses this untapped urge to create will sculpt a handsome niche market for herself. Women who don't express their creativity (71% vs. 44% who use their creativity) want to be more influential in their careers (30%), politics (16%), with children/ grandchildren (12%), and on social issues such as homelessness and the environment (9%).

Exhibit 6-4.   Profiles by household income

Women who use their creativity and those who do not

	yes (233)	no (465)
$40-$50,000	31%	29%

(cont.)

(Ex. 6-4 cont.)

$50-$75,000	39%	41%
$75-$100,000	16%	18%
$100,000+	6%	8%

Women who work for pay and those who do not

	yes (500)	no (178)
$40-$50,000	28%	35%
$50-$75,000	44%	30%
$75-$100,000	17%	18%
$100,000+	8%	12%

Sexually appealing women and those who say they aren't

	yes (624)	no (54)
$40-$50,000	29%	37%
$50-$75,000	42%	33%
$75-$100,000	17%	20%
$100,000+	9%	4%

Women who want to change themselves and those who don't

	yes (331)	no (364)
$40-$50,000	30%	30%
$50-$75,000	40%	41%
$75-$100,000	18%	17%
$100,000+	7%	8%

Source: *The Lear's Report: A Self-Portrait of the Woman Who Wasn't Born Yesterday*, conducted for *Lear's* by Louis Harris and Associates

Gay Market

Affluence out of the closet—gay consumers are a seriously neglected, seriously wealthy market. Simmons' Proprietary Data gives an inside view of the gay market. This study of the primary readers of eight gay publications verifies that the gay consumer has a very high income level, a very high educational level, usually no dependents and, consequently, very high discretionary income. Conducted in October 1988, this survey establishes the demographic profile and purchasing habits of readers of the eight leading gay newspapers in the U.S.

As extraordinary as it may seem, the statistics on gays that are still generally used are derived from the Kinsey study (1948), which states that ten percent of the population is predominantly or exclusively gay. This means at least 25 million people (about as large as the entire U.S. black population), but it's a conservative figure since individuals in the 1940s were less likely to be candid about their sexual orientation than they are today; the percentage is higher in urban areas. The average household income for readers of the top eight gay newspapers is $55,430 according to the Simmons' study, compared to the U.S. Census Bureau's figure for average U.S. households—$32,144. Individual employment income for gays is $36,800, or triple the national average (exhibit 6-5).

Exhibit 6-5.   Income for readers of gay publications vs. national averages

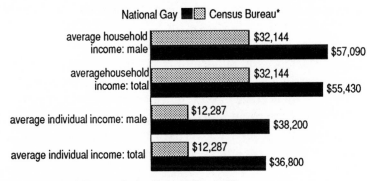

National Gay ■ ▓ Census Bureau*

average household income: male	$32,144 / $57,090
average household income: total	$32,144 / $55,430
average individual income: male	$12,287 / $38,200
average individual income: total	$12,287 / $36,800

*Money, Income & Poverty Status in the U.S.—1987

Source: Simmons Proprietary Research for Rivendell Marketing Co.

The same comparison holds true when household income of gays is compared to the household income of Simmons' adult male readers. For example, the survey shows 45% of adult gays with a household income of $50,000+ compared to 20% of adult male respondents with the same income on the national level. And in the upper bracket of household income $100,000+, gays rate 13% compared to total male respondents' 3%; put in other terms, gay readers shown to earn $100,000+ surpass the national average of males by 427%. Furthermore, gay publication readers' average age is 36; 74% fall between the ages of 25 and 44; readership is 86% male.

In addition to an economic elite, the survey also depicts an educational and employment elite—60% of gays are college graduates vs. 18% of the U.S. population—that's 331% times the national average. Nearly all (97%) are employed, vs. 63% of the U.S. population; this is a rate equal to 153% of the national average. Equally impressive in terms of the potential consumer is the gay occupational profile. Gays hold professional/managerial positions in the U.S. at 308% above the national average; New York's gays take the lead, with an index of 390%.

The medium can be more important than the message. As advertisers know from marketing to other minority groups, ads placed in specialty publications deliver far more impact. An advertiser willing to invest in advertising its product in a gay publication signals to that gay reader a vote of confidence, a vote of trust in that consumer's freedom to choose—whether a lifestyle, a service or a product. It is a potent public relations move. It can make a sale—a big step towards brand loyalty. The survey also states that readers of the top eight gay newspapers rely heavily on both the advertising and editorial content. Eighty-six percent of readers of gay publications say they would be likely to purchase nationally advertised products featured in their newspapers. In the last year, an average of 63% relied on advertising or editorial seen in their local gay paper in their choice of leisure activities, 53% purchased a product or service advertised in their local gay paper, and 45% mentioned to others products or services seen in their local gay paper.

Exhibit 6-6.   Average HHI for selected income brackets: readers of gay publications vs. *Simmons' 1988 Study of Media and Markets* averages

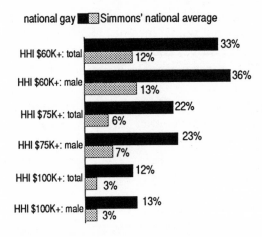

Source: Simmons Proprietary Research for Riverdell Marketing Co.

Readers of gay publications (comparisons are to Simmons' national average figures for adult males):*

- 84% dine at a restaurant in the average month; an average of 16 times per month. Two-thirds went to a bar or dance club an average of eight times per month; drink 6.2 times as much imported champagne; 73% shop for liquor or wine by brand name, and 53% order by brand when out;
- purchase 4.5 times as many albums, over 8.3 times as many CDs, three times as many cassettes. In one year they purchase an average 18 albums, 19 CDs, 9.5 prerecorded cassettes, and 14 blank cassettes;
- 46% bought pre-recorded video cassettes in the last year (1.8 times the national average), an average of 10 per year. Four-fifths (79%) rented video cassettes (twice the national average), an average of 33 per year;
- 77% own a VCR or plan to buy one in the coming year, 13% for video cameras, 7.6% for a laser video disc player. More than 43% own a CD player or plan to buy one, and over 62% own or plan to own a component stereo system;
- 39% attended a pop/rock concert in the last year (3.8 times average), 67% a live theater performance (6.3 time average), 29% a classical music concert (6.5 times average), and 18% attended an opera.

*Source: Simmons Proprietary Research for Rivendell Marketing Co.

Exhibit 6-7. College grads: readers of gay publications vs. *Simmons' 1988 Study of Media and Markets* averages

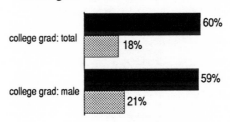

The papers surveyed: *Bay Area Reporter* (San Francisco), *Bay Windows* (Boston), *Dallas Voice* (Dallas), *Frontiers* (Los Angeles), *Montrose Voice* (Houston), *New York Native* (New York), *Philadelphia Gay News* (Philadelphia), *Windy City Times* (Chicago).

Asian-American Market

The Asian influx is an affluence influx. *Market Opportunities in Retail: Asian American Consumers*[107] reports that as a group, Asian-American households enjoy a higher income than the U.S. average, the median Asian household income being $27,300, vs. $26,400 for the total population. Although Asian-Americans are 11% more likely than the average to live in a less than $10,000 per year household (mostly new immigrants, particularly Vietnamese), they are 34% more likely to live in $75,000+ households. Marketers will have a long time to court Asians, too, because their households are young—median age is 33.2 versus 38.1 for the country.

This youthful population reflects the fact that those Asians who came at the beginning of the Asian Wave now have children. These indexes will even out as the generations replenish themselves here in the U.S. Asian households are larger than others—averaging 3.4 people versus 2.8 for the nation; this results from the above average presence of young children as well as aging adults at home. While 34% of the U.S. population lives in two-person households, 20% of Asians live in four-person households.

Education is a time-honored value for Asian consumers, and their formal schooling extends more than two years longer than others'. Median years of education for Asians is 14.9; median for the U.S. is 12.8. As we have seen, their future potential earnings—based on their high educational attainment—are great (exhibit 6-8).

Exhibit 6-8.   Education profile: Asian Americans vs. total
                U.S. population (index 100=U.S. average)

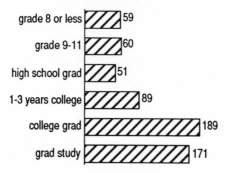

Source: *Market Opportunities in Retail: Asian American Consumers,*
           Deloitte & Touche/Impact Resources

With a head full of education and a pocket full of money, what do Asians do? Things like finding new hobbies and buying new technologies. Asians snap up new high-tech toys at rates far exceeding the average American. Those pieces which entertain and teach are more popular than those which merely help save time (personal computer vs. microwave, for example) (exhibit 6-9).

Asians are likely to own foreign cars. That's if they drive at all. In comparison to other Americans, they use public transportation 2.6 times more often, largely because of their urban concentration (exhibit 6-10).

Exhibit 6-9.   Index for Asian American ownership (index of 100=U.S. average)

Outdoor activities		Home communication/technology	
Photography/video	138	CD player	163
Exercise/play sports	109	Home personal computer	158
Travel	105	Telephone answering machine	116
Snow skiing	96	VCR	111
Go to beach	91	Rent videos	100
Go to sporting events	87	Microwave	97
Camp/fish/hike/hunt	85	Cable	80
Boating/sailing	61		

Source: *Market Opportunities in Retail: Asian American Consumers,* Deloitte & Touche/Impact Resources

---

Exhibit 6-10.   Asian-Americans and transportation

Car preference		Commuter preference	
Foreign car	169	Public transportation	261
No car/no answer	136	Drive self	101
American car	68	Other	86
		Car pool	69

Source: *Market Opportunities in Retail: Asian American Consumers,* Deloitte & Touche/Impact Resources

---

Childless Households

Having a single child eats up 30% of the household budget—having three or more demands half the household budget. By some counts, it now costs a parent almost $200,000 to raise a child to age 18, *before* college tuition. Little ones mean big bucks to affluents and non-affluents alike. So, those who have no children, *and* have an affluent mindstyle, are particularly juicy prospects for many marketers—their levels of discretionary money are substantially higher.

The Upper Deck[108] (the top 10% of households ranked by income) from Mediamark presents two segments of childless affluents and dubs them No Strings Attached and Two Careers. Marketers tend to lump these two groups together, just by the fact that children don't figure in the picture, but childless affluents (half of all affluent households) are quite dissimilar. Some high-income, no-kids households only have one high income, and these are older, wealthier homeowners with a higher concentration of males than females.

These one-income, no-kids households (OINKs) are most concentrated in the $100,000+ income range (index=111, or 11% higher representation than median affluent households). This lifestyle group has the highest concentration of people 55 years old and older (index=173). They are college and postcollege graduates, and though they are more likely to be married (index=111) than single (index=60), OINK households are most likely to consist of just one or two adults (index=264). They are homeowners whose residences tend to be worth over $200,000.

Multiple income, no kids (MINKs) households are those in which there are two or more income earners, none of which are high earners. MINK households earn under $100,000 a year, tend to consist of more women than men, and tend to be younger than the more established OINK households—they are highly represented in the 18-34 age segment. They are half as likely as the median affluent household to have a postgraduate degree (index=53) and there is a 24% greater likelihood that no one in the household has a college degree. There is significantly less incidence of marriage (index=60), and a 112% higher concentration of single people. These households tend to consist of three or four people who don't own their residence.

MINK households show a low concentration for newspaper reading and TV watching, and high activity for magazines and radio, while OINK households show low usage of radio and magazines.

Common Millionaires

The word millionaire has always seemed to mark some magical plateau of almost unimaginable wealth; for most Americans a game of

Monopoly is their only chance to act like a millionaire. According to *New York* magazine, in 1980, a meager 4,114 Americans were millionaires ($1 million or more adjusted gross annual income). But by 1986, nearly 36,000 Americans were into seven figures—almost nine times the estimate from six years prior. Then again, a million bucks isn't what it used to be. Do people with a million bucks *feel* like a million bucks these days? How does the profile of an exclusive club change when the doors are thrown wide open?

It is easier to be a millionaire today than ever before. Robert Heller calls it the "democratization of wealth," or "the common millionaire." In his book, *The Age of the Common Millionaire* (E.P. Dutton/Penguin USA), Heller claims the common millionaire "creates himself by skimming the cream off the general pool of wealth. The wider and deeper the pool, the smaller the amount of skimming required to fill the same size money pot." He reports increasing numbers in the millionaire club; he says that according to the Federal Reserve Board, 1.3 million U.S. households have with net worths in excess of a million dollars.

The creation of wealth is a whole new ball game today. During the heyday of Rockefeller the First, one had to create an equivalent amount of assets in order to create wealth. In the not-so-distant days of Boesky, wealth was defined by pieces of paper labeled as "less than investment grade ... wealth represented by real assets could be gained in exchange for no assets at all." The Common Millionaire places on the market not that which he owns, but that which he will one day own. *The precariousness of this proverbial crap shoot makes for a different kind of contemporary millionaire than in days of yore.*

What is the niche market of American millionaires like today? Heller says "The Common Millionaire lives in the same way as the good bourgeois citizen." He cites the middle-class origins of the newly rich as influencing their lifestyles; still, he says, a taste for the finer things has spread inexorably.

The news for marketers from Heller: "The key change in the 'Age of the Common Millionaire' is that higher taste and higher turnover can go hand in hand. Lead the masses up-market and you can hope to win mass sales at upscale prices."

Surprising Pockets of Wealth

One niche of affluence in America (lawyers) won't surprise you if you've ever had anything to do with the U.S. legal system; the other niche (lottery winners) won't surprise you if you've ever watched on television as someone even more average-looking than yourself (you thought) stepped up to win a million dollars.

Perhaps you think that we've given you the old bait-and-switch, but the real element of surprise hiding in this section is a niche mindstyle. If you get to it—using your imagination, hunches, and daily observations to identify pockets of wealth within the consumer population— you won't be in a field crowded with marketers. Rather, you will have room to take advantage of your novel approach—and your very real (if unusually grouped) affluent consumer segment.

For example: how many of us know—or think we know—that, yes, lawyers always seem to make a lot of money. Attorneys are a very appealing affluent market. But do you have any idea how appealing they are, or—most important for your purposes—how similar lawyers are to each other? The *American Bar Association Journal's* "Reader Profile—A Study of Influence and Purchasing in Business and Consumer Markets" finds its subscribers to be among the wealthiest Americans, with an average personal income of $117,000 and average total household income of $131,800. Subscribers average income is over $100,000, and average net worth is $664,000. Legal eagles' homes are worth an average of $258,300, and one in five lawyers owns a second vacation/weekend home.

The majority of lawyers (80%) are male, and their median age is 39 years. Over three-quarters (78%) are married, and about half (46%) have children. Demographically speaking, lawyers already share the traditional affluent profile, and represent a ready-made affluent pool. Lawyers are also among the nation's best credit card customers (exhibit 6-12).

We hope that a few tidbits about this segment will inspire you to find out more about this heretofore unheralded niche group of affluent consumers; we also know that it will inspire a string of associations (and possible other professional niche groups) for you to label, research, and address. Is there a doctor in the $250,000 household income house?

Exhibit 6-11. Personal and household income

	ABA Journal subscriber	Total U.S.	Index
Personal			
$100,000+	30%	1%	6,020
$75-$99,999	15%	1%	2,157
$50-$74,999	24%	2%	1,017
$35-$49,999	13%	6%	202
$25-$34,999	7%	11%	64
<$25,000	4%	42%	9
HHI			
$100,000+	48%	3%	1,920
$75-$99,999	20%	4%	567
$50-$74,999	19%	12%	165
$35-$49,999	7%	20%	35
$25-$34,999	3%	19%	16
<$25,000	2%	44%	5

Source: "Reader Profile—A Study of Influence and Purchasing in Business and Consumer Markets," *American Bar Association Journal*

Exhibit 6-12. Percent who have or use

	ABA journal subscribers	Total US	Index
AmEx green	41%	6%	672
AmEx gold	27%	3%	979
AmEx platinum	1%	.6%	233
CarteBlanche	2%	n/a	n/a
Car rental card	18%	n/a	n/a
Diners Club	8%	2%	447
Discover	13%	8%	163
MasterCard	50%	21%	234
MasterCard gold	35%	3%	1300
Visa	57%	28%	199
Visa gold	16%	3%	582
Visa preferred	11%	2%	713

Source: "Reader Profile," *ABA Journal*

Luck will be the only lady (or man) who can predict this next niche group—you probably won't be able to drop in at this millionaire club to target the regulars. But this group of potential affluents represent some startling numbers: the lottery millionaire is becoming a demographic to be reckoned with.

More than 20 multimillion-dollar lotteries now take place across the country each week, creating some 100 new millionaires each month, says USC marketing professor Jagdish Sheth. This means at least

120,000 more lottery millionaires will be added to the ranks of more than a million American millionaires by the end of the century. "What's interesting about lotteries," explains Sheth, "is that they redistribute resources, not from the rich to the poor, but from the poor to the poor. The poor are the largest players and the largest recipients of lottery funds." Moreover, preliminary studies show that lottery millionaires have a greater tendency than do other tycoons to redistribute their wealth among family members and charities.[109]

Chapter

VII

Outlining the Next Generation

Gazing into our crystal ball for the future picture of affluent consumers, we see . . . some familiar faces. A whole new crop of affluents may be making their presence increasingly known, but they are not a brand new group. Rather, *the forces affecting affluent consumers of today are shaping those same affluent consumers of tomorrow.*

Trends develop slowly, at a glacial pace. Many trend mavens will announce dramatic new directions for affluents, conjuring mediagenic labels that get them a lot of free publicity. When you encounter these proclamations, take them with 50 carats worth of salt.

The future of affluence is being written now in a slow and steady hand. Values and lifestyles are indeed evolving, but the expressions of these trends will emerge over the course of years, not from one issue of a magazine to the next. We will point out the future directions that we feel confident about based on research; we won't hype you with fads promoting themselves as trends. We will focus on those aspects of the current affluent market that stand out in bold relief; those lines will form the outlines for images of affluence in the future.

You will recognize some themes of affluence mentioned throughout this book—the value of time, the impact of children on the affluent family structure and lifestyle, and the increasing bifurcation of American society (with the parallel polarization of wealth). We'll extrapolate on these themes in this chapter as well, because we believe they will play a large role in defining affluents and affluent behavior in the coming decade.

Harder to measure quantitatively—but with just as much impact on affluents—are the images that affluents will have of themselves as affluents. Make no mistake: as the stratification of American society (and the economy) intensifies, the affluents will be more aware of themselves as affluents—and more anxious than ever to *think* of themselves as affluents. For that matter, consumers left out of the traditional categories of affluence will also be anxious to get whatever piece of the *attraction* of affluence they can.

This leads to some of the biggest news about the future of affluence: image advertising that markets the attraction of affluence. This will be important for affluents and for wannabee affluents alike (your whole affluent market). *Marketers using image advertising will be able to read, feed and define the mindstyle of affluence for future affluents.* You will find a caution from us, however. The emerging values of 1990s affluents play down the fashionable, stylish, glitzy parts of affluence, and play up the more practical, reliable, and confident aspects.

Affluent image-making leads to the second big trend coming around the marketing bend: the trickle-down effect that affluent preferences for certain products and services will have on all consumer markets. Consider this last point as fair warning: if you think the field of marketers concentrating on the affluent market is big (and growing) now, wait until the word gets out that this group of consumers—*your* group of affluent consumers—will be *the* alternative in the demise of mass marketing. Affluent consumers will become the most attractive targets for all marketers, as affluents' tastes, lifestyles, and preferences trickle down to become the standard which all consumers will seek to emulate. This will develop to a major marketing change. Within a few years we feel you will begin to see traditional mass market products, household cleansers and the like, pitched to affluents with the trickle down as part of the plan.

That said, there is also a word of encouragement: as the trickle-down effect gains in importance, your affluent market could stretch in size out of proportion with any of the ways we have to define that market now. The wildest dreams of all consumers about living the affluent way—helped along by increasing publicity for and about the affluent market—have the potential of increasing your audience significantly.

The Age Wave—Maturing Baby Boomers and Baby Busters

The age wave is going to wash over all markets. The nation's median age is rising, and the population in the second half of life is beginning to swell. Affluence is not a kid's game, and the affluent market will be nurtured by an aging nation.

Maturing Baby Boomers

Like the boa constrictor who swallowed an elephant, the nation is moving a huge generation through its system. The Baby Boom generation is usually referred to as a monolithic entity by marketers. However, in regard to affluence, it must be divided at the very least into two parts—older Boomers (now in their late thirties and early forties), and younger Boomers (now turning thirty or in their thirties). These two groups have had very different financial experiences and are going to have different relationships with affluence.

The older Boomers have had it easier. When they were starting their first households, housing prices and mortgage rates were low, and they bought houses in record numbers. The demand they created drove up housing prices at an unprecedented rate, at a time when mortgage rates were also rising. So, when the younger Boomers came to buy their first homes, they were at a deep disadvantage. Down payments were prohibitive for many and house prices and mortgage rates were high. Many kept renting. Rents, however, also escalated, and the younger Boomers found it hard to save enough for a downpayment.

The situation was further aggravated by the fact that salary increases weren't keeping up with increasing housing costs. This hurdle accounts in large part for the decreasing homeownership rate in the U.S. The situation is beginning to ease for younger Boomers as the housing market starts to soften; and they are likely to go on a home-buying spree of their own. These different experiences of younger and older Boomers partly explains their different attitudes toward money—young Boomers are much more earnest and intent about money, older

Boomers take money more for granted, preferring to focus on experiences that money can buy. These prevailing differences are likely to sustain into their affluent years; youngers will be more cautious and financially conservative, olders more affluent overall, and more experientially inclined.

There is little agreement on the likely spending behavior of the Boomers in coming years. Predictions range from Scrooge-Boomers to prodigal sons and daughters. Media oversimplifications haven't added any clarity. The free-spending yuppie image is mostly apocryphal (there were far more Yuffies, young urban failures, than Yuppies in the 1980s). Baby Boomers have saved money at a rate that is actually not far below that of previous generations, and when increases in costs for housing, and slowed wage increases are taken into account, the Boomer saving rate is close to that of previous generations.

The Baby Boom generation will become even more important to the affluent market in the 1990s (see exhibit 7-1).

Two basic reasons for this:

- Boomers have yet to enter their big-earning years. Their available amounts of discretionary income will steadily increase in the 1990s. Their increasing available cash will far outstrip the increases in any other segment.
- Boomers will set the values for the nation to an even greater degree than they have in the past. Their demographic weight will be enhanced by the social clout they will gain as they take over the top leadership in almost every area of the nation. They will run the preponderance of political, industrial, financial, cultural, and recreational institutions in the U.S.

Fairchild[110] finds very few indicators to suggest that Boomers will become big savers as they approach their peak saving years of 45-49. The International Association for Financial Planning[111] finds that the "emerging affluent" (respondents 45 years old or younger who earn between $50,000-$79,999 annually) tend to feel financially insecure—half say that their net worth is short of where they want it to be, and over one-quarter say it's harder now to pay all expenses and have something left over. Saving for retirement and for their children's education are their top two long-term financial goals. Examining yesterday's hype about their savings, and today's widely differing predictions about tomorrow's savings and spending, it is likely that the Boomers will actually save and spend in percentages similar to past generations. As they earn their way into their peak-income years (which older Boomers will reach before the end of the century), Boomers will split their dollars between Barclay's and Bloomingdale's much as their parents did.

Exhibit 7-1.   Are Baby Boomers "very important" to luxury marketing? Percent of luxury product executives saying yes for the:

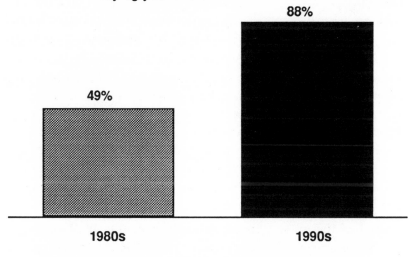

Source: *Luxury Marketing in the 1990s*, The Prestige Marketing Group

Consumers & Innovation[112] suggests that the aging of the population will probably have a negative impact on the diffusion of technological innovation—products such as smart houses, personal computers, and the all-in-one laser disc player. But that's not necessarily so. For one thing, Boomers are familiar with technological innovations that they need to control time; their children have grown up with VCRs and Nintendo, and are learning about computers in school. When the Baby Boom begins to hit its peak earning years around the turn of the century, it's going to be the first and biggest tech-comfortable generation. Boomers will be interested in technological innovations, and will try them. If they like one, everyone will hear about it, and the well-established pattern will continue—the products that make it with the affluent Boomers will trickle down through the socioeconomic categories. They get cheaper and everyone gets one.

Management Horizons supports this point of view with their observation, "The Boomlet is likely to have a positive impact on the diffusion of technological innovation as Boomers strive to give their children an edge over their peers." And, incidentally, you don't have to wait until the year 2000—today's mature market, which is not particularly comfortable with high-tech gadgetry, is comfortable using the technological innovations in health care.

Baby Busters
After the Baby Boom comes the Bust. The U.S. birth rate declined between 1964 and 1976, creating an age group of fewer members. This Bust generation is now entering adult years, and because of its smaller size, it will create a new income environment. More educated than any generation in history, Busters will be sought after by business. There is already a scarcity of qualified applicants to fill the entry-level needs of businesses, and the numbers of those in the employment pool will remain low, and actually diminish until near the end of the century. This pressure will increase the competition for the qualified Busters, and will drive up entry-level wages and benefits.

In simplest terms, this means fewer young adult households through the end of the century, but more affluent young households. As *American Demographics* predicted in 1987, "The median income of young householders should rise from $22,790 to $28,080 in the next 14 years, a gain of 23% after accounting for inflation. Assuming a 1.5% annual growth in household income between 1985 and 1999, the number of affluent young householders—those with annual incomes of $50,000 and above—should nearly double, from 2.4 million in 1986 to 4.2 million by 2000."[113]

Image Advertising
Today's new affluents have a different sense of themselves *as affluents*. In past generations, affluents have perceived themselves as a part of a long-standing tradition that had its particular ways and means. Those were the good old days, when the world of American affluence was young—before old money was old; when affluence was a combination of wealth and social position.

Today's affluents, newly empowered by the unprecedented explosion of affluence and the growing social diversity of wealth, feel they have a different identity. They are less encumbered by tradition than any affluent market in history, and many see themselves as different from prior generations of affluents. Many of today's affluents are first-generation affluents. This sense of newness makes them susceptible to definitions of affluence presented successfully by marketers and advertisers. *Image advertising will be the linchpin in marketing products and services to the new affluent market.*

Affluents are actively seeking reflections that define them as affluents. Successful marketers will define the idea of what old money is to the multitude of affluents who are enjoying their buying power for the first time. They will also present fresh alternatives to young affluents—even those who grew up in affluence—who want to define a new tradition of affluence for themselves. You will run into the paradox of affluence again and again: a group of diverse consumers who yearn for an identity; that is at once part of a grand legacy of wealth and, at the same time, represents their very individual expression of their brave new mindstyle and lifestyle.

One of the clearest examples of this phenomenon is the overwhelming image campaign launched by Ralph Lauren. From presenting the classic American look in his line of men's and women's sportswear, the designer moved to include more in his designing empire. Only in the new age of "old" American affluence could a clothes designer hawk everything from bed linens to table flatware to furniture, extending the authority of his opinion to cover every aspect of the affluent life his photographs can capture. Each Lauren photograph presents a complete vignette—a moment captured from a lifestyle of affluence. For a price—and in this case, it's a pretty high price—you can purchase something new that will speak of your place in the tradition of affluence. You can have the immediate gratification of purchasing tradition. If you didn't grow up with it, you can remedy that quirk of fate with one trip to the image store.

Affluents will be excited by any aspect of their lives that says affluence—look at the boom in upscale faucet sales. Every product is a potential mirror to show them a glimpse of themselves as affluent. For example: Dutch Boy paint has shown that it's possible to move a basic item into the upscale arena with the right kinds of marketing messages. Targeted to 18- to 34-year-old fashion-conscious consumers, Dutch Boy's messages, emphasizing color and quality, have run on such TV shows as "Thirtysomething" and "Late Night with David Letterman" and in such magazines as *Country Living* and *Metropolitan Home*.

Think about it for a moment: it's a product that will only show its label for the duration of a paint job, and only friends and neighbors who happen to stop by while the affluent is painting will see the can. But the key to moving something like housepaint into the realm of affluence is that the affluent consumer will know that it is affluent paint—the kind other affluents use (after all, the affluent painter saw or read about this paint in media aimed at affluents).

This eagerness makes affluents more trend-prone than ever. "Creative brand management" is the ticket, says McKinsey & Co.[114] Well-planned spin-offs and image exploitation can keep the cash rolling in while protecting the integrity and sophistication of the luxury brand name.

Roads to Success

- Consolidate design and manufacture;
- Intensify marketing;
- Strengthen distribution management; and
- Integrate levels of management.

It's all in the image. It goes without saying that the product or service must be one of quality, that it must serve efficiently and reliably. All consumers expect this. But to attract the upper crust, you must entice their egos. The ego that presumes: I'm special and privileged, I'm on top, I'm a leader, my surroundings are exclusive and luxurious, I have more choices than the mass, my tastes are better, I work hard, I *need a reward*, and certainly not least, I *deserve a reward*. It's that simple. Price and performance must then reflect the attitude. Affluents are willing to pay the price to send THE message "This is who I am, who I want to be, who I want you to think I am."[115] Marketing must promote this image; every product must be a mirror in which the affluent see an affluent image of themselves reflected.

Advertising copy for the affluent should be similarly imagistic. Affluents are smart, and like to have advertising reflect their cleverness.

You can take shortcuts of logic; you can be a bit disjointed—they get involved in making a leap of logic, if it is *genuinely* clever. Yesterday's hip words will repel the affluent—either be on the cutting edge or use straightforward phrases. They like advertising games; they are so ad-savvy that you can goof on ads themselves as successfully as Joe Isuzu did. They like to be surprised; use words they don't expect.

Don't condescend, over-promise, or hype; don't sound uncool, pompous, ordinary, dated, intellectual. Shoot straight, fast, and fun.

Symbolism

Symbolism is an important intangible affecting affluence. Certain symbols emerge and come to *mean* affluence to all Americans—really to all the civilized world. Madison Avenue has been behind many of these successful images, and the power of such images (not to mention the wealth they generate) cannot be overestimated—we've seen a Cuisinart in a Cretan stone house. It is worth pointing out the key underlying factor in these successful images—yearning for something unknown.

Few people realize that the word symbol derives from an ancient Greek custom. At the end of a pleasurable visit, a host would break a ring or coin, and give part to the departing guest. This was the symbol on—something valuable you held that reached across a void toward completion, and inherent in the symbol is yearning for this completion. There is a yearning for the good life (symbolized as the American dream) throughout the global village. An affluent image that can tap into this yearning for fulfillment can become a cultural symbol. And a cultural symbol becomes a product everyone not only wants but thinks they *need*.

What do you do when you have everything you need, and you can buy a lot of what you may want? The only problem standing in your way is deciding *what* you want. You choose an array of goods and services to set the stage that presents your personal image. Your belongings are a shortcut language to transmit your personal meaning to the viewing audience, which is everyone. This stage set of goods is not necessarily an expression of the real you; it is more the expression of images you think will impress others—the you that you want them to think you are. This image you've carefully constructed does not reflect either your values or your viewers' values, but a composite of what you think will most impress them.

You buy the objects that fit the image—this is the crux of the affluent lifestyle and the main motivation to buy. Because time is the commodity in the shortest supply for affluents, talk gets very expensive, and possessions become the affluent language. The stage that affluents set is a way to shorten the interpersonal communications load. In the quest to transmit more meaning, every new purchase *must* fit in with, and seamlessly enhance, what is already owned.

Prestige

An old word for this new emphasis on letting the objects do the talking is prestige. Prestige is derived from possessing products or attributes which others desire but don't or can't have. It is derived from a feeling of being present on the minds of others, of being somehow visible to the invisible masses. It is derived from a sense of elevation through the hierarchy of social importance to a level of security which soothes an otherwise questioning ego. Underlying any description of prestige, however, is its fundamental derivation: *praestrigiae*, the Latin word for deception.

Mikhail Gorbachev went to visit a typical Soviet apartment and was impressed with its display of apparent opulence. What he didn't see was that the day before he arrived, a moving truck full of new furniture had delivered the plush interior; the day after, the same truck took it all away. What was in the truck? Prestige. Controlled deception.

Like all theater, prestige could not exist without an audience. If stranded on a deserted island, one would not find prestige. (If, however, one found a buried treasure and returned to show it to friends and perhaps a treasure dealer, then one might.) Only a social backdrop—a cultural context— determines prestige. Both affluents and affluent product marketers repaint this social backdrop regularly—that is part of what keeps this drama (some might say comedy) interesting and unpredictable.

American Express, which uses prestige as a marketing tool all over the world, believes other marketers can follow its lead. What bestows a product or service with prestige? A combination of high cost, limited supply (or the perception thereof), and high quality.

Setting the price of a prestige item is a tricky business, since an error in either direction spells serious marketing trouble. The cost to consumers must be high enough to weed out a large segment of the population (hence part of the prestige), but not so high as to limit the customer base to an unprofitable level. Given the delicate interplay of variables, other players in the market become the calibration against which prestige prices are judged. Taken together, the prices for any service or product create a "cost curve." A prestige item must be at the top—but not so far above the rest that, in the mind of the consumer, it breaks the curve and enters a separate sphere of competition.

In the normal course of doing what they do, consume, consumers constantly select those items and services which they desire from a range of choices. Prestige marketing often turns that selection dynamic around: the provider selects the consumer. This adds to the image of exclusivity central to prestige. Being qualified leads to a feeling of entitlement, no matter what is being judged—income, talent, appearance, or some other attribute. That not everyone can qualify potentially affirms the importance of those who do.

Consumers do not set out with the express purpose of buying into an item's prestige aura; to do so would, in a sense, blow their cover. That is what the non-affluents do—make an effort to afford a piece of prestige as others have defined it. Buying a prestige item ought to display an affluent consumer's intelligence and discretion, not a need for recognition. Ironically, then, the message consumers want to hear is, "prestige for those who are above worrying about prestige," a postmodernist sort of marketing cry. It may be gauche to buy prestige directly, but it's perceived as sheer good taste to buy prestige which derives from quality. Price must be justified on such a basis.

Prestige marketing logic works something like this: you have the money; therefore, already you're worth more than someone who can't afford the product or service. You are among the select few who qualify for the opportunity to spend your money on a given item. You're a trendsetter; you're dipping into the future. This isn't something the average Joe is going to have—but you can be sure he wants to have it. Not only are you empowered by your money and your select qualifications, but you exhibit the intelligence and good taste to make the right purchasing decisions. The prestige message is clear: You're Special.

Also implied in the message is a crucial subtext: there's a world of people out there who aren't special. You are their hero.[116]

When you introduce your ideas of prestige products and services to the affluent market, you are simultaneously going to be shaping the desires and tastes of other consumer audiences as well. If the affluents turn to you—consciously or subconsciously—to set the ideas about affluence, other consumers will turn to affluents to set the standard for taste and luxury. This trend will be self-perpetuating, especially as the images of Old Money capture the affluent market. For all that Old Money implies—and especially the ideas of continuity, stability, and security—will be some of the most sought-after *mental* commodities of the 1990s, by affluents and non-affluents alike.

With the dissolution of a monolithic mass market, look to the affluents to predict mass consumer appeal. There will be a trickle-down effect from the pace they set in terms of purchases and preferences, as non-affluents yearn for the kinds of things that affluents seem to have in abundance. As a matter of fact, affluents themselves will still yearn for those very same things.

Now, a final word of caution: you are going to have to be good. Affluents are becoming less willing to be influenced by advertising. They're hyped-out. In fact, in a Prestige Marketing study, top luxury executives see advertising as significantly less effective for the 1990s. It fell from the most important tool of the 1980s to the number three for the 1990s (exhibit 7-2).

We feel you will do better if you let the simplifying values inform the advertising you do. Reduce your reliance on celebrity endorsers. Make your advertising images simple, clever, and product-oriented as opposed to style-oriented. Pack the image punch we've been describing in this chapter—but sock it to them with a velvet boxing glove.

Exhibit 7-2.   What is the most effective marketing tool

	1980s	1990s
Advertising	35%	18%
Public relations	31%	36%
Direct mail/marketing	17%	27%
Direct sales	7%	9%
Sales promotion	3%	9%

Source: *Luxury Marketing in the 1990s*, The Prestige Marketing Group

Preservation

Part of the romance and the attraction of Old Money that today's affluents will want to hang on to—even cling to—in what promise to be turbulent financial times in the near future, is the security of keeping what they've earned thus far. This will be true of older and younger affluents alike. If the 1980s were years filled with the pressure to get more, the 1990s will be the decade of making sure that you keep what you have.

Money doesn't always mean security—we see this in many surveys. Affluents are worried about institutions, about the future of the economy, about the environment, about having enough money for their children's education, their retirement, and about the ability of institutions to handle the nation's social problems. Affluents are scared—the explosive recent growth in their markets may seem too good to be true—even to them. As they watch some of the most successful entrepreneurs of the previous decade, Donald Trump and Michael Milken the most visible among them, fall because their empires were built on real estate speculation or the aptly-named junk bonds, they wonder if their status has been hastily built on similarly shaky underpinnings.

The undercurrent to entrench and stabilize the gains of the past decade will lead to the emergence of some new values—values Old Money has quietly known all along. In their report "The Era of the Influents," *Town & Country* offers some watchwords for the affluent preservation values of the coming decade:

- Enlightened consumption;
- Savings;
- Value for the dollar;
- Taking care of people—your own and others; and
- Preservation of nature, capital, society.

These values will be in sync with the trends we've seen begin to take hold already. Their most obvious expression will appear in the form of image advertising that offers a sense of continuing tradition with the purchase of new status items boasting an implied history of affluent usage. Their subtler expression will probably be in an increased emphasis on the preservation of lifestyle *within the affluents' families*. (We part company here with many researchers and trend-spotters, but we suspect that the much-vaunted "we" in the new decade will not go much farther than the four walls of the affluent household.) Affluents' tendency to keep their financial portfolio diversified suggests that they are embedding the foundations for their future success in more than one institutional rock.

Just as excess is a sign of success when the only way to go is up, hanging on will become just as impressive when it becomes obvious that the upward momentum of the previous decade may have just met the gravity of the coming decade.

Affluents and Philanthropy

The decade of the 1990s has already been labeled with many titles. While these banners are catchy, they are usually inaccurate. They do, however, reflect general public feeling and have the effect of refocusing everyone's view of what they see in society. To some degree they have a self-perpetuating gravity of their own.

Several labels like the "decency decade," the "we decade," "new community," and the "era of a thousand points of light," all point to the same impulse. They speak of a shift toward a decade in which Americans will take greater care of one another. The affluent are prominently included in this equation; in fact, their levels of charitable giving are one of the most significant bulwarks of this argument.

Don't get us wrong, we think the affluent care about the welfare of the remaining five-sixths of the populace. They want life to be good for them too. However, examine the facts before you count on the beneficence of the upscale. Make sure you know which points of light the affluent are drawn toward before you rely on their generosity.

First, know that the highest earners (over $100,000 a year in household income) give about half as much to charitable causes on a percentage of income basis as those living at or below the poverty line—about 6% for the poor, less than 3% for the top earners.

Second, the majority of philanthropic giving by the affluent goes to institutions that address themselves to affluent interests—cultural institutions, private universities, private hospitals. Only a minority of upscale giving goes to institutions that directly aid the struggling sectors of the population.

Third, the tax advantages of charitable giving are a key, if not primary, motivation in philanthropic giving. As the revisions in the tax codes in recent years have somewhat diminished their tax advantages, patterns of giving have changed. The Internal Revenue Service reports that donations of those earning a half a million dollars a year or more fell in 1988 to one third of the 1980 average—from $47,432 in 1980 to $16,062 in 1988.

So, while you may expect a thousand points of philanthropy to improve the lot of the struggling sector somewhat, you shouldn't expect the decency decade to mean a bonanza for decent social causes. The facts we see suggest a modest increase in concern among the affluent for the less-advantaged in society. This increase is roughly proportionate to the increasing severity in the social problems themselves. We feel the affluent will indeed give more to charitable causes in this decade. However, the increase will result more from the natural transition of the Baby Boomers' aging into the more-socially-minded middle years than from a new national sense of community.

In fact, Robert B. Reich in his new book, *The Worth of Nations: Preparing Ourselves for 21st Century Capitalism*, argues that the top earners are becoming progressively more isolated from the rest of society. He sees the upscale further withdrawing into their own protected enclaves, using their affluence and high-tech conveniences to minimize their contact with the rest of the population.

There are now more private security guards in the U.S. than there are public police officers.

Pragmatism
Tape this word above your desk—it will be a major key to the affluent. Politically they are becoming less party-affiliated, less doctrinaire, and are looking for what works. Socially, the liberal-conservative axis is becoming more balanced. Affluents are less big government in their view, but want the homeless housed and the environment improved, and they want the federal government to do it. They are fairly liberal on many social issues—abortion, homosexuality; they are fairly conservative on economic issues.

They often ask for more information and less hype in advertising; they feel they can decide based on the facts—the same will hold true for their judgment of political candidates. To sell them anything, you must convince them that it works, that it makes sense. Bear in mind that they are savvy enough with advertising to be skeptical of claims. Skeptical is perhaps the most apt word for their attitude toward advertising—they've heard it all before; yet, they are not cynical. Cynicism (the belief that people and fate are basically malevolent) is more the trap of the struggling classes; one of the luxuries of affluents is the belief that goodness is predominant, and that they can make things work out.

Affluence will get down-to-earth. The watchwords will be value and quality; supplanting fashionable and status as key marketing hooks (exhibit 7-3).

Greater Power for Brands
A strong brand image will become more important. The luxury marketers agree—57% feel brand considerations were important in luxury marketing in the 1980s; 54% feel it will be important for the 1990s.

We feel that brand image will become more important in the 1990s, for three reasons:

- Commercial clutter will increase in the coming years. More products will be pitched, in more ways, and with more creative and intrusive means. This clutter will push against the grain of affluents' turn toward simplicity and lower stress. As a result, affluents will turn to the known quality brands.
- Affluents will be convenience driven for their 1990s shopping. They will find less pleasure in shopping, and will have less time to gather information before they make major purchases. These pressures will lead them to the known brands—brands they know they can trust and feel good about.
- Established brands fit in with the values of the 1990s. Just as the admired images will come to be old money and traditional hard work, so the brands in favor will be those that say established, proven, trustworthy.

Greater Importance of Segmentation
Addressing the diverse segments within the affluent market will become standard operating procedure in the 1990s. This marketing

Exhibit 7-3. Which of the following were "very important" to luxury marketing in the 1980s and the 1990s

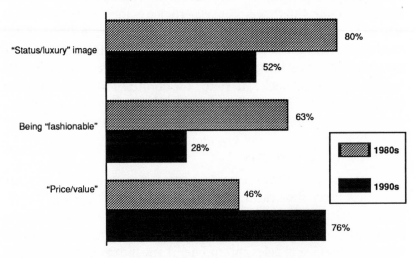

Source: *Luxury Marketing in the 1990s*, The Prestige Marketing Group

trend will not merely mean targeting the niche affluents we discussed in previous chapters; it will be a broader change. Just as mass marketers came to realize there was no viable, monolithic mass American market in the 1980s, so affluent marketers will realize that the affluent market is merely the sum of its diverse parts.

The Prestige Marketing study[117] suggests one part of this trend. The luxury marketers were asked specifically about the importance of three particular age groups to their marketing in the 1990s as opposed to the 1980s. Each of the age groups become much more important in the 1990s. The Baby Boomers were a "very important demographic group for the luxury market" to 49% in the 1980s, and to 88% in the 1990s; seniors were "very important" to 38% in the 1980s and to 68% for the 1990s; and the "MTV generation" was rated very important to 12% in the 1980s, and to 37% for the 1990s.

Be segment-minded in the 1990s.

Time
Time-scarcity is a pressing issue with affluents; it's probably *the* pressing issue—and it's increasing in importance. It leads affluents to

buy all sorts of time-saving products and services. Free time is status; affluent images rarely include someone working hard or under stress—affluence provides freedom from these facts of life. And not just to the affluent. Middle Americans often experience employment as a necessary evil, a job not a career; affluence is relief from that evil. (That dream fuels the hundreds of worldwide lotteries.) Create an image of abundance of time, images of leisure (affluents like active-leisure), and consumers will flock to it. Here's the quintessential affluent time-fantasy—Malcolm Forbes said his perfect weekend consisted of two days vegging-out reading magazines, and two spent playing with his toys—hot air balloons and big motorcycles. Note that his kind of affluent weekend lasted *four* days.

Even though, statistically, entrepreneurs log more work hours than any other kind of workers, the current affluent-image has it that owning your own business is the best kind of work. Owning a business means power in the public mind (though many business owners might disagree), and gives entrepreneurs the ultimate bonus—time. Note that the entrepreneurial reality (having little time away from work) is exactly the opposite of the collective image of entrepreneurship (having time at your command)—reality can't hold its own against a wished-for image of affluence. However, an image that is contrary to reality has less staying power, and will be eroded over the short run rather than the long.

A study on households with annual incomes of at least $100,000 by Doyle Graf Raj shows that *necessities* to the affluent are mostly those devices which permit them to most efficiently control their time: 42% say they need a computer, 57% a microwave, 49% a phone answering machine, 36% a VCR, 27% cable TV, 25% a financial advisor, 19% an overseas vacation, 14% a car phone, and 12% a vacation home, while only 8% consider a swimming pool a necessity.

Children

Affluents are having fewer babies per couple and are having them later in their lives (further into their high-earning years). We see an evolution in social values coming that will make babies more important in the lives of affluents. Though there will be *fewer* babies, they will be more significant in the lives of their parents. The now hard rails of the Mommy-track will soften, and a parallel Daddy-path will be demanded by affluents.

Affluent dads will become more active in child rearing—they will be *do-dads*. Do-dads will begin to emerge as a sizeable, lucrative market. This will happen when emerging affluent, active, Boomer dads reach a sizeable proportion of the father pool, in the mid-1990s. Proactive advertisers and marketers will begin to address this new target segment within the next few years, to expand the already-lucrative audience of new mothers. Do-dads will actually do what they have been telling researchers for years that they are willing to do—they will reduce their work hours to have more family time. A baby will be a status symbol.

Incidentally, only-children are more likely to become affluent than those with siblings. Two reasons: there are more one-child families among the ranks of upper-income parents, and new research finds that only-children have higher IQ scores and get 20% more years of schooling than kids with siblings. With education as the number one predictor of affluence, only-kids are the most likely to become affluent adults.[118]

The higher the income the more likely the family is to be using organized child care. Working-mother families with annual incomes over $45,000 are twice as likely as working-mother families with yearly incomes of less than $15,000 to use organized child care facilities, 34% vs. 16%, respectively (exhibit 7-4).

Exhibit 7-4.   Children under 5 in organized child care facilities (by monthly income, Fall 1987)

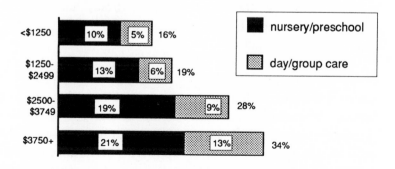

Source: *Who's Minding the Kids? Child Care Arrangements*, Winter, 1986-87, The Census Bureau

The amount of money couples spend on their children varies wildly, but as a rule higher-income households spend more on their children than others. In general, an upper-income couple (before-tax income of more than $46,900) spends twice as much on Junior than less wealthy parents—$160,080 compared to $114,150 for middle income families (before-tax income between $28,000-$46,900), and $81,810 for lower-income families (before tax income of less than $28,300) (exhibit 7-5).

Exhibit 7-5. Estimated expenses on a child by spending category (through age 17) figures in 1989 dollars

	<$28,300 HHI	$28,000-$46,900 HHI	$46,900+ HHI
Housing	$ 27,990	$ 37,860	$ 57,840
Food	$ 16,890	$ 21,150	$ 25,530
Transportation	$ 13,320	$ 20,520	$ 27,180
Clothing	$ 7,620	$ 9,600	$ 11,610
Health	$ 3,870	$ 4,950	$ 6,150
Education & Care	$ 12,120	$ 20,070	$ 31,770
Total	$81,810	$114,150	$160,080

Source: "Expenditures on a Child by Husband-Wife Families," *Family Economics Review* 1990 Vol. 3, No. 3

Annual expenditures for children in affluent homes range from $8,330-$9770, with older children costing slightly more than younger ones. That's based on a two-child household. With only one child, add 21% to each figure, and with three children, subtract 22%. Throughout the traditional 18-year childrearing period, upscale parents will spend an estimated $160,000 to bring a kid to adulthood. Exhibit 7-6 shows what that looks like year-by-year for a child born in 1989 and reaching age 18 in 2006.

Go on Green
Environmentalism will become more important to the affluent consumer. Already more than half of affluents claim to have made an environmentally-motivated purchase in the past year. They will make such purchases more often as the time passes and as they are presented with more green choices. In the Prestige Marketing study, 20% of the luxury marketers rated the environment as a very important issue for the 1980s; 53% see it as an important issue for the 1990s.

Exhibit 7-6.	Future cost of rearing a child in three household income groups (assuming inflation rate of 6 percent)

Year	Age	HHI <$28,300	HHI $28,300-$46,900	HHI $46,900+
1989	<1	$ 4100	$ 5850	$ 8330
1990	1	$ 4350	$ 6200	$ 8830
1991	2	$ 4610	$ 6570	$ 9360
1992	3	$ 5240	$ 7370	$10,480
1993	4	$ 5550	$ 7810	$11,110
1994	5	$ 5890	$ 8280	$11,780
1995	6	$ 6240	$ 8750	$12,310
1996	7	$ 6620	$ 9280	$13,050
1997	8	$ 7010	$ 9830	$13,830
1998	9	$ 7200	$10,170	$14,360
1999	10	$ 7630	$10,780	$15,220
2000	11	$ 8090	$11,430	$16,140
2001	12	$ 9840	$13,480	$18,670
2002	13	$10,430	$14,290	$19,790
2003	14	$11,060	$15,150	$20,980
2004	15	$12,510	$17,060	$23,410
2005	16	$13,260	$18,090	$24,820
2006	17	$14,060	$19,170	$26,310
Total		$143,690	$199,560	$278,780

Source: "Expenditures on a Child by Husband-Wife Families," *Family Economics Review* 1990 Vol. 3, No. 3

The more educated an American is, the more likely he or she is to be an active environmental consumer. The more educated an American is, the more likely she or he is to be a mindstyle affluent.

Here's a rough sketch of the psychology of green purchasing among affluent consumers. They feel pressure to be pro-environmental. They give to eco-groups, but not as much as they feel they should. They know about the various aspects of environmental degradation. They hear about ecology issues regularly in the media, which is used with increasing dexterity by the environmental organizations to publicize the smorgasbord of current and future crises. All of this exposure generates:

- Regular reminders of the problems and their severity (including, most importantly, their potential impact on personal health); and,
- Guilt. Guilt that they are doing some things that are not pro-environmental (commuting alone in the car, using Pampers, not

recycling newspapers, etc.); guilt that they are part of the problem.

As a result, affluent consumers are constantly seeking ways in which to make acceptable trade-offs. They are looking for products or activities with which they can do something green—suffering the attendant cost in either finances or convenience. Suffering a little relieves the guilt. They are actively seeking offerings that allow them to change their repertoire of activities to replace guilt with green. If you can offer a green-guilt affluent an easy trade-off, you will make a loyal customer. However, the green must be genuine for a false pro-environmental claim will create serious damage among the affluent when it is exposed. With the current vigilance of the environmental groups, bogus products will be exposed.

For example, Mobil introduced its Hefty degradable trash bags with a pro-green flourish. A firestorm of criticism from environmental groups in response to the product claims made the public aware that the bags would not degrade under real-life conditions, and that the claim was misleading. Mobil promptly withdrew the claim and the product, suffering marketing and publicity black eyes in the process. Don't let your product meet a Hefty fate.

Recession

As this book goes to press, the last of the holdout economists have admitted that the U.S. economy has entered a recession. Let's pause for a moment to consider the effect that a recession is likely to have on the affluent market.

We feel that there are two consumer trends that are relatively insulated from a mild recession: *environmentalism* and *affluence*. Environmentalism will continue to grow for three reasons:

- The pressure caused by environmental degradation will increase Americans' personal concern, forcing greater guilt and consequently greater willingness to trade some portions of convenience to address the necessities of protecting the environment.

- Progressively more green choices will be offered that are either cheaper or as convenient as their nongreen alternatives.

- The leaders of the environmental movement are the leaders of the nation, the upscale, influential, educated opinion shapers—their influence will continue to trickle down.

The upscale are relatively well-insulated against the modest damage to their finances that a downturn creates, so the trend toward greater affluence will continue even through a mild recession. The likely hit most affluents will take is not a blow to the investment portfolio, but a decrease in the rate at which their earnings will increase. This will engender only a slight increase in caution, and falls in line with the trends for the 1990s that we have previously discussed: the re-trenchment toward caution, greater emphasis on quality and value, and less importance for status goods that announce affluent status.

Also, a mild recession will have more impact on the marginal-affluent than the real-affluent—those who became affluent in the 1980s from dual-incomes, who are struggling to maintain their neo-affluent lifestyle. Many of these are indeed mindstyle affluents. They will be less eager to undertake further debt to bankroll the next impulse. There will be a noticeable retrenchment in their consumer behavior in a recession that lasts more than half a year. More established affluents will be relatively unchanged by a light-to-modest recession. A sustained recession, however, will hit all affluents, even the mid-to-upper group.

When addressing affluents during a recession you should:

- Be practical. It is important to make the product seem fun, but it must not seem frivolous or flashy.

- Stress quality above all; reinforcing the concept of value as a quality-and-price combination. Recession will make affluent consumers want to reduce frivolous consumption; if you can present an upscale practical image, they will feel they are buying out of personal necessity.

- Try to become the "one luxury you deserve." In serious financial times affluents will not cut out luxuries altogether, they will merely buy fewer of them.

Chapter
VIII

Conscientious Consumption

"Me, marketer. You, affluent."

We recognize that in the jungle out there, real-affluents are the most desirable of catches and the most elusive of prey. They slip in and out of sight before you can blink; they camouflage themselves in the midst of other consumer segments. They seem to change their spots at will. And sometimes, you could almost swear that they are hiding all around you, making survey noises that attract your attention—until they know you're after them, when they thumb their noses, turn tail, and run. It's enough to make you want to conk them in the head and drag them back to the traditional realm of mass market research—where a marketer's a marketer and the consumer sheep are afraid not to buy what they think everyone else is buying.

Yes, affluents pose problems for marketers and researchers. You can't approach them the way you would a quantifiable group of consumers. The real-affluents are not captured in traditional marketing categories, and their vital statistics, the ones that target mindstyle affluents, are not available in standard market research. You can't take research from the shelf and expect it to deliver the mindstyle affluent market.

"Off the shelf" is not an affluent concept—that's one of the blessings and the curses of marketing to them. They defy standard categorization, yet respond to fresh approaches that speak to them personally. The real-affluent market is an enormous group of consumers, eager to try new products, new ideas, new lifestyles, and willing to spend a lot of money on the innovative and the luxurious. Whether or not the individuals that constitute this market share the same demographic characteristics—all share an affluent mindstyle.

As we prepared this book, we were well aware that we couldn't give you the perfect answer you wanted—"here are the real-affluents, here's precisely how to reach them." We would be delighted to hand them to you on a silver platter. If anyone could, we would—it just is not that easy.

But affluent marketing is as much a process as a result. We offer you the truth—the research doesn't provide you with the perfect answers, and you will have to develop an ongoing process to collect and interpret your way to mindstyle affluence. The current research is improving, however, and newer methods for addressing the complex individuality of affluents will provide for more accurate pinpoint targeting.

As the research on the affluent market continues to sharpen, and affluents become a better-defined market, the hunting grounds will be crowded with marketers. The time to go after the affluent market is now. While the unprecedented numbers of new-affluents of the 1980s are trying to define themselves as affluents; while values are in flux. Now, while competitors are marketing with gut feel, old notions, and off-the-shelf research and ideas—running after affluents, but not keeping up with them.

As the mass market breaks into smaller pieces, the ideal of affluence will continue to represent a constant in both the marketplace and in the way of life: the American dream of success, the American *spirit* of success. All consumers—no matter how much money they have to spend—can recognize that dream. All consumers can share that dream by participating, once in a while or most of the time, in the affluence.

Will affluence have a place in the "New World Order," in an America full of Carebears and under-defined points of light shining through the conspicuous consumption of the 1980s? You bet it will. Conspicuous consumption is evolving into what looks like conscientious consumption, *caring* consumption, experiential consumption— it will still be socially, morally, and environmentally sound to be consuming.

As the bifurcation of American society continues and it becomes almost painfully clear (even to the sensitive affluents) that the haves and the have-nots are getting farther apart, don't expect affluents to renounce their worldly goods. Don't expect other consumers to stop wanting to be just like the affluents.

Expect, rather, for the affluent to hang on with both fists to the lifestyle they forged for themselves during the 1980s. (You may hear talk that people who indulged themselves in the free-for-all market economy of the last decade are waking up in this decade, and that they are waking up sorry. Not so.) They will understand that ostentation may be out; they will, nevertheless, consume quietly and surely—putting a modern spin on the idea of classic Old Money that doesn't have to *show*, but merely has to *enjoy*.

Also expect the not-so-affluent to continue to emulate the affluent in every way they can manage. There is a recession, and there are plenty of dashed hopes for many people in the middle and upper-lower classes of our economy. But deprivation will not lead to desperation; it will turn instead to a renewed emphasis on money, and, once again, back to the affluent.

Endnotes

Chapter 1

1. Tom Black, Associate Publisher, Advertising Director, *Smithsonian*.
2. *Market Opportunities in Retail, Affluent American Consumers*, Deloitte & Touche/Impact Resources.
3. *Cahners' Economic Index of Affluence*, Cahners Economic.
4. *The Clustering of America*, Michael J. Weiss, Harper & Row.
5. "Who Pays for College," *American Demographics*, February 1990.
6. *Economic Status Across Generations: Prospects for the Future*, The Urban Institute.
7. *The 1988 Affluent Market Factbook*, Payment Systems, Inc.
8. *The Upper Deck 1989*, Mediamark Research Inc.
9. *Market Opportunities in Retail: Affluent American Consumers*, Deloitte & Touche/ Impact Resources.
10. *Affluence 1988-1989*, Mendelsohn Media Research Inc.
11. *The Affluent Market*, Find/SVP.
12. *Americans Widely Disagree on What Constitutes "Rich,"* Vol. 55, No. 9, The Gallup Poll.
13. *American Demographics*, June 1989.
14. "Changing Times Personal Prosperity Index," *Changing Times*.

15. *Inside Affluent America*, George Lesnick, Yankelovich Clancy Shulman.
16. *Demographics in the U.S.: Segmenting of Demand*, National Association of Realtors.
17. *Policy and Research Report*, The Urban Institute.
18. *Consumer Expenditure Survey: Quarterly Data from the Interview Survey, 2nd Quarter 1989*, Report 790.
19. *A Marketer's Guide to Discretionary Income*, Census Bureau/The Conference Board.
20. *The Get Set*, Simmons Market Research Bureau.
21. *The National Fitness Study, 1989: A Demographic, Behavioral and Psychographic Profile of Active and Inactive Americans*, National Sporting Goods Association.
22. *Americans Widely Disagree on What Constitutes "Rich,"* Vol 55, No. 9, The Gallup Poll.
23. *Inside Affluent America*, George Lesnick, Yankelovich Clancy Shulman.
24. IDS Financial Services/Yankelovich Retirement Study.
25. "Subjective Discretionary Income," Thomas C. O'Guinn and William D. Wells, *Marketing Research Magazine*, March 1989, The American Marketing Association.
26. *The Upper Deck 1988*, Mediamark Research, Inc.
27. *The Upper Deck 1988*, Mediamark Research, Inc.
28. *The Up Market*, December 1987, Management Horizons.
29. *1988 Survey of Adults and Markets of Affluence*, Mendelsohn Media Research, Inc.
30. *The Lifestyle Market Analyst*, National Demographics and Lifestyles/Standard Rate and Data Service.
31. *Consumer Innovators 1988*, Mediamark Research, Inc.
32. *MA*RT Spenders (45-64)*, Impact Resources.
33. *The Get Set 1989*, Simmons Market Research Bureau, Inc.
34. *Consumers & Innovation*, 1988, Management Horizons.
35. *VALS II*, SRI International.

Chapter 2

36. *1988 Survey of Adults and Markets of Affluence*, Mendelsohn Media Research, Inc.
37. *Money Income and Poverty Status in the U.S.*, 1989, Census Bureau.

38. *The Up Market*, Management Horizons.
39. *Consumer Market Developments*, Fairchild Publications.
40. *Shifting Tax Burdens Leave all but Wealthy Worse Off*, #101-30, Democratic Study Center.
41. *The Affluent Handbook*, December 1987, Starch INRA Hooper.
42. *A Marketer's Guide to Discretionary Income*, Census Bureau/ The Conference Board.
43. *Working Woman*, May 1989.
44. *Wall Street Journal*, June 19, 1989.
45. Challenger, Gray & Christmas, Inc., press release August 7, 1989.
46. *Black Enterprise*, September 1989.
47. *The Franchise Marketing & Sales Survey 1989-'90*, DePaul University/Francorp, Inc.
48. "The Era of the Influents," *Town & Country*.
49. *Critical Consumer Trends Impacting Financial Services Marketing in the 1990s*, Joseph Plummer, DMB&B.
50. *Financial Planners*, February 1988, The Securities and Exchange Commission.
51. "The New Generation of Affluent Consumers," *Private Banking*, Winter 1990.
52. "Voice of the Consumer 1988," *American Banker*.
53. "Americans and Their Money," *Money*.
54. *Affluent Consumers: A Special Report*, Deloitte & Touche/Impact Resources.
55. *Home Equity Study*, September 1989, The Gallup Organization.
56. *Americans Widely Disagree on What Constitutes "Rich,"* Vol 55, No. 9, The Gallup Poll.

Chapter 3

57. *Quality of Service Study* June 1989, The Gallup Organization/ Bank Advertising News.
58. *The Public Pulse*, September 1988, The Roper Organization, Inc.
59. *Inside Affluent America*, George Lesnick, Yankelovich Clancy Shulman.
60. *Old Money, The Mythology of America's Upper Class*, Nelson W. Aldrich, Jr., Random House.
61. "The Era of the Influents," *Town & Country*.
62. *American Demographics*, October 1990.

63. *Luxury in the Nineties: A Study Assessing the Meaning of Luxury Among Opinion Leaders*, Yankelovich Clancy Shulman/ Nissan Motor Corp., USA.
64. *The Bruskin Report*, August 1989, R.H. Bruskin Associates.
65. *Target Marketing*, September 1989.
66. *The Upper Deck 1989*, Mediamark Research, Inc.
67. *The People, the Press, & Politics 1990: A Times Mirror Political Typology*, Times Mirror Center for People & the Press.
68. "The Era of the Influents," *Town & Country*.
69. "The Era of the Influents," *Town & Country*.
70. *1989 Survey of Adults and Markets of Affluence*, Mendelsohn Media Research, Inc.
71. Scott Paper Company, March 1990.
72. *Environmental Consumerism in the U.S.*, Abt Associates, Inc.
73. *The New Greening of America*, Cambridge Reports/Research International.
74. *The Environment: New Concerns, New Choices*, Cambridge Reports' *Trends and Forecasts*.
75. *The Environment: New Concerns, New Choices*, Cambridge Reports' *Trends and Forecasts*.
76. "Americans and Their Money," *Money*.
77. "Americans and Their Money," *Money*.
78. *Giving and Volunteering in the U.S. 1990*, Independent Sector.

Chapter 4

79. *The Lifestyle Market Analyst*, National Demographics and Life-styles/Standard Rate and Data Service.
80. *The Crown Royal Report on American Entertaining*, Research and Forecasts, Inc.
81. *The Crown Royal Report on American Entertaining*, Research and Forecasts, Inc.
82. *Affluent Travelers*, Reed Travel Market Reports, U.S. Travel Service Information.
83. *Frequent Leisure Travelers: A Study of Markets and Media 1990*, Erdos & Morgan/MPG.
84. *Frequent Leisure Travelers: A Study of Markets and Media 1990*, Erdos & Morgan/MPG.
85. *Frequent Leisure Travelers: A Study of Markets and Media 1990*, Erdos & Morgan/MPG.

86. *Market Opportunities in Retail: Affluent American Consumers*, Deloitte & Touche/Impact Resources.

87. *Personal Health and Chemical Avoidance*, Cambridge Reports' Trends and Forecasts.

88. *Market Opportunities in Retail: Affluent American Consumers*, Deloitte & Touche/Impact Resources.

89. *Golf Participation in the United States: 1988*, Dr. Gordon Benson, National Golf Foundation.

90. *The National Fitness Study, 1989: A Demographic, Behavioral and Psychographic Profile of Active and Inactive Americans*, National Sporting Goods Association.

91. *The National Fitness Study, 1989: A Demographic, Behavioral and Psychographic Profile of Active and Inactive Americans*, National Sporting Goods Association.

92. *Perceived Stress in a Probability Sample of the United States*, Carnegie Mellon University psychologist Sheldon Cohen.

93. *The Environment: New Concerns, New Choices*, Cambridge Reports' *Trends and Forecasts*.

94. *Attitudes Toward Nutrition in Restaurants: Assessing the Market*, National Restaurant Association.

95. *New Vehicle Purchasers: Who They Are and How They Buy*, Newspaper Advertising Bureau.

96. "1988 Buyers of New Cars Summary Report," *Newsweek*.

97. *Affluent Consumers: A Special Report*, Deloitte & Touche/Impact Resources.

Chapter 5

98. Simmons Market Research Bureau data, as cited by *Media Matters*.

99. *The Public Pulse*, March 1989, The Roper Organization, Inc.

100. *The Up Market*, Management Horizons.

101. "Marketing Luxury Cars 1989", subscriber study, *Fortune*.

Chapter 6

102. *Cahners Economics' Index of Affluence*, Cahners Economics.

103. "The Who and How-to of the Nifty 50-Plus Market," *Grey Matter Alert*, Grey Advertising Inc.

104. "The Who and How-to of the Nifty 50-Plus Market," *Grey Matter Alert*, Grey Advertising Inc.

105. *Consumer Market Developments*, Fairchild Publications.
106. "Do You Know the Spenders in Your Market," *Retail Market Analysis Report*, June 1988, Touche Ross.
107. *Market Opportunities in Retail: Asian American Consumers*, Deloitte & Touche/Impact Resources.
108. *The Upper Deck*, Mediamark Research, Inc.
109. "Marketing to the Year 2000," *Adweek*, Judith Newman.

Chapter 7

110. *Consumer Market Developments*, Fairchild Publications.
111. *Americans Cope With Their Finances 1988*, International Association for Financial Planning.
112. *Consumers & Innovation, 1988*, Management Horizons.
113. *American Demographics*, October 1987.
114. *The Luxury Industry: An Asset for France*, McKinsey & Company, Inc., France.
115. Rose Anne Moore, Manager, Marketing Research, Saab-Scania of America, Inc., in presentation at the Affluent Consumer Conference sponsored by the Marketing Institute.
116. "Cross-cultural Perspectives on the Dynamics of Prestige," Richard T. Garfein, *The Journal of Services Marketing*, Vol. 3, No. 3, Summer 1989, Grayson Associates.
117. *Luxury Marketing in the 1990s*, The Prestige Marketing Group.
118. Judith Blake, demographer, University of California, as cited by *U.S. News & World Report*, March 6, 1989.

Information Sources

ABA Journal
750 North Lake Shore Drive
6th Floor
Chicago, IL 60611
(312) 988-5000

Abt Associates, Inc.
55 Wheeler Street
Cambridge, MA 02138
(617) 492-7109

Adweek's Marketing Week
49 East 21st Street
New York, NY 10010
(212) 529-5500

American Banker
One State Street Plaza
New York, NY 10004
(212) 943-6700

American Demographics
108 North Cayuga Street
Ithaca, NY 14850
(800) 828-1133

American Health
80 Fifth Avenue
New York, NY 10011
(212) 242-2460

American Marketing Association
250 South Wacker Drive
Chicago, IL 60606
(312) 648-0536

Backer Spielvogel Bates
Worldwide, Inc.
The Chrysler Building
405 Lexington Avenue
New York, NY 10174
(212) 297-7000

Black Enterprise
130 Fifth Avenue
New York, NY 10011
(212) 242-8000

Bozell, Jacobs, Kenyon, &
  Eckhardt (Bozell)
40 West 23rd Street
New York, NY 10010
(212) 727-5210

R.H. Bruskin Associates
303 George Street
New Brunswick, NJ 08903
(201) 349-0781

Builder
Hanley Wood
1 Barker Avenue
White Plains, NY 10601
(914) 682-2808

Cahners Economics
275 Washington Street
Newton, MA 02158
(617) 630-2105

Cambridge Reports, Inc.
675 Massachusetts Avenue
4th Floor
Cambridge, MA 02139
(617) 661-0110

Census Bureau
Public Information Office
Room #2705-3
Washington, DC 20233
(202) 763-4040

Center for Health Statistics
3700 East-West Highway
Hyattsville, MD 20782
(301) 436-8500

Challenger, Gray & Christmas
150 South Wacker Drive
Chicago, IL 60606
(312) 332-5790

Changing Times
220 East 42nd Street
New York, NY 10036
(212) 398-6320

The Conference Board
845 Third Avenue
New York, NY 10022
(212) 759-0900

Democratic Study Center
499 South Capitol
Suite 113
Washington, DC 20003
(202) 863-0083

Direct Marketing Association
6 East 43rd Street
New York, NY 10017
(212) 689-4977

Donnelly Marketing
Information Services
70 Seaview Avenue
P.O. Box 10250
Stamford, CT 06904
(203) 353-7267

Erdos and Morgan/MPG
116 East 27th Street
New York, NY 10016
(212) 685-9393

Ernst & Young
787 Seventh Avenue
New York, NY 10019
(212) 830-6000

Esquire
1790 Broadway
New York, NY 10019
(212) 459-7500

Fairchild Publications
7 East 12th Street
New York, NY 10003
(212) 741-4000

Forbes
60 Fifth Avenue
New York, NY 10011
(212) 620-2200

Fortune
Time & Life Bldg.
Rockefeller Center
1271 Avenue of the Americas
New York, NY 10020
(212) 522-1212

Francorp, Inc.
20200 Governors Drive
Olympia Fields, IL 60461
(708) 481-2900

The Gallup Organization
100 Palmer Square, Suite 200
Princeton, NJ 08542
(609) 924-9600

Grey Advertising
777 Third Avenue
New York, NY 10017
(212) 546-2000

IDS Financial Services
219 East 44th Street
New York, NY 10017
(212) 573-9500

Impact Resources
125 Dillmont Drive
Columbus, OH 43235
(614) 888-5900

Industry Week
122 East 42nd Street
New York, NY 10068
(212) 867-9191

International Association for
    Financial Planning
2 Concourse Parkway, Suite 800
Atlanta, GA 30328
(404) 395-1605

Journal of Services Marketing
Grayson Associates
108 Loma Media Road
Santa Monica, CA 93103
(805) 564-1313

Management Horizons
570 Metro Place North
Dublin, OH 43017
(614) 764-9555

The Marketing Institute
331 Madison Avenue
New York, NY 10017
(212) 883-1770

Media Dynamics, Inc.
322 East 50th Street
New York, NY 10022
(212) 753-2674

The Media Report
New Electronic Media Science
    Inc.
P.O. Box 1173
Woodstock, NY 12498
(914) 339-6477

Mediamark Research, Inc. (MRI)
341 Madison Avenue
New York, NY 10017
(212) 599-0444

Mendelsohn Media Research,
   Inc.
352 Park Avenue South
New York, NY 10010
(212) 684-6350

Money
1271 Avenue of the Americas
New York, NY 10020
(212) 586-1212

National Association of Realtors
430 North Michigan Avenue
Suite 250
Chicago, IL 60611
(312) 329-8292

National Demographics &
   Lifestyles
1621 Eighteenth Street
Denver, CO 80202-1211
(800) 525-3533

National Golf Association
1150 South U.S. Highway 1
Jupiter, FL 33477
(800) 872-1150

National Restaurant Association
1200 Seventeenth Street, N.W.
Washington, DC 20036
 (202) 331-5900

National Sporting Goods
   Association
1699 Wall Street
Mt. Prospect, IL 60056
(312) 439-4000

Newspaper Advertising Bureau
1180 Avenue of the Americas
New York, NY 10036
(212) 704-4547

Newsweek
444 Madison Avenue
New York, NY 10022
(212) 350-4000

The Nightly Business Report
P.O. Box 2
Miami, FL 33261

Nissan Motor Corporation USA
18501 South Figueroa Street
Carson, CA 90248
(215) 532-3111

Opinion Research Corporation
One Penn Plaza, Suite 1632
New York, NY 10119
(212) 557-6616

Payment Systems, Inc.
352 Park Avenue South
New York, NY 10010
(212) 684-6350

The Prestige Marketing Group
104 Fifth Avenue
11th Floor
New York, NY 10011
(212) 255-7403

Private Banking
Faulkner & Gray, Inc.
106 Fulton Avenue
New York, NY 10038
(212) 766-7800

Professional Builder
1350 Touhy Avenue
Cahners Plaza
Des Plaines, IL 60017
(312) 635-8800

The Public Pulse
(see listing for The Roper Organization)

Reed Travel Market Reports
500 Plaza Drive
Secaucus, NJ 07096

Rivendell Marketing Company
Box 1268
Plainfield, NJ 07061
(212) 242-6863
(201) 754-4348

The Roper Organization, Inc.
205 East 42nd Street
17th Floor
New York, NY 10017
(212) 599-0700

Sales & Marketing Management
633 Third Avenue
New York, NY 10017
(212) 986-4800

Securities and Exchange
   Commission
Public Reference Room
450 Fifth Street, NW
Washington, DC 20549
(202) 272-7450

Security Industry Association
120 Broadway, 35th Floor
New York, NY 10271
(212) 608-1500

Simmons Market Research
   Bureau
380 Madison Avenue
New York, NY 10017
(212) 916-8900

Sirota Alper & Pfau
1675 Third Avenue
New York, NY 10128
(212) 722-8054

Smithsonian
420 Lexington Avenue
New York, NY 10017
(212) 490-2510

SMRB Newsletter
(See listing for Simmons Market
Research Bureau)

SRI International
333 Ravenswood Avenue
Menlo Park, CA 94025
(415) 326-6200

Standard Rate & Data Service
3002 Glenview Road
Wilmette, IL 60091
(708) 256-6067

Starch INRA Hooper
205 East 42nd Street, 17th
   Floor
New York, NY 10017
(212) 490-3197

Target Marketing
322 Eighth Avenue
New York, NY 10001
(212) 620-7330

Times Mirror Center for People
& the Press
1875 Eye Street, N.W.
Washington, DC 20006
(202) 293-3126

Touche Ross
1633 Broadway
New York, NY 10019
(212) 492-2891

Town & Country
1700 Broadway
New York, NY 10019
(212) 903-5328

University of California at Los
Angeles
405 Hilgard Avenue
Los Angeles, CA
90024-1492
(213) 825-4321

Urban Institute
2100 M Street, N.W.
Washington, DC 20037
(202) 833-7200

U.S. Commission on Civil
Rights
1121 Vermont Avenue, N.W.
Washington, DC 20425
(202) 376-8582

The Wall Street Journal
200 Liberty Street
New York, NY 10281
(212) 416-2000

Working Woman
342 Madison Avenue
New York, NY 10173
(212) 390-9818

Yankelovich Clancy Shulman
8 Wright Street
Westport, CT 06880
(203) 227-2700

Young & Rubicam
285 Madison Avenue
New York, NY 10017
(212) 210-3000